P9-DBM-029
DATE DUE

THE DAILY TELEGRAPH BOOK OF CAROLS

Chosen, edited and introduced by

Ian Bradley

Continuum
The Tower Building
11 York Road
London SE1 7NX

80 Maiden Lane
Suite 704
New York, NY 10038

www.continuumbooks.com

First published 2006

British Library Cataloguing-in-Publication Data
A catalogue record for this book is available from the British Library.

ISBN 0-8264-9240-1

Typeset by BookEns Ltd, Royston, Herts.
Printed and bound by MPG Books Ltd, Bodmin, Cornwall

CONTENTS

In loving memory of my mother

MARY CAMPBELL BRADLEY

Born 12 March 1910, Died 3 August 1998

'Sleep in heavenly peace'

INTRODUCTION

Even in our supposedly secular and post-Christian times, carols are as much a part of Christmas as turkeys, trees, tinsel, television specials and excessive expenditure on what John Betjeman memorably called 'those tissued fripperies'. They may now first assail us from shopping mall and supermarket sound systems around the end of October but for many people Christmas proper only begins with the sound of the boy treble intoning the first verse of 'Once in Royal David's city' in the live broadcast of the nine lessons and carols from King's College, Cambridge, on the afternoon of Christmas Eve. The intervening weeks are filled with the sound of carols, whether sung live in school concerts and end-of-term services, at church events which attract once-a-year worshippers, in homes and on the streets, or played on national and local radio stations.

Yet although it now seems almost unthinkable to celebrate (or survive) the festive season without them, carols originally had nothing to do with Christmas, nor even with Christianity. They were among the many pagan customs taken over by the medieval church which used them initially as much in the celebration of Easter as of Christmas. The subsequent development of the carol as a distinctive genre standing somewhere between the hymn, the folksong and the sacred ballad and having as its subject matter the story and significance of Jesus' birth serves as an interesting pointer to several major currents in religious, social and cultural history over the last five hundred years. Born out of late medieval humanism, carols were suppressed by Puritan zealots after the Reformation, partially reinstated at the Restoration, sung by Dissenters and radicals to the distaste of the established churches in the eighteenth century, rediscovered and reinvented by Victorian antiquarians and romantics, and re-written in the late twentieth century to fit the demand for social realism and political correctness. As well as reflecting the mood of their times, some of our best-loved carols also contain coded comments on contemporary events, including, perhaps, the 1745 Jacobite rebellion and the revolutions across Europe in 1848.

The derivation of the word 'carol' has been the subject of much speculation. It probably goes back through the old French '*caroler*' and the Latin '*choraula*' to the Greek '*choros*', a circling dance often accompanied by singing and associated with dramatic performances, religious festivities and fertility rites. The carol of classical times was a major element in popular celebrations to mark the passing of the winter solstice and the coming of spring. The coming of Christianity may well have increased the carol's pagan connotations with its lively dance rhythms providing a marked contrast to the restrained and measured chants of the new religion. The Church was for long uneasy about the performance of such popular singing dances and the '*caraula*' was explicitly proscribed in a decree of the mid-seventh century Council of Chalon-sur-Saone. The singing of carols was further condemned by the Council of Avignon in 1209 and as late as 1435 by the Council of Bale. The earliest known reference to the carol in English literature, which dates from around 1300 and uses the word in its modern spelling, has no religious connotations and seems to denote simply a round dance.

Although the Church came relatively early to see the advantages of incorporating elements of pagan customs such as the Roman Saturnalia and the Germano-Celtic Yule in its celebration of Christ's nativity, it took much longer to be persuaded of the merits of carols. It was not until the austerity of early medieval Christianity had been tempered by the new spirit of imagination and romance associated with the twelfth-century renaissance that they were taken up as Christian folksongs. The new humanism also brought a change of emphasis away from death and judgement towards a more incarnational focus on the humanity and personality of Jesus, in which the cradle became almost as important an object of devotion as the Cross.

Francis of Assisi is often credited with being instrumental in bringing about this new interest in the feast of the Nativity and devotion to Christ as the Babe of Bethlehem. He was for long regarded as the instigator of the cult of the Christmas crib but recent scholarship has shown that there was singing and dancing around cribs at Christmas time in several Italian churches more than a century before he set one up at Grecchio in 1223. There is no doubt, however, that he and his followers promoted the image of the baby lying in a manger surrounded by animals that was to feature prominently in so many carols. Franciscans were also more directly involved in Christianising the carol. Members of the Order of Friars Minor established by Francis in 1209 were at the forefront of developing the '*lauda*', a vernacular Italian religious folk song with a dance rhythm which is often regarded as the prototype of the Christmas carol. From Italy this new style of popular sacred song spread to France and Germany where numerous carols were written during the fourteenth century, the best known being '*In dulci jubilo*' (No. 37 in this collection), an intermingling of Latin and German phrases traditionally attributed to the Dominican mystic, Heinrich Suso.

It was almost certainly through Franciscans that Christmas carols came to the British Isles. The earliest extant English Christmas carol, 'A child is boren amonges man' is found in a set of sermon notes written by a Franciscan friar before 1350. Collections of poems produced by friars in Kildare around the same time and in Scotland in 1372 contain lullabies to the infant Jesus.

The period from around 1400 to 1550 was the heyday of the English carol, by now established as a popular religious song generally on the theme of Christ's nativity. Among those still sung which date from this time are 'Adam lay ybounden' (No. 4), 'A child this day is born', 'A virgin most pure' (No. 3) and 'On Christmas night all Christians sing' (No. 58). The development of open-air religious drama inspired the writing of carols to be sung during performances of the mystery plays, like the well-known Coventry Carol, 'Lullay, lulla, my little tiny child', (No. 49) which comes from the Pageant of the Shearmen and the Tailors performed in that city between 1400 and 1450. The more worldly aspects of Christmas were also celebrated in song. The Boar's Head carol (No. 75), first found in a fifteenth-century manuscript, is one of several from this period which dwell on the pleasures of festive eating and drinking.

The distinguishing feature of the traditional (by which is generally meant late medieval and Tudor) English carol has often been taken to be its burden, or refrain, usually a couplet, repeated after every stanza. It is an indication both of the carol's origins in folk song and dance and its greater suitability for exuberant performance in home or street than lugubrious chanting in church. In content, as well as in verse structure and musical style, the carol is distinct from the hymn, generally eschewing theology in favour of narrative and focusing on the drama of the Nativity with its cast of innkeepers, shepherds, wise men, stars and beasts in the manger rather than on the direct praise of God.

Carol-singing in the later Middle Ages was not just a popular extra-ecclesiastical activity, however. The Church saw its appeal and potential and acknowledged that it provided more appetizing fare for most worshippers than the monotonous tones of Gregorian chant or the severity of ancient Latin office hymns. Carols were brought into the church's liturgy. The Christmas Day offices had, in fact, long included the angels' hymn to the shepherds beginning 'Glory to God in the highest' recorded in St Luke's account of the Nativity. This was taken as a scripturally authorised precedent for including other carols in Christmas services. A mid-sixteenth-century poem provides a colourful picture of Christmas Day devotions on the eve of the Reformation:

Three masses every priest doth sing upon that solemne day,
With offerings unto every one, that so the more may play.
This done, a woodden childe in clowtes is on the altar set,
About the which both boyes and gyrles do daunce
and trymly jet;
And Carols sing in prayse of Christ, and, for to
helpe them heare,

The organs answere every verse with sweete and solemn cheare.
The priestes do rore aloude; and round about the parentes stande,
To see the sport, and with their voyce do helpe them and their bande.

The Reformation curbed carol-singing in British churches. In Germany its effects were very different. Martin Luther's enthusiasm for congregational singing led him to write several Christmas hymns in the style of folk songs with strong popular tunes. The established churches of England and Scotland chose rather to follow Calvin's aversion to all but metrical psalms being sung in the sanctuary. As a result carols were no longer heard in church although they continued to be sung elsewhere. Indeed, their popularity was such in the early seventeenth century that one late Victorian antiquarian speculated that the word 'carol' was derived from the Latin name (*Carolus*) of Charles I. In 1619 Launcelot Andrewes used his first Christmas sermon as bishop of Winchester to extol the glories of a day celebrated 'as well as at home with *Carolls*, as in the Church with Anthemes'. An account of domestic Christmas festivities in 1631 describes 'the evergreen ivie trimming and adorning the portals ... and the usual *carols*, to observe antiquitie, cheerefully sounding'.

Most Puritans shared the early church's view that carol singing was essentially a pagan activity. In Scotland it was regarded with particular suspicion and was often among the activities confessed by those accused in the witchcraft trials in the sixteenth and seventeenth centuries. Oliver Cromwell was determined to outlaw the practice despite the eloquent tribute paid to the original angels' carol by his friend and supporter, John Milton, in *Paradise Lost*:

His place of birth a solemn Angel tells
To simple shepherds, keeping watch by night;
They gladly thither haste, and by a quire
Of squadron'd Angels hear his *carol* sung.

Another defender of carol singing was the Anglican divine, Thomas Warmstry, whose 1648 tract, *The Vindication of the Solemnity of the Nativity of Christ*, argued that '*Christmasse Kariles*, if they be such as are fit for the time, and of holy and sober composures, and used with Christian sobriety and purity, are not unlawfull, and may be profitable, if they be sung with grace in the heart'. However, his arguments failed to sway members of the Long Parliament who included carols in the various measures prohibiting Christmas festivities which were passed during the period of the Commonwealth and Protectorate.

The Restoration of 1660 ended the official prohibition on the singing of Christmas carols and was greeted by the publication of a volume of *New Carolls for this Merry Time of Christmas*. However, the established churches remained in thrall to Calvinistic principles with regard to what could appropriately be sung in church. Throughout most of the eighteenth century the only Christmas hymn officially permitted in Church of England services was the paraphrase of St Luke's account of the Nativity, 'While shepherds watched' (No. 99), written by Nahum Tate around 1698. Towards the end of the century it was joined on the 'approved list' by 'Hark, the herald angels sing' (No. 32), the heavily altered version of Charles Wesley's 'Hark, how all the welkin rings' (No. 31).

Carols do seem to have survived in some of the more remote country churches where they were sung in the florid fuguing style favoured by west gallery bands and choirs. Oliver Goldsmith noted that churchgoers in the north of England parish where he set *The Vicar of Wakefield* (1766) 'kept up the Christmas carol'. In general, however, carol-singing reverted to being an extra-ecclesiastical activity, focused on the home, the streets and Dissenting chapels. New carols continued to be written – that rich blend of Christian and pagan imagery, 'The holly and the ivy' (No. 78), made its first appearance in 1710 – but they tended to be the work of those distanced from both the political and religious Establishment. In the 1740s the plainchant scribe at the English Catholic college at Douai in France, John Wade, a fervent Jacobite, wrote '*Adeste, fidelis*' (No. 5), later translated as 'O come, all ye faithful' (No. 53). The dedication '*Regem nostrum Jacobum*' and Stuart cyphers on the manuscript have led some historians to speculate that the carol may have been intended to rally Jacobites in Britain on the eve of Bonnie Prince Charlie's rising.

Although carols were out of official ecclesiastical favour, they were still regularly heard in the streets of towns and villages at Christmas time. The tradition of wassailers going from door to door singing and drinking the health of those whom they visited went back to medieval times. Indeed, it probably had pre-Christian origins in the fertility rites with which the first carols had been associated. In the English west country wassailers went through the orchards around Twelfth Night singing and shouting loudly to drive out evil spirits and pouring cider over the roots of trees to encourage fertility. Wassailing later became associated with 'luck visits' made around the neighbourhood and general merry making, fortified by copious quantities of alcohol. It also merged with the tradition of 'waits' or watchmen who went through the streets of urban areas sounding a horn or crying out to mark the passing hours of the night. Increasingly the name 'waits' became applied to parties of singers and musicians who went from house to house at Christmastide in both towns and country areas. A book on *Popular Antiquities*, published in 1795, noted that in Newcastle upon Tyne and other places in the North of England boys and girls went round on the nights leading up to Christmas, including Christmas Eve, 'knocking at the doors and singing their Christmas Carols'. A correspondent to the *Gentleman's Magazine* in 1811 wrote that while staying in the North Riding of Yorkshire he had been awaken about six o'clock on Christmas morning 'by a sweet singing under my window'. An American visitor to Yorkshire in 1820 reported a similar experience on Christmas Eve:

> I had scarcely got into bed when a strain of music seemed to break forth in the air just below the window. I listened, and found it proceeded from a band, which I concluded to be the waits from some neighbouring village. They went round the house playing under the windows.

Despite this evidence suggesting that carol-singing was still flourishing, at least in the north of England, there was considerable concern in other parts of the country in the early 1800s that the tradition was dying out. The repertoire seems to have shrunk with many of the pre-Reformation carols dropping out of use. They were preserved thanks to the labours of a small group of antiquarians and folksong collectors. In 1822 Davies Gilbert, MP for Bodmin in Cornwall, published the first modern collection of traditional carols. He clearly saw them as belonging to a past world that had all but disappeared, noting that they had been sung 'in Churches on Christmas Day, and in private houses on Christmas Eve, throughout the West of England up to the latter part of the late century' and giving a lyrical description of what had happened on Christmas Eve in the 'Protestant West of England' until the late eighteenth century:

> At seven or eight o'clock in the evening cakes were drawn hot from the oven; cyder or beer exhilarated the spirits in every house; and the singing of Carols was continued late into the night. On Christmas Day these carols took the place of Psalms in all the churches, especially at afternoon service, the whole congregation joining; and at the end it was usual for the Parish Clerk to declare, in a loud voice, his wishes for a merry Christmas and a happy new year to all the parishioners.

A similar sense of the need to preserve a tradition on the verge of extinction inspired William Sandys, a London solicitor and antiquarian who also had strong Cornish connections, to publish a collection of *Christmas Carols Ancient and Modern* in 1833. While acknowledging that carols were still being sung 'in the Northern counties and some of the Midland', he noted that 'the practice appears to get more neglected every year'. Among the carols preserved by Sandys and Gilbert which might otherwise have fallen into oblivion were 'God rest you merry, gentlemen' (No. 26), 'The first Nowell' (No. 77) and 'I saw three ships come sailing in' (No. 35). Other important collections included the wassail songs transcribed in 1843 by John Broadwood from his Sussex parishioners, the *Little Book of Carols* (1846) and *Old*

Christmas Carols (1863) published by Edward Rimbault, an organist who founded the Musical Antiquarian Society, and the *Songs of the Nativity* assembled in 1868 by William Henry Husk.

Carols played an important role in the Victorian reinvention of Christmas as a largely domestic festival full of sentimentality and good cheer. A huge number of new carols were written in the mid-nineteenth century, many in a pseudo-traditional style. Even the pioneer socialist William Morris provided a pastiche medieval carol with the refrain 'The snow in the street and the wind at the door' (No. 61). It was the Victorians, rather than Bing Crosby, who invented the concept of the White Christmas, bringing snow into the Nativity story with Christina Rosseti's 'In the bleak mid-winter' (No. 38) and Edward Caswall's 'See amid the winter snow' (No. 69). Moralizing was also a feature of the Victorian carol, most famously exemplified in Cecil Frances Alexander's injunction in 'Once in Royal David's City' (No. 60) that 'Christian children all must be mild, obedient, good as He'. American writers were equally infused with the sentimental spirit of the Victorian Christmas, producing 'Away in a manger' (No. 10), 'O little town of Bethlehem' (No. 55), 'We three kings of Orient Are' (No. 94) and 'It came upon the midnight clear' (No. 40). This last carol was written by Edmund Sears, a Unitarian minister in Massachusetts, in 1849 and it may have been the disruptions in Europe and the United States over the previous twelve months that he had in mind when he penned the lines 'O hush the noise, ye men of strife, and hear the angels sing'.

Thomas Hardy's novel *Under the Greenwood Tree*, published in 1872, contributed to the aura of romantic nostalgia with which the practice of carol singing became invested in the later nineteenth century. It lamented the passing of the old Mellstock gallery band who had gone out at Christmas time enjoining the Wessex villagers to 'remember Adam's fall' (No. 68) and 'Arise and hail the sacred day' (No. 8). In fact, the very forces which Hardy blamed for killing off the traditional waits and wassailers, Tractarian clergy with their robed choirs and organs, literally brought carols in from the cold and into church. The Oxford Movement finally ended the reign of metrical psalmody in the

Church of England and introduced hymns and carols into the liturgy. Among those who led the way in this innovation was J.M. Neale whose 1853 *Carols for Christmas-tide* included translations of medieval Continental carols as well as his own 'Good King Wenceslas' (No. 29), a highly fanciful account of the philanthropic activities of the tenth-century Bohemian prince. Another important collection, *Christmas Carols Old and New*, produced in 1871 by H.R. Bramley, fellow of Magdalen College, Oxford, and John Stainer, the college organist, did for carols what *Hymns Ancient and Modern* had done for hymns, making them easily accessible to clergy and organists and bringing them into the mainstream of Anglican worship.

In 1878 the cathedral choir in the newly created diocese of Truro switched from its usual practice of singing around the city on Christmas Eve to holding a service in church at 10pm. It included two lessons, prayers and a sermon interspersed with carols. Two years later the service was expanded to a festival of nine lessons and carols, providing a model that was taken up in 1918 at King's College, Cambridge and subsequently by many parish churches and cathedrals.

The early decades of the twentieth century saw renewed efforts to collect long-lost carols by those involved in the folklore revival. Cecil Sharp's *English Folk Carols* appeared in 1911 and Ralph Vaughan Williams' arrangements of traditional west country carol tunes in 1919 and 1920. Percy Dearmer's *Oxford Book of Carols* (1928) brought together numerous pre-Reformation texts and tunes, including carols for Lent, Passiontide, Easter and summer, with more recent items often culled from literary sources, while omitting anything that smacked of Victorian sentimentality. Its successor, The *New Oxford Book of Carols* (1992) is a more scholarly volume reflecting the considerable contemporary interest in recovering and researching old tunes and texts.

Carols are not just for antiquarians and scholars, however. They belong to a living tradition which is constantly being added to with new material. The last three decades have seen modern expressions of the Christmas story in Michael Perry's 'Calypso

Carol' (No. 70), Sydney Carter's 'Every Star Shall Sing a Carol' (No. 19) with its references to space travel and John Bell's 'Funny kind of night' (No. 23) which speaks of 'Tax collectors, child inspectors, all in disarray'. A carol written in 1992 by Michael Forster, a Baptist minister, portrays Mary as a 'blessed teenage mother' (No. 50). Whatever feelings these and other modern lyrics stir up among traditionalists, there is no doubt that they conform to Percy Dearmer's oft-quoted definition of carols as 'songs with a religious impulse that are simple, hilarious, popular and modern . . . set in such language as shall express the manner in which the ordinary man at his best understands the ideas of his age'.

Hilarious for rather different reasons, and perhaps less happy, are some of the recent attempts to re-write classic carols to eliminate gender-exclusive or overtly Christian language. With the arrival of the politically correct, multi-faith carol, purged of any reference to men, Christ, cribs or angels, we have come back where we started – with carols disconnected from Christmas or Christianity.

The 100 carols printed in this book represent a selection that is inevitably personal but also chosen to reflect the richness and variety of the genre. It covers the full spectrum of the carol tradition both chronologically and geographically, ranging from fifteenth-century boar's head to 1990s teenage mother, and from Czech folk song to Caribbean calypso. I have taken note of indicators of popularity and included all of the Top Twenty carols chosen by viewers of *Songs of Praise* and listeners to local radio stations in a large-scale BBC poll conducted in 2005.

Like the *Daily Telegraph Book of Hymns*, this is a words-only collection but don't let that inhibit you from singing your way through it. Most of the tunes are very well-known and will be dancing round in your head as you read the carols. Those that aren't you can always make up and so follow in a long tradition of improvised and spontaneous carol-singing. Tidings of comfort and joy!

1
A GREAT AND MIGHTY WONDER

The first item in this collection provides a good example of the many different strands from which our Christmas hymns and carols have been woven together. The words originally come from seventh-century Greece (via a translation into English in the mid-nineteenth century), the tune from sixteenth-century Germany and the two were married at the beginning of the twentieth century when the text was re-shaped in its present form.

We owe this stately re-telling of the Christmas story to John Mason Neale (1818–66), one of the great figures in the story of English hymnody who was responsible for several carols, notably 'Good King Wenceslas' (No. 29). Brought up in a strictly evangelical household, Neale fell under the spell of the Oxford Movement while a student at Trinity College, Cambridge and was ordained as a priest in the Church of England in 1841. The following year he became vicar of Crawley in Sussex. He was appalled when in the middle of his first evening service there the churchwarden climbed up on the altar in order to open the east window. Neale deplored such liturgical laxity and greatly enhanced the atmosphere of reverence and solemnity during worship. His Anglo-Catholicism brought him into conflict with many of his parishioners and with his diocesan bishop and in 1846 he was forced to quit parish ministry for the quiet backwater of the wardenship of Sackville College, a group of almshouses near East Grinstead. He spent the last twenty years of his life there, surviving on a pittance of £27 a year. For most of this period he was barred from administering the sacrament of Holy Communion and from saying the Divine Office by his bishop who disliked the 'spiritual haberdashery' involved in Neale's introduction of a rood screen and vested altar with cross and candlesticks in the college's chapel. At least this enforced leisue gave Neale plenty of time to devote himself to his great passion, the translation of the office hymns of the early church.

Neale had a particular interest in the Eastern Orthodox Church and hoped to awaken his fellow-Anglicans to its liturgical and devotional riches by translating ancient Greek hymns. 'A great and mighty wonder' first appeared in his *Hymns of the Eastern Church* (1862). It is based on a poem by St Germanus (634–734) which was sung as a hymn in the Greek liturgy for Christmas Day. In an uncharacteristic lapse, Neale erroneously attributed it to St Anatolius.

Germanus' original hymn had two stanzas, the order of which was inverted by Neale in his six verse translation. The first stanza began with the verse that Neale renders 'While thus they sing their monarch' and the second with 'A great and mighty wonder'. The third verse of Neale's original translation, accurately reflecting the closing lines of the Greek poem, ran:

And we with them triumphant
Repeat the hymn again!
'To God on high be glory
And peace on earth to men!'

The hymn, as it appears on page 16, was fashioned out of Neale's translation by the editors of the *English Hymnal* (1906). In order to set it to the melody of the German folk carol, *'Es ist ein' Ros entsprungen*', they used Neale's original third verse as a refrain, omitting its first line.

It took some time for 'A great and mighty wonder' to gain wider currency. The *English Hymnal* version appeared, shorn of its last verse, in the revised edition of *Hymns Ancient and Modern* (1950), and complete in the *Baptist Hymn Book* of 1962 and the *Church Hymnary, Third Edition* (1973). The *New English Hymnal* contains the full version, while the New Standard edition of *Hymns Ancient and Modern* includes verses one to four.

For *Songs of Praise* (1931) Percy Dearmer substantially amended Neale's hymn. The first verse was re-written to bring it more in line with the theme of the German words originally associated with the tune:

A great and mighty wonder,
A full and blessed cure!
The Rose has come to blossom
Which shall for ay endure.

Dearmer also changed the first two lines of the second verse to 'The Word has dwelt among us/The true light from on high!' and substituted 'succour' for 'ransom' in the first line of verse four.

The compilers of *Carols for Today*, the collection made by the Jubilate Hymns group in 1986, have made further revisions, including changing the first verse to:

A great and mighty wonder,
Redemption drawing near!
The Virgin bears the infant,
The Prince of peace is here.

They also changed the last line of the refrain to 'And peace on earth.Amen', presumably to excise the supposedly sexist, gender-specific language in the original. The Jubilate version appears in *Baptist Hymns and Worship* (1991).

All modern hymn-books follow the *English Hymnal* in setting 'A great and mighty wonder' to the tune ES IST EIN' ROS. Further information on this tune can be found in the introduction to 'Lo! How a rose e'er blooming' (No. 46). Its use for the *English Hymnal* adaptation of Neale's verses in 1906 marked the tune's first appearance in Britain.

A great and mighty wonder,
A full and holy cure!
The Virgin bears the Infant
With virgin honour pure:

Repeat the hymn again!
'To God on high be glory
And peace on earth to men!'

2 The Word becomes incarnate,
And yet remains on high;
And cherubim sing anthems
To shepherds from the sky.

3 While thus they sing your Monarch,
Those bright angelic bands,
Rejoice, ye vales and mountains,
Ye oceans, clap your hands!

4 Since all he comes to ransom,
By all be he adored,
The infant born in Bethlem,
The Saviour and the Lord.

5 And idol forms shall perish,
And error shall decay,
And Christ shall wield his sceptre,
Our Lord and God for ay.

2

A SONG WAS HEARD AT CHRISTMAS

It is appropriate that the second item in this collection should be the work of a contemporary hymn writer. Carols are not just quaint olde worlde museum pieces which rely for their appeal on the nostalgia factor and properly belong to the burgeoning heritage industry. New ones are constantly being written to re-tell the story and significance of Jesus' birth in a way that brings its eternal life-enhancing message fresh and alive today.

This one is the work of a man who has been amongst the most prolific hymn writers in Britain over the last forty years. Timothy Dudley-Smith, who is still probably best known for his fine modern paraphrase of the Magnificat, 'Tell out, my soul the greatness of the Lord' (No. 122 in the *Daily Telegraph Book of Hymns*), has so far written and published over 250 hymns and carols, many of which appear in current hymn-books.

Born on Boxing Day 1926 in Manchester, Timothy Dudley-Smith grew up in Derbyshire where his poetry-loving father was a schoolmaster. He was educated at Tonbridge School in Kent and Pembroke College, Cambridge, where he found himself writing comic verse ('which, though I did not know it, is an invaluable part of learning the trade'). After theological studies at Ridley Hall, Cambridge, he was ordained into the Church of England in 1950 and served as a curate on the outskirts of London. A period running the Cambridge University Mission and Boys' Club in Bermondsey was followed by a stint as editor of *Crusade*, a monthly Christian magazine founded as part of the follow-up to Billy Graham's 1955 London crusade. From 1959 to 1973 he worked with the Church Pastoral Aid Society. Thereafter he was Archdeacon of

Norwich and, from 1981 to 1992, Suffragan Bishop of Thetford. He and his wife, Arlette, now live in retirement near Salisbury.

Most of his hymns have been written on annual family holidays in Cornwall. This one was composed in August 1978. The author notes 'Originally planned as "A star there was at Christmas", this text was written and then extensively re-worked over a week-end while on holiday in Cornwall; verse 3 in particular being redrafted on a walk to Porthoustock quarry'. 'A song was heard at Christmas' first appeared in print on the official Christmas card of the Lord Mayor of Norwich, Dr J.P.English, in December 1978. Dr English, who was the Dudley-Smiths' family doctor, had asked his hymn-writing patient for a carol that he might use on his mayoral card. The author sent several and this one was chosen.

The text appears here as Timothy Dudley-Smith originally wrote it and as it appears in his volume of collected hymns published in 1984 under the title *Lift Every Heart*. In several hymnbooks the third line of verse two has been changed to 'That all might know the way to go' and the fourth line of verse four to 'The Son of God made man'. In an interesting note on the subject of inclusive language at the end of *Lift Every Heart*, the author quotes these changes in a list of permitted variations and says that they may be substituted for the original lines at the discretion of editors.

Much of the strength of this hymn derives from the way it builds on four simple Christmas images - the song, the star, the tree and the child - to make some profound theological points and take the Christian message beyond the story of the Nativity. The third verse is particularly effective in linking the Christmas tree to the Cross of Calvary. There is, of course, a long tradition in Christian thought of linking the tree of life and the tree of death. Stars are a recurring theme in Dudley-Smith's Christmas verses - he has told me that his own favourite is 'Stars of heaven, clear and bright' which powerfully evokes the mysterious meeting of earth and heaven in Christ's Nativity. Its first verse runs as follows:

Stars of heaven, clear and bright,
Shine upon this Christmas light,
Vaster far than midnight skies
Are its timeless mysteries.
Trampled earth and stable floor
Lift the heart to heaven's door-
God has sent to us his Son,
Earth and heaven meet as one.

'A song was heard at Christmas' has been set to a number of tunes. The author's own preferred one is J.B. Dykes' ALFORD, to which it is set in a booklet of his carols published in 1983 in the United States with the title *A Song was heard at Christmas*. *Hymns for Today's Church* offers both the traditional CHERRY TREE CAROL and David Wilson's HOLY APOSTLES.

A song was heard at Christmas
To wake the midnight sky:
A saviour's birth, and peace on earth,
And praise to God on high.
The angels sang at Christmas
With all the hosts above,
And still we sing the newborn King
His glory and his love.

2 A star was seen at Christmas,
A herald and a sign,
That all might know the way to go
To find the child divine.
The wise men watched at Christmas
In some far eastern land,
And still the wise in starry skies
Discern their Maker's hand.

3 A tree was grown at Christmas,
A sapling green and young:
No tinsel bright with candlelight
Upon its branches hung.
But he who came at Christmas
Our sins and sorrow bore,
And still we name his tree of shame
Our life for evermore.

4 A child was born at Christmas
When Christmas first began:
The Lord of all a baby small,
The Son of God made man.
For love is ours at Christmas,
And life and light restored,
And so we praise through endless days
The Saviour, Christ the Lord.

3

A VIRGIN MOST PURE

These verses introduce us to the rich genre of traditional English ballad carols. They appear in numerous early carol collections with a bewildering variety of different versions of both words and music.

The earliest known version of the text is in a book produced in the aftermath of the restoration of the monarchy in 1660 and almost certainly associated with the revival of carol singing following its outlawing during the period of the Commonwealth and Protectorate. *New Carolls for this Merry Time of Christmas*, published in London in 1661 and surviving now only in a single copy preserved in the Bodleian Library, Oxford, contains a version with thirteen 11-syllable verses which begins 'In Bethlehem city, in Jewry it was' with the refrain 'Rejoice and be merry' at the opening and 'Therefore be merry' after each stanza.

The editors of the *New Oxford Book of Carols*, that magisterial work of reference of which I have made much use in the preparation of my own more modest collection, note that 'the refrain-verse-refrain form would suggest a sixteenth-century origin at the latest, and the evidence of the text itself supports a sixteenth-century date'. In the eighteenth century a new first verse seems to have been added:

A virgin unspotted, the prophet foretold,
Should bring forth a Saviour, which now we behold,
To be our Redeemer from death, hell and sin,
Which Adam's transgression involved us in.

A six-stanza version of the carol, which differs in several major respects from that printed overleaf, appeared in William Chappell's *Popular Music of the Olden Time*, published in the

1850s. Chappell identified the tune to which it was sung as one associated with a song entitled 'Admiral Benbow' and noted that it was sung by carollers at Marden, near Hereford.

We owe the version of the carol printed on page 24, which is the one most commonly sung today, to the work of the two pioneer early nineteenth-century collectors who played so important a part in preserving traditional English folk carols at a time when they were beginning to disappear. 'A virgin most pure' was one of eight carols with tunes published by Davies Gilbert in 1822. It is his version, which almost certainly comes from the West Country, which I have chosen to reproduce in this book. A similar version appeared in William Sandys' *Christmas Carols, Ancient and Modern* in 1833. Sandys included this extra verse which is not found in Gilbert's version:

Three certain Wise Princes they thought it most meet,
To lay their rich offerings at our Saviour's feet;
So then they consented, and to Bethlehem did go,
And when they came thither, they found it was so.

Like other ballad carols, 'A virgin most pure' narrates the Christmas story in a straightforward way, closely following the account in Luke's Gospel. Although it is in several carol collections, it has found its way into virtually no modern hymn-book and is more often sung by choirs than congregations. This is perhaps largely because the several tunes to which it has been set all seem to have a disconcerting number of flats and semitones and be rather too plaintive and fussy for such a jolly carol. There is a more robust and merry tune dancing round in my head to which I am sure I have heard it sung but I cannot find it in any printed source and maybe I have simply invented it.

A virgin most pure, as the prophets do tell,
Hath brought forth a baby, as it hath befell,
To be our Redeemer from death, hell and sin,
Which Adam's transgression hath wrapped us in.
Aye, and therefore be you merry,
Rejoice and be you merry,
Set sorrows aside!
Christ Jesus, our Saviour,
Was born on this tide.

2 In Bethlehem in Jewry a city there was,
Where Joseph and Mary together did pass,
And there to be taxed with many one more,
For Caesar commanded the same should be so.

3 But when they had entered the city so fair,
The number of people so mighty was there
That Joseph and Mary, whose substance was small,
Could find in the inn there no lodging at all.

4 Then were they constrained in a stable to lie,
Where horses and asses they used for to tie;
Their lodging so simple they took it no scorn
But against the next morning our Saviour was born.

5 The King of all kings to this world being brought,
Small store of fine linen to wrap him was sought;
When Mary had swaddled her young Son so sweet,
In an ox's manger she laid him to sleep.

6 Then God sent an Angel from heaven so high,
To certain poor shepherds in fields where they lie,
And bid them no longer in sorrow to stay,
Because that our Saviour was born on this day.

7 Then presently after, the shepherds did spy
A number of Angels appear in the sky,
Who joyfully talked, and sweetly did sing,
'To God be the Glory, Our Heavenly King.'

4
ADAM LAY YBOUNDEN

This is another carol which is largely confined to the choir repertoire and has not found its way into general hymn-books. Its distinctly archaic character perhaps makes it unsuitable for congregational singing but it has appealed to a number of modern composers who have set it for choirs and it has been a popular item in the Christmas Eve services of nine lessons and carols at King's College, Cambridge.

The words come from a fifteenth-century manuscript in the British Library which also includes another carol that has been set for choir use, 'Lullay, my liking' (also known by its first verse 'I saw a maiden').

'Adam lay ybounden' is unusual, although not unique, among Christmas hymns and carols in never mentioning Jesus or his birth. Its emphasis is almost entirely on the Original Sin embodied in Adam's disobedience to God in taking the apple from the tree of the knowledge of good and evil, as recounted in the third chapter of Genesis. The anonymous author of the carol pictures the taking of the apple as a happy fault, without which there would have been no 'queen of heaven' (Mary) and, by implication, no Nativity and Incarnation of God on earth.

This carol introduces a feature found in a number of medieval carols - the mingling of Latin phrases with the vernacular text (on this practice see the notes to 'In dulci jubilo', No. 37). It belongs to an age when Latin was the main liturgical language and everyone would have been familiar with phrases such as '*Deo gracias*'. The word moun in the third line of the last verse means must.

No contemporary tunes for this carol survive but it has been set to music by a distinguished trio of twentieth-century English composers. Peter Warlock's 1925 setting can be found in the *Oxford Book of Carols* (1928), John Ireland's in the *University Carol*

Book (1961, paperback edition 1978) and Boris Ord's in the *New Oxford Book of Carols* (1992). Ord (1897-1961) was organist and director of music at King's College, Cambridge, from 1929 to 1958 and wrote it for the service of lessons and carols there. I have to say that of the three I prefer Warlock's which strikes me as the simplest and cleanest.

Adam lay ybounden
Bounden in a bond:
Four thousand winter
Thought he not too long

2 All for an apple,
An apple that he took,
As Clerkes finden written in their book.

3 Ne had the apple taken been,
The apple taken been,
Ne had never our Lady
A been heavene queen.

4 Blessed be the time
That apple taken was;
Therefore we moun singen:

'Deo gracias!
Deo gracias!
Deo gracias'

5

ADESTE, FIDELES

There is so much to say about this carol that I have separated the Latin original from its best-known English translation, 'O come, all ye faithful' (No. 53) and treated them as two separate items.

Until the middle of the twentieth century it was widely believed that this great Latin hymn calling the faithful to worship the new-born Christ was the work of the thirteenth-century mystic Bonaventura. However the discovery of a mid-eighteenth-century manuscript in 1946 by Maurice Frost, vicar of Deddington in Oxfordshire and a noted hymnologist, and research over the next three years by his friend Dom John Stéphan of Buckfast Abbey led both men to conclude that the author of '*Adeste, fideles*' was John Francis Wade (1711-86).

Wade was an English Roman Catholic who spent much of his life at the English College at Douai in France where he worked copying plainchant manuscripts and teaching Latin and church music. The college had been founded in 1568 to educate English Roman Catholics for the secular priesthood. Wade's signature appears on six manuscripts containing the words and tune of '*Adeste, fideles*' and dated between 1750 and 1761. The text seems first to have appeared in print in Britain in 1760 in an edition of *The Evening Office of the Church*, one of a number of books believed to have been published anonymously by Wade, and its first known publication in America was in a broadside of 1795.

The manuscript discovered by Frost and worked on by Stéphan, which can be dated to between 1740 and 1744, is in the same handwriting as the others although it lacks both date and signature because the title page is missing. Stéphan christened this earliest known copy of the hymn 'the Jacobite manuscript' because it includes the words '*Regem nostrum Jacobum*', presumably referring to James Francis Edward Stewart, son of James VII of Scotland and II of England, and best known as 'the Old Pretender', in a plainchant setting of '*Domine salum fac Regem*'. Like other groups of English Roman Catholic exiles abroad in the mid-eighteenth century, the students at Douai were loyal to the Stuart cause and celebrated a weekly sung Mass for the military success of Prince Charles Edward Stewart, the Young Pretender, and the return of the Old Pretender to the British throne.

In 1990 Bennett Zon, a historian of music, gave a paper to the Catholic Family History Society in which he speculated that '*Adeste, fideles*' might even have been written as a coded Jacobite call to arms on the eve of the 1745 rebellion. He pointed out that half-hidden Jacobite imagery, including Scottish thistles and the initials of the Stuart pretenders, often appeared in Wade's musical transcriptions and manuscripts. Twenty years after the defeat of Bonnie Prince Charlie at Culloden, Wade was still writing '*Domine salvum fac Regem nostrum Carolum*' rather than '*Georgium*' for English Catholic congregations to sing.

It seems slightly far-fetched to suggest that '*Adeste, fideles*' was written to alert Jacobite sympathizers in Britain of the impending arrival of the Young Pretender in 1745, although I have to confess that I have myself toyed with this theory in several articles and entitled a BBC Radio 2 programme on the unusual stories behind carols which I made in 1996 'O Come, All Ye Jacobites' on the strength of it! It does seem to be the case, however, that Wade's hymn (if he was, indeed, the author which seems highly likely but is not absolutely certain) was initially largely confined to Roman Catholic circles in Britain and that it was at least if not more popular on the Continent, especially in France. There is a tradition that it was sung for the first time in the Channel Row Dominican Priory, Dublin, shortly after the Jacobite uprising of 1745. A manuscript of the carol dating from 1750 and now in the possession of Stoneyhurst College contains the name of King Joseph of Portugal and was probably used in the English College in Portugal. The carol's popularity in Britain in the late eighteenth century seems to have had much to do with its use in the chapel of the Portuguese Embassy in London where it was regularly sung in the late 1790s and well into the nineteenth century it was known as the 'Portuguese hymn'.

All the early manuscripts apparently written by Wade contain just four verses (the first, second, seventh and eighth of those that appear in the extended version printed on page 32). Verses three, five and six seem to have been added by Abbé Etienne Borderies, who wrote them in his native France in 1794, having come across the hymn during his exile in England in the previous year. His three stanzas, together with the original four, were published in the *Office de S.Omer* in 1822. The fourth verse, presumably added for the Feast of the Epiphany, also appears to be of French origin and is first found in a *Thesaurus Animae Christianae* published in Belgium around 1850. In France, where '*Adeste, fideles*' remains very popular, only verses one, three, four and five are usually sung, with the fifth verse generally coming before the fourth.

'*Adeste, fideles*' has undergone two textual modifications. The 'Jacobite manuscript' contains the phrase '*Venite adorate*' (Come and worship) in the refrain but in Wade's later manuscripts this is replaced by the more liturgically correct '*Venite adoremus*' (O come, let us worship). Stéphan suggested that Wade made this change after objections were raised to his original and more grammatical words by his superiors. The alteration brings the hymn more in line with the refrain of the Christmas matins invitatory, '*Christus natus est nobis/Venite adoremus*' which may well have been the inspiration for the hymn. In later printed versions of the hymn the phrase in verse seven '*Cantent nunc Io*' (which, in Erik Routley's words 'means something very like "let the angelic choir shout Hooray"') is replaced by the more demure '*Cantent nunc hymnos*'.

In his fine book, *The Folk Carol of England*, David Brice writes:

> It is no exaggeration to say that the 'Adeste Fideles' is the most popular Christian song in the whole of our English carol repertory. In the vernacular, it is in every sense a true carol, it has all the ingredients of a carol by which it is distinguished from the hymn, and it is unique in that it was inspired by the stanza-burden form of the Invitatory prayer from Matins of the Divine Office. It was born in the very heart of the liturgy, and in this sense may be called a liturgical carol - if there is such a thing.

Although carol singing had become extinct by the end of the seventeenth century, yet strangely enough, it was precisely at a time of persecution while the Church was in hiding that England produced the carol that more than any other has endeared itself to the hearts of Christians the world over. Without being a folk-song it is an international possession.

There is so much to be said about the tune ADESTE FIDELES, that I will reserve my remarks on it for the note introducing 'O come, all ye faithful' where there is rather less to be said about the words.

Prosa in Nativitate Domini

Adeste, fideles, laeti triumphantes;
Venite, venite in Bethlehem:
Natum videte Regem Angelorum.
Venite adoremus,
Venite adoremus,
Venite adoremus Dominum.

2 Deum de Deo, lumen de lumine,
Gestant puellae viscera,
Deum verum, genitum, non factum.

3 En grege relicto, humiles ad cunas
Vocati pastores approperant:
Et nos ovanti gradu festinemus.

4 Stella duce Magi Christum adorantes
Aurum, thus et myrrham dant munera:
Jesu infanti corda praebeamus.

5 Aeterni Parentis splendorem aeternum
Velatum sub carne videbimus,
Deum infantem pannis involutum.

6 Pro nobis egenum et foeno cubantem
Piis fovaemus amplexibus:
Sic nos amantem quis non redamaret?

7 Cantet nunc Io chorus Angelorum,
Cantet nunc aula caelestium:
Gloria in excelsis Deo.

8 Ergo qui natus die hodierna,
Jesu, tibi sit gloria,
Patris aeterni Verbum caro factum.

6

ALL MY HEART THIS NIGHT REJOICES

Several great Christmas hymns and carols have come out of the German Lutheran tradition. Indeed, an English translation of a Christmas hymn by Martin Luther himself, '*Von Himmel hoch da komm ich*' appears later in this collection (No.21).

'All my heart this night rejoices' is the best-known translation of a hymn by the seventeenth-century Lutheran pastor, Paul Gerhardt, '*Frohlich soll mein Herze springen*', which first appeared in fifteen stanzas in Johann Cruger's *Praxis Pietatis Melica* (1656).

Paul Gerhardt was born at Grafenhainichen, near Wittenberg, in 1607. He served for 15 years as a pastor in Berlin and spent the years from 1669 until his death in 1676 as Archdeacon of Lübben. He wrote a large number of hymns, including '*O Haupt voll Blut und Wunden*' (O Sacred head, surrounded).

John Julian, the Victorian clergyman who edited the first and so far the only dictionary of hymnology, described Gerhardt's hymn as 'a glorious series of Christmas thoughts, laid as a garland on the manger at Bethlehem'. Erik Routley in his book *The English Carol* noted that this is the only familiar carol from the culture of seventeenth-century Protestant pietism 'which came very near the borders of Catholicism in some of its religious habits'. It has a strong devotional streak and a deeply personal quality which contrast with the objective, narrative approach more normally found in Christmas carols.

Several English translations of Gerhardt's verses were made in the mid-nineteenth century. They include 'Let the voice of glad thanksgiving' by A.T. Russell (1848), 'All my heart with joy is springing' by Dr Kennedy (1863) and 'Lightly bound my bosom ringing' by Dr M. Loy (1880). The most successful and enduring, described by Julian as 'a beautiful but rather free translation' was made by Catherine Winkworth.

Catherine Winkworth was the foremost translator of German hymns into English in the nineteenth century. Among her other translations still in common use are 'Praise to the Lord, the Almighty, the King of Creation', 'Now thank we all our God' and 'Christ the Lord is risen again'. Born in London in 1827, she spent most of her life in the vicinity of Manchester where her father was a successful businessman, although she later moved to Clifton, near Bristol, where she took an active interest in women's education. She died suddenly on a visit to the Savoy in 1878.

Her translation ran to ten verses – she omitted stanzas three, four, five, 13 & 14 of Gerhardt's original – and first appeared in the second series of her *Lyra Germanica* in 1858. It is this version which is given below. Set to the fine tune BONN, which had been written in 1666 by Johann Ebeling, a contemporary of Gerhardt, for another hymn, *Warum sollt ich mich denn gramen?,* six of Miss Winkworth's verses (one, four, five, six, nine and ten)were turned into a hymn by the editors of *Church Hymns* (1874).

In modern hymnals this hymn is usually restricted to four verses – one, four, five and ten of the original. In the last verse the opening line has been changed to 'Thee, O Lord, with heed I'll cherish'. The *Presbyterian Hymnal* (the hymnbook of the Presbyterian Church of the USA) turns this into a Christmas morning hymn by changing the first line to 'All my heart today rejoices'. It also updates and de-sexes the third verse to read:

Hark! a voice from yonder manger,
Soft and sweet, does entreat:
'Flee from woe and danger;
Come and see; from all that grieves you
You are freed; all you need
I will surely bring you.'

This hymn has a great sweep to it, beginning in Bethlehem and ending in heaven. The second and third lines of the last verse echo Romans 6.8 and 2 Timothy 2.11 ('If we have died with Christ we shall live with him too').

Christmas – A Song of Joy at Dawn

All my heart this night rejoices,
As I hear, far and near,
Sweetest angel voices:
'Christ is born', their choirs are singing,
Till the air, everywhere,
Now with joy is ringing.

2 Hark! a voice from yonder manger
Soft and sweet, doth entreat,
'Flee from woe and danger!
Brethren, come from all doth grieve you
You are freed; all you need,
I will surely give you.'

3 For it dawns, – the promised morrow Of his birth who the earth Rescues from her sorrow.
God to wear our form descendeth,
Of his grace to our race
Here His Son he lendeth.

4 Come, then, let us hasten yonder!
Here let all, great and small,
Kneel in awe and wonder!
Love Him who with love is yearning:
Hail the star that from far
Bright with hope is burning.

5 Yea, so truly for us careth,
That his Son all we've done
As our offering beareth;
As our Lamb who, dying for us,
Bears our load, and to God
Doth in peace restore us.

6 Ye who pine in weary sadness,
Weep no more, for the door
Now is found of gladness.
Cling to Him, for He will guide you
Where no cross, pain or loss
Can again betide you.

7 Hither come, ye heavy-hearted;
Who for sin deep within,
Long and fore have smarted;
For the poisoned wounds you're feeling
Help is near, One is here
Mighty for their healing!

8 Hither come, ye poor and wretched;
Know His will is to fill
Every hand outstretched;
Here are riches without measure,
Here forget all regret,
Fill your hearts with treasure.

9 Blessed Saviour, let me find Thee!
Keep Thou me close to Thee,
Cast me not behind Thee!
Life of life, my heart Thou stillest,
Calm I rest on Thy breast,
All this void Thou fillest.

10 Heedfully my Lord I'll cherish,
Live to Thee, and with Thee
Dying, shall not perish,
But shall dwell with Thee for ever.
For on high, in the joy
That can alter never.

7

ANGELS FROM THE REALMS OF GLORY

There cannot be many writers of carols who have been imprisoned for their political views. The author of this one, James Montgomery, served two periods in gaol in the 1790s, first for printing a song supporting the storming of the Bastille in the French Revolution and then for his supposedly biased reporting of a reform riot in Sheffield.

Montgomery was born in 1771 in Irvine, Ayrshire, where his father was serving as a Moravian missionary. Five years after his birth the family moved to a Moravian settlement near Ballymeena in County Antrim and at the age of seven he was sent to board at the Moravian seminary at Fulneck in Yorkshire. He spent the rest of his life in Yorkshire, working first in shops in Mirfield and Wath, near Rotherham, and then in newspaper journalism in Sheffield. He took over as editor and publisher of the radical *Sheffield Register* in 1794 when its proprietor fled to France to escape imprisonment over the paper's strong support for the French Revolution. Montgomery edited the paper, whose name he changed to the *Sheffield Iris*, for 31 years. When it was taken over by a rival in 1825, he devoted himself to writing religious verse.

Montgomery moved from Moravianism first to Methodism and eventually to Anglicanism. A prolific hymnwriter, he also revised the work of others – it is his version of John Byrom's 'Christians awake, salute the happy morn' (No. 16) that we sing today. Among his 400 or so hymns are such enduring classics as 'Hail to the Lord's Anointed' and 'Stand up and bless the Lord' (Nos.48 & 116 in the *Daily Telegraph Book of Hymns*).

'Angels from the realms of glory' first appeared in the *Sheffield Iris* on Christmas Eve 1816. It attracted little attention there and it was only when it appeared in 1825 in his collection *The*

Christian Psalmist and as the first of 'Three New Carols for Christmas Day' in *The Christmas Box or New Year's Gift* published by the Religious Tract Society that it began to be sung in churches.

The hymn appears on page 41 as Montgomery wrote it. His last verse was deemed too strong meat by hymnbook editors and did not find its way into any major hymnal. Many books simply print the first four verses but some have followed the editors of *Hymns Ancient and Modern* who for the 1950 revised edition added a new fifth verse taken from another of Montgomery's hymns which appeared in *The Christmas Box*, 'Come, behold the virgin mother':

Though an infant now we view him,
He shall fill his Father's throne,
Gather all the nations to him:
Every knee shall then bow down:

In Britain, 'Angels from the realms of glory' is nowadays almost universally sung to the French carol tune IRIS with its florid sequential 'Gloria'. This particular marriage was effected in 1928 by the editors of the *Oxford Book of Carols*. Before then, Montgomery's hymn was sung to a variety of tunes, including LEWES by John Randall, published c.1774, WILDERSMOUTH or FENITON COURT by Edward Hopkins and Henry Smart's majestic REGENT SQUARE, which is still its most common tune in the United States of America.

The tune now known as IRIS (the name being taken from Montgomery's radical Sheffield journal) belongs to a French carol '*Les anges dans nos compagnes*', said to be 'an old noël from Lorraine' but not found in any printed source before the 1840s. The tune, which may well go back to the eighteenth century, first seems to have appeared in print in England in 1860 when it was attached to a translation of the French carol by James Chadwick (1813–82), Roman Catholic Bishop of Hexham and Newcastle, 'The angels we have heard on high'. A slight modification of Chadwick's translation, 'Angels we have heard on high'. Sung to IRIS has established itself as a popular carol in its own right, especially in the United States. It begins:

Angels we have heard on high,
Sweetly singing o'er the plains
And the mountains in reply,
Echoing their joyous strains.
Gloria in excelsis Deo.
Gloria in excelsis Deo.

There have been several other English translations of '*Les anges dans nos compagnes*' which have achieved a measure of popularity sung to IRIS. One taken up in the West Country begins 'Bright angel hosts are heard on high' and another written in 1910 by G.R. Woodward, beginning 'Shepherds in the field abiding', appeared in *Hymns Ancient and Modern Revised* (1950).

The editors of the *Oxford Book of Carols* seem to have chosen to set 'Angels from the realms of glory' to the tune of the French carol largely because of the coincidental similarity of their opening stanzas. Indeed, they note that Montgomery's hymn 'reads almost like an early nineteenth-century translation of the opening verses of "*Les anges dans nos campagnes*"'. The editors of the *New Oxford Book of Carols* are scathing about this choice of tune and describe their predecessors' substitution of the refrain '*Gloria in excelsis Deo*' from '*Les anges*' for Montgomery's 'Come and worship Christ the new-born King' as 'incongruous'. Incongruous it may be, but it is also understandable: there is certainly no doubt that it is easier to sing 'Gloria' than 'Come and worship' to the great run of notes that IRIS provides for the refrain.

Erik Routley was also uneasy about the use of IRIS for this hymn, writing in *The English Carol*:

Since G.R. Woodward's admirable carol, "Shepherds in the field abiding", which begins with a line borrowed from Montgomery, is available for that tune, and accommodates its Gloria without change, an ordinary hymn tune is probably better for "Angels from the realms of glory"; but having said as much, I am at a loss where to find a hymn tune carol-like enough to do justice to Montgomery, and hymnbook-editors have certainly not come to a mind on this point.

Half a century after those comments were made, IRIS remains firmly embedded as the tune for 'Angels from the realms of glory' and I doubt very much if it can be shifted. REGENT SQUARE fits the text well but has the effect of making it more of a four-square hymn and less of a carol.

A New Carol for Christmas Day

Angels, from the realms of glory,
Wing your flight o'er all the earth;
Ye who sang creation's story,
Now proclaim Messiah's birth:
Come and worship,
Worship Christ, the new-born King.

2 Shepherds, in the field abiding
Watching o'er your flocks by night,
God with man is now residing,
Yonder shines the infant Light:

3 Sages, leave your contemplations:
Brighter visions beam afar:
Seek the great Desire of Nations;
Ye have seen his natal star:

4 Saints before the altar bending,
Watching long in hope and fear,
Suddenly the Lord, descending,
In his temple shall appear:

5 Sinners, wrung with keen repentance,
Doomed for guilt to endless pains;
Justice now repeals the sentence,
Mercy calls you, – break your chains.

8

ARISE AND HAIL THE SACRED DAY!

This item introduces us to the repertoire of gallery carols dating from the period between c.1740 and 1860 when the music in most English country churches and chapels was led by a small band of singers and instrumentalists who were usually installed in a purpose-built gallery at the west end of the church.

West Gallery musicians, who were usually drawn from the ranks of certain families of artisans and tradesmen, were a law unto themselves and operated in almost complete independence of the clergy. Congregations turned to face the west gallery for the singing of psalms but often did not get much chance to sing unless they could fathom the complex fuguing style with its repetitive entries and orchestral 'symphonies' favoured by the gallery musicians who doubled as the village band and moved easily from sacred to secular tunes.

The novelist Thomas Hardy, whose father and grandfather both played the bass viol in gallery bands in Dorset country churches, wrote several eloquent laments for the passing of the west gallery tradition when it was swept away in the mid-nineteenth century by Tractarian clergymen anxious to bring more order and decorum to worship. His novel *Under the Greenwood Tree* tells of a High Church clergyman determined to replace the artisan fiddlers by a choir sited in the nave and clad in surplices accompanied by a demure schoolmistress on the organ.

This particular carol is one of those mentioned in the novel as being sung by the Mellstock Choir on Christmas Eve. As the four men and seven boys prepare to set off round the farms, old William Dewey, the bass player, issues a word of warning about sticking to the right parts:

'You two counter boys, keep your ears open to Michael's fingering, and don't ye go straying into the treble part along o'

Dick and his set, as ye did last year; and mind this especially when we be in "Arise and hail".'

'Arise and hail' seems first to have appeared in print in *The Gentleman's Magazine* of November 1748 where it is described as 'a hymn for Christmas Day, the words by Mr Oats, set to music by Mr.T. Wright, both of Devonshire'. It is this version which I reproduce on page 45. According to Julian's *Dictionary of Hymnology*, it subsequently appeared in the Liverpool Liturgy of 1763, in a Bristol Baptist collection of 1769 and in a three-part version in Joseph Stephenson's *The Musical Companion*, published in Poole, Dorset, in 1775. 'Arise and hail' was taken up in a number of late nineteenth-century revivalist hymnbooks, notably Hall & Lasar's *Evangelical Hymnal* of 1880, where it was given a chorus 'O then let heaven and earth rejoice'. It does not appear in any contemporary hymn-book that I have come across although it is to be found in *The Book of Christmas Carols* published in 1996 by Aurora Publishing of Bolton. Here, as in most other surviving versions of the carol, the first verse has 'earthly things' instead of 'meaner things' in line three and refers to 'our' rather than 'thy' woes in line four.

Shorter versions are found in three of the four West Gallery carol books collected and preserved by the Hardy family and now housed in the Dorset County Museum in Dorchester. The most complete appears to have been copied down after 1845, when the gallery bands at Stinsford and Puddletown had been disbanded, and the tradition of Christmas Eve carolling had also ceased. Its inclusion as 'Christmas piece' in collections which are otherwise largely made up of songs and dances suggests that it was sung domestically in the Hardy household during the Christmas season.

The first verse in the Hardy carol books is similar to that in the *Gentleman's Magazine*, except for the changes noted above. The second and third verses, however, show substantial differences:

If angels on that sacred morn
Our Saviour, Jesus Christ, was born
Poured forth their seraph's songs

How should a people, then, on earth,
Triumph in honour of his birth
To whom all praise belongs?

Then let us with the angels join
And praise the glorious power divine
With hallelujah high,
With endless thanks to God above
In showing forth his boundless love
To all eternity!

The above version of the carol, with the tune that accompanies it in the Dorest books, appears in the *New Oxford Book of Carols*. It has been recorded as a duet with fiddle accompaniment on compact disc (SAYDISC CD-SDL 360, 1986) by the Mellstock Band, one of the groups which have done so much to revive West Gallery music. In the recording, the last line of the second verse is sung as 'The praise to him belongs'.

A hymn for Christmas Day

Arise, and hail the sacred day!
Cast all low cares of life away,
And thought of meaner things;
This day, to cure thy deadly woes,
The Sun of Righteousness arose
With healing in his wings.

2 If Angels on that happy morn
The Saviour of the world was born,
Poured forth seraphic songs;
Much more should we of human race
Adore the wonders of His grace,
To whom that grace belongs.

3 How wonderful, how vast His love,
Who left the shining realms above,
Those happy seats of rest;
How much for lost mankind He bore,
Their peace and pardon to restore,
Can never be expressed.

4 While we adore His boundless grace,
And pious joy and mirth take place
Of sorrow, grief, and pain,
Give glory to our God on high,
And not among the general joy
Forget good-will to men.

5 O then let Heaven and earth rejoice,
Creation's whole united voice,
And hymn the Sacred Day,
When sin and Satan vanquished fell,
And all the powers of death and hell,
Before his sovereign sway.

9

AS WITH GLADNESS MEN OF OLD

Strictly speaking, this is not a Christmas carol at all but a hymn about the wise men's visit to see the baby Jesus which properly belongs to the season of Epiphany. In the popular mind at least, however, Christmas and Epiphany have become conflated, and it seems entirely appropriate to include this item in a book devoted to Christmas hymns and carols. In his book *The English Carol*, Erik Routley describes 'As with gladness' as one of two Epiphany hymns 'so closely associated with the Christmas season that they are almost thought of as carols'. The other is Reginald Heber's 'Brightest and best are the sons of the morning' (No. 13).

'As with gladness' is the work of William Chatterton Dix who was born in 1837 in Bristol where his father was a surgeon. Educated at Bristol Grammar School, he pursued a mercantile career and became manager of a marine insurance company in Glasgow. He retired back to Bristol and died there in 1898. Dix wrote a large number of hymns, including 'Alleluia! sing to Jesus', 'Come unto me, ye weary' and the harvest hymn 'To thee, O Lord, our hearts we raise'.

'As with gladness' was written in 1860 while Dix was ill and first published the following year in a small collection of his work, *Hymns of Joy and Love*, which he circulated privately. Its popularity really became assured when it was chosen for inclusion in the first edition of *Hymns Ancient and Modern* (1861). It subsequently found its way into nearly every major denominational hymnbook and was commended in a lecture on English Church Hymnody in 1866 by Lord Selborne, a distinguished hymnologist and future Lord Chancellor, as 'a work so admirable in every respect'.

The version which appears here is that printed in the 1875 edition of *Hymns Ancient and Modern* and subsequently adopted in all other hymnals. In Dix's original 1860 version the second line of verse two read 'To that lowly manger-bed', the fourth line of the same verse began 'Him Whom' and the second line of verse three 'At that manger'. The changes were made to make the hymn more Scripturally accurate, reflecting the fact that the Gospel story on which the hymn is based (Matthew 2:9-11) records the wise men coming to a house rather than a manger. Dix approved the changes and desired that they should be permanently incorporated.

The tune universally associated with this hymn is derived from a chorale melody by Conrad Kocher, who was organist of the Stiftskirche in Stuttgart from 1827 to 1865. It originally appeared in his *Stimmen aus dem reiche Gottes* (1838) set to the hymn *'Treuer Heiland, wir sind hir'*. The music editor of *Hymns Ancient and Modern*, W.H. Monk, chose this melody to accompany 'As with gladness' in the first edition and harmonized and arranged it to fit the hymn. The tune is called DIX despite the fact that Dix himself apparently never liked it.

As with gladness men of old
Did the guiding star behold,
As with joy they hailed its light,
Leading onward, beaming bright;
So, most gracious Lord, may we
Evermore be led to thee.

2 As with joyful steps they sped,
Saviour, to thy lowly bed,
There to bend the knee before
Thee whom heaven and earth adore;
So may we with willing feet
Ever seek thy mercy-seat.

3 As they offered gifts most rare
At thy cradle rude and bare,
So may we with holy joy,
Pure and free from sin's alloy,
All our costliest treasures bring,
Christ, to thee our heavenly King.

4 Holy Jesus, every day
Keep us in the narrow way,
And, when earthly things are past,
Bring our ransomed souls at last
Where they need no star to guide,
Where no clouds they glory hide.

5 In the heavenly country bright
Need they no created light;
Thou its light, its joy, its crown,
Thou, its sun which goes not down;
There for ever may we sing
Alleluias to our King.

10

AWAY IN A MANGER

This is undoubtedly one of the most popular of all Christmas hymns and carols. It came ninth in the 2005 BBC *Songs of Praise* poll, while a survey in the run-up to Christmas in 1996 found that it occupied joint second place with 'O come, all ye faithful' in the nation's list of Top Ten carols. It also must be said that it is one of the most unScriptural – there is no mention in any of the Gospels of cattle (nor, indeed, of any other animals) being present at Jesus' birth and there is certainly no suggestion that Jesus did not cry as a baby. That assertion seems to belong to heresies such as Apollinarianism and Gnosticism which denied that Jesus was fully human.

Although it has been kept out of successive editions of several hymn-books, including *Hymns Ancient and Modern* and *The English Hymnal*, 'Away in a manger' remains a firm favourite amidst all the best efforts of New Testament scholars and theologians to demythologize the Christmas story. So it should. Its sentiments, while simple, are admirable and it expresses an altogether childish (in the best sense of the word) prayer for Jesus to stay by us. A more serious assault may come from the devotees of political correctness and multiculturalism. A report in the *Observer* in December 1991 reported under the headline 'Away with the manger, no crib is correct' that 'children in Bradford may have sung the traditional version of "Away in a manger" for the last time. Religious education advisers have asked schools to consider changing the words of Christmas carols to make them acceptable to non-Christian pupils.' Other carols on the list to be de-Christianized included 'Silent Night', 'Once in Royal David's City' and 'Hark! the Herald Angels Sing' although 'Jingle Bells' was given a clean bill of health.

At least if 'Away in a manger' is sanitized into oblivion, no author's posthumous reputation will suffer as a result. Some older books used to suggest that Martin Luther was the author but there is no evidence to support this attribution. The hymn's authorship is unknown but it almost certainly comes from late nineteenth-century America. The first two verses first appeared anonymously in the *Little Children's Book for Schools and Families* published in Philadelphia in 1885 and the third in a collection of *Vineyard Songs* published in 1892.

'Away in a manger' has been set to more than forty tunes in hymn and song books. In Britain the most popular tune is undoubtedly CRADLE SONG by the American Gospel song writer W.J. Kirkpatrick (1838-1921). A carpenter from Philadelphia, he became musical director of Grace Church in that city and compiled 87 books of Gospel songs. His other enduring tune is that for Priscilla Owens' 'Will your anchor hold'. In the United States a number of other tunes are still in regular use, notably perhaps James Murray's MUELLER, written in 1887, and found in both the 1989 *United Methodist Hymnal* and the 1990 *Presbyterian Hymnal.*

Away in a manger, no crib for a bed,
The little Lord Jesus laid down his sweet head.
The stars in the bright sky looked down where he lay,
The little Lord Jesus asleep on the hay.

2 The cattle are lowing, the Baby awakes,
But little Lord Jesus no crying he makes
I love thee, Lord Jesus! look down from the sky,
And stay by my side until morning is nigh.

3 Be near me, Lord Jesus; I ask thee to stay
Close by me for ever, and love me, I pray.
Bless all the dear children in thy tender care,
And fit us for heaven, to live with thee there.

11

BEHOLD, THE GREAT CREATOR MAKES

This is one of a number of very fine poems written in the seventeenth century which were turned into congregational hymns by the editors of the *English Hymnal* of 1906. Others include George Herbert's 'Teach me my God and King' and John Bunyan's 'Who would true valour see'(*Daily Telegraph Book of Hymns* Nos. 120 & 146).

'Behold, the great Creator makes' was the work of Thomas Pestel (c.1584–1659), an Anglican clergyman who served as chaplain to Charles I and was incumbent of Packington, near Ashby-de-la Zouch in Leicestershire. In 1644 he resigned his living and was succeeded by his son, alnother Thomas. Both men fell foul of the Puritans and Thomas junior was ejected from his living by the Westminster Assembly in 1646 for using illegal ceremonies in church.

Educated at Queen's College, Cambridge, Pestel was a noted minor poet. The verses which make up this carol first appeared in a longer poem entitled 'A Psalm for Christmas Day Morning' in his *Sermons and Devotions Old and New* (1659). It began somewhat unpromisingly:

Fairest of morning light, appear,
Thou blest and gaudy day,
On which was born our Saviour dear;
Arise, and come away!

The early stanzas continued in similarly pedestrian fashion but at the fifth verse the poem took off and became much more original and striking in its imagery. The Christmas hymn which first appeared in *The English Hymnal* and has subsequently been taken up in several denominational hymnbooks is made up of verses five to nine of the original.

Erik Routley, who acknowledges the 'unusual and vivid beauty' of the verses chosen by the editors of the *English Hymnal*, comments in his book on *The English Carol* that Pestel is 'undecided whether he is writing a psalm-like paraphrase of conventional piety, or whether he is writing an imaginative lyric'. Routley also accuses Pestel of penning two phrases which could be taken as being theologically unsound: 'Which he will wear for aye' (the last line of the last verse) suggests the Apollinarian heresy to certain sensitive souls, and 'God in cradle lies' the patripassian heresy to others.

There is, I think, little justice in either of these charges. The notion that God eternally takes the robe of virgin flesh (which does not conform with my understanding of Apollinarianism but I will spare readers a disquisition into fourth-century Christological controversies) seems perfectly consistent with the doctrine of the pre-existence and continuing presence of Christ in the Godhead. The picture of God lying in a cradle squares with the notion of divine kenosis, or self-emptying, expressed in Philippians 2.7 and taken up in the hymn 'Thou didst leave thy throne' (no.87 in this collection). With its arresting opening couplet about God making himself a house of clay, 'Behold, the great Creator makes' does seem to me to be one of the most strongly Incarnational (and therefore 'Christmasy' in the real sense) of all carols.

The modern-language *Carols for Today* produced by the Jubilate Hymns group in 1985 updates lines 3-4 of verse 1 to 'A robe of human form he takes/For ever from this day' and changes the second verse to:

Hear this! the wise eternal Word
As Mary's infant cries
A servant is our mighty Lord,
And God in cradle lies.

Ralph Vaughan Williams, the distinguished music editor of *The English Hymnal* set 'Behold the great Creator makes' to the tune of a fifteenth-century carol, 'This endris nyght'. I have not included that carol in this book. It has numerous variants - different versions can be found in the *Oxford Book of Carols*, the *University Carol Book* and the *Galliard Book of Carols*. It generally begins as follows:

This endris night I saw a sight,
A star as bright as day,
And ever among a maiden sang;
'Lullay, by by, lullay'.

Other modern hymnal editors have set 'Behold, the great Creator makes' to the tune KILMARNOCK, written around 1830 by Neil Dougall, a singing teacher based in the Clyde port of Greenock.

Psalm for Christmas Day

Behold, the great Creator makes
Himself a house of clay,
A robe of virgin flesh he takes
Which he will wear for aye.

2 Hark, hark! the wise eternal Word
Like a weak infant cries;
In form of servant is the Lord,
And God in cradle lies.

3 This wonder struck the world amazed,
It shook the starry frame;
Squadrons of spirits stood and gazed,
Then down in troops they came.

4 Glad shepherds ran to view this sight;
A choir of angels sings,
And eastern sages with delight
Adore this King of Kings.

5 Join then, all hearts that are not stone,
And all our voices prove,
To celebrate this Holy One,
The God of peace and love.

12

BETHLEHEM, OF NOBLEST CITIES

This is another hymn which properly belongs to the season of Epiphany rather than that of Christmas. It is a translation of part of a long Latin poem by Aurelius Clemens Prudentius (348–c.413).

One of the most prolific early Christian poets, Prudentius was born in northern Spain and trained as a lawyer. At the age of 57, after serving in the Roman Imperial Court, he felt the call of the cloister and entered a monastery. Among the books of hymns which he wrote as a monk was the *Liber Cathemerinon* which provided hymns for the twelve hours of the day. The last hymn in this collection, which ran to 208 lines, began '*Quicumque Christum quaeritis*' and dealt with the Transfiguration, the Epiphany and the massacre of the Holy Innocents. Found in a fifth-century manuscript in the *Bibliotheque Nationale* in Paris, it was taken up for liturgical use in the Roman Catholic Church when the Roman Breviary was revised after the Council of Trent in the mid-sixteenth century. A section of the poem beginning with the words '*O sola magnarum urbium*' was prescribed to be sung at the service of Lauds during Epiphany:

O sola magnarum urbium
Major Bethlem, cui contigit
Ducem salutis caelitus
Incorporatum gignere.

In the aftermath of the Oxford Movement in the mid-nineteenth century when the Church of England was recovering many of the early Latin and Greek poems of the early and medieval church for liturgical use, a number of English translations were made of this section of Prudentius' poem to make an Epiphany hymn. The translation which appears on page 59, and is the basis for the versions found in modern hymnbooks, was made by Edward Caswall for his *Lyra Catholica* in 1849. Other translations made around the same time include W.J. Copeland's 'That mightiest cities mightier far' (1848), W.J. Blew's 'Fair queen of cities, star of earth' (1852) and R.C. Ingleton's 'Of noblest cities thou art queen' (1868). Altogether Julian cites 13 translations of Prudentius' Epiphany hymn from this period but only Caswall's proved enduring.

Caswall was a classic product of the Oxford Movement. Born in 1814 in Yately, Hampshire, where his father was vicar, he fell under the spell of John Henry Newman and the Tractarians while an undergraduate at Brasenose College, Oxford. In 1840 he became perpetual curate of Straford-sub-Castle, Wiltshire, but seven years later he resigned his living and was received into the Roman Catholic church. After the death of his wife in 1850 he became a priest, spending the next 28 years in the Oratory of St Philip Neri at Edgbaston which had been founded by Newman. Among other translations which he made of ancient Latin hymns in the Roman Breviaries are 'At the Cross, her station keeping', 'Jesus, the very thought of Thee', 'My God, I love Thee, not because' and 'When morning gilds the skies'.

Some modern hymn-books have hardly altered Caswall's verses. They include the *Celebration Hymnal* (1978) used in many Roman Catholic churches and the *New English Hymnal* (1986) favoured in High Anglican circles. Both these books print the first three verses exactly as he wrote them although in the first line of the fourth 'Solemn things' is substituted for 'Offerings' and in the last verse of the fifth 'praise eterne' is replaced by 'endless praise'.

In most other modern hymnals, the third and fourth lines of verse two are rendered 'To the world its God announcing/Seen in fleshly form on earth' which gives a rather different sense. The 'lambent beauty' has also disappeared with verse three being generally recast to:

Eastern sages at his cradle,
Make oblations rich and rare;
See them give, in deep devotion
Gold and frankincense and myrrh.

The fourth verse is usually rendered:

Sacred gifts of mystic meaning:
Incense doth their God disclose,
Gold the King of kings proclaimeth,
Myrrh his sepulchre foreshows.

The compilers of the first edition of *Hymns Ancient and Modern* changed the first verse of Caswall's hymn to:

Earth has many a noble city;
Bethl'em, thou dost all excel:
Out of thee the Lord from heaven
Came to rule his Israel.

This remains the first stanza of the hymn in the current New Standard edition of *Hymns Ancient and Modern* (1984) which also retains an altered final verse introduced by the compilers of the first edition which serves to underline the hymn's Epiphany associations:

Jesu, whom the Gentiles worshipped
At thy glad Epiphany,
Unto thee with God the Father
And the Spirit glory be.

There are several other textual variants to be found in hymn-books but I suspect that patient and even obsessive readers have had enough of them. It is something of a relief to turn to the tune, STUTTGART, which has remained a constant companion since it was first coupled to this hymn by the compilers of the first edition of *Hymns Ancient and Modern* in 1861. It is based on a melody which first appeared in a Lutheran collection published in Gotha in 1715 accompanying the hymn *'Sollt' es gleich bisweilen scheinen*' and is thought to have been the work of Christian Friedrich Witt (c.1660-1716), Kapellmeister at Gotha.

O sola magnarum urbium

Bethlehem, of noblest cities
None can once with thee compare;
Thou alone the Lord from heaven
Didst for us incarnate bear

2 Fairer than the sun at morning
Was the star that told his birth;
To the lands their God announcing
Hid beneath a form of earth.

3 By its lambent beauty guided,
See the eastern kings appear;
See them bend, their gifts to offer-
Gifts of incense, gold and myrrh.

4 Offerings of mystic meaning:
Incense doth their God disclose,
Gold a royal child proclaimeth,
Myrrh a future tomb foreshows.

5 Holy Jesu, in thy brightness
To the Gentile world displayed,
With the Father and the Spirit
Praise eterne to thee be paid. Amen.

13

BRIGHTEST AND BEST ARE THE SONS OF THE MORNING

I have generally avoided including in this collection items which are already to be found in the *Daily Telegraph Book of Hymns*. This explains the absence from this volume, for example, of four Advent hymns, which are regularly sung in churches in the run-up to Christmas, 'O come, o come, Emmanuel', 'On Jordan's bank the Baptist's cry', 'Hark the glad sound', 'Wake, O wake! with tidings thrilling' and also of Charles Wesley's magnificent 'Lo, he comes with clouds descending', which although found in the Advent sections of many hymnbooks, is really about Christ's second coming.

There are, however, two items in this collection which also appear in the *Daily Telegraph Book of Hymns.* They are 'From heaven you came, helpless babe' (No.22) and this one, 'Brightest and best are the sons of the morning'. It is here because Epiphany hymns (of which there are no others in the *Daily Telegraph Book of Hymns*) have come, rightly or wrongly (and probably rightly) to find their way into the Christmas sections of many hymn-books and one could argue that no collection of Christmas hymns and carols is complete without this one. The great twentieth-century hymnologist, Erik Routley, in fact saw 'Brightest and best' as being more of a carol than a hymn. Commenting on the controversy which it generated over whether it incites star worship, he wrote:

> Perhaps the truth is, though he hardly knew or intended it, that Heber was writing a carol. The carols are not afraid of astrology. But in the end it is a matter of values. To Heber the delicate adjective and the smooth rhythm were of more value than the hard-wearing commonplace and the aptly-inserted Biblical tag, and the result is a precious devotional

lyric, even if by the standards of Wesley's style or Calvin's theology it hardly reaches the dignity of being a true hymn.

'Brightest and best' was the first hymn written by Reginald Heber (1783–1826), who was one of the first hymn writers in the Church of England. Born into an aristocratic family in the village of Malpas on the Cheshire-Shropshire border where his father was rector, he was educated at Whitchurch Grammar School and privately in Neasden, North London. He went on to Brasenose College, Oxford where he won the University prize for Latin verse three years running. He was elected to a fellowship at All Souls College and after an extensive Grand Tour of Europe became rector of Hodnet in Shropshire.

Heber spent sixteen years as a parish priest and it was during this period that he wrote most of his 57 hymns, which include such favourites as 'Holy, Holy, Holy, Lord God Almighty'. He wrote a hymn for nearly every Sunday and for each solemn day and feast day in the Church of England calendar. 'Brightest and best' was written for the Feast of the Epiphany. It was published in 1811 in the *Christian Observer*, a journal associated with the Evangelical wing of the Church of England. Heber tried to get a book containing hymns written by himself and others authorized for use in the Church of England but he was refused permission by both the Bishop of London and the Archbishop of Canterbury. It was only in 1827, a year after his death, that his widow was given permission to publish his *Hymns written and adapted to the weekly Church Service*.

The phrase 'sons of the morning' which Heber uses to such spectacular effect in the first line of this hymn has its origins in Isaiah 14.12 where it is used in the singular to describe Lucifer. Perhaps because of their unease about this association, the editors of the *Presbyterian Hymnal* produced for use in the Presbyterian Church of the United States of America in 1990 changed the opening line to 'Brightest and best are the stars of the morning'. Their alteration makes more explicit another Biblical allusion, which was almost certainly in Heber's mind, the reference in Job 38.7: 'When the morning stars sang together, and all the sons of

God shouted for joy'. Several hymnal editors have refused to include the hymn on the grounds that it seems to be addressed to the 'Star of the East' referred to in the third line of the first verse and therefore encourages star worship. Edom, referred to in the second line of verse three, was the mountainous land to the south of Moab, stretching down to the Gulf of Aqaba on the Red Sea. It has been suggested that its odours referred to here were those of frankincense.

'Brightest and best', which originally seems to have been sung to an old Scottish ballad tune WANDERING WILLIE, has been set to a bewildering variety of different tunes in British hymn-books. Those of us responsible for the fourth edition of the *Church Hymnary* plumped for WAS LEBET, WAS SCHWEBET, a German melody first found in a manuscript in Uttingen in 1754 to which it goes particularly well, with EPIPHANY by Joseph Francis Thrupp (1827–67), vicar of Barrington, Cambridge, as an alternative tune. EPIPHANY is the preferred choice of the compilers of *Baptist Hymns and Worship* (1991) and the excellent *Hymns and Prayers for Dragons* produced for use at the Dragon School, Oxford. It also appears in the United Reformed Church's *Rejoice and Sing* (1991). It first appeared in Thrupp's *Psalms and Hymns*, published in 1863, and is sometimes called EPIPHANY HYMN (as, for example, in Jubilate Hymns' *Carols For Today*), possibly to distinguish it from another tune called EPIPHANY by E.J. Hopkins (1818–1901) to which Heber's hymn has also been sung. *Hymns Ancient and Modern* favours BEDE, adapted from an aria in Handel's *Athalaih* of 1733 by Sir John Goss (1800–1880). The Methodist *Hymns and Psalms* offers JESMIAN written by George Thalben Ball (1896–1987) for the 1951 *BBC Hymn Book* (this is also in *Rejoice and Sing*) and SPEAN written by John Frederick Bridge (1844–1924) for *The Quiver* magazine in 1878 and named after the Scottish river where he enjoyed fishing. This last tune has long been popular with Methodists. On the evidence of the *Church Hymnal*, Irish Anglicans like ST NINIAN by John Bacchus Dykes (1823–76) or LIEBSTER EMMANUEL, a harmonization by J.S. Bach of a German melody first published in 1679.

Brightest and best of the sons of the morning,
Dawn on our darkness, and lend us thine aid;
Star of the east, the horizon adorning,
Guide where our infant Redeemer is laid.

2 Cold on his cradle the dew drops are shining;
Low lies his head with the beasts of the stall;
Angels adore him in slumber reclining,
Maker and Monarch and Saviour of all.

3 Say, shall we yield him, in costly devotion,
Odours of Edom, and offerings divine,
Gems of the mountains and pearls of the ocean,
Myrrh from the forest or gold from the mine?

4 Vainly we offer each ample oblation,
Vainly with gifts would his favour secure;
Richer by far is the heart's adoration;
Dearer to God are the prayers of the poor.

14

CHILD IN THE MANGER

This deservedly popular carol belongs in origin to the Gaelic bardic tradition of the Western Highlands and islands of Scotland. Its fresh lyrical style, at once so simple and yet so richly poetic, exemplifies the distinctive spirituality of the Celtic Christian tradition which has been so widely rediscovered and taken up in recent years.

The Gaelic verses on which it is based were written by Mary MacDonald, née MacDougall (1817–90) who spent all her life in a small corner of the island of Mull. She was born at Ardtun, near Bunessan, in the south-west corner of the island known as the Ross of Mull and married Neill MacDonald, a crofter from nearby Knockan. Like others of her family, Mary, who had no English education, was a noted Gaelic poet and wrote several hymns and songs which she sang as she sat at her spinning wheel. A strong Baptist, she also wrote a satirical poem on the evils of tobacco, of which she thought her husband smoked too much.

Mary MacDonald entitled her Nativity hymn '*Leanabh an aigh*', or 'The Child of Aigh', *aigh* being a Gaelic word which means happiness, good fortune, power and wonder. While serving as a locum minister on the tiny Hebridean island of Berneray in the winter of 1995, I had the pleasure and privilege of learning it in Gaelic with the children of the 12-strong primary school.

In the mid-1880s part of '*Leanabh an aigh*' was translated into English by Lachlan Macbean (1853–1931), a Highland-born journalist who edited the *Fifeshire Advertiser* and was a considerable Gaelic scholar. He included it in his book *Songs and Hymns of the Gael*, which was first published in 1888. There the hymn ran to four verses with the following stanza coming between the first and second verses of the version printed below:

Monarchs have tender
Delicate children,
Nourished in splendour,
Proud and gay;
Death soon shall banish
Honour and beauty,
Pleasure shall vanish,
Forms decay.

The next verse then began 'But the most holy', providing a contrast and pointing a moral which is lost in the shorter version of the hymn which has, understandably, found its way into so many hymnbooks.

In his *Songs and Hymns of the Gael* Macbean set 'Child in the manger' to the tune BUNESSAN to which it has been sung ever since and which must surely account for a good part of its popularity. It was noted down by Alexander Fraser from the singing of a wandering Highland singer in the 1880s. In the 1920s it was given a new lease of life when Percy Dearmer, preparing his new hymnbook *Songs of Praise*, suggested to Eleanor Farjeon that she might like to write a hymn of thanksgiving for each new day to fit the tune. The result was 'Morning has Broken', which first appeared in *Songs of Praise* in 1931 and went on to spend several weeks in the Top Ten in both Britain and the United States in the early 1970s thanks to a recording by Cat Stevens (see *The Daily Telegraph Book of Hymns*, No.86).

Leanabh an aigh

Child in the manger,
Infant of Mary,
Outcast and stranger,
Lord of all!
Child who inherits
All our transgressions,
All our demerits,
On him fall.

2 Once the most holy
Child of salvation
Gentle and Lowly
Lived below;
Now as our glorious
Mighty Redeemer,
See him victorious
O'er each foe.

3 Prophets foretold him,
Infant of wonder;
Angels behold him
On his throne;
Worthy our Saviour
Of all our praises;
Happy for ever
Are his own.

15

CHILD OF THE STABLE'S SECRET BIRTH

For more than thirty years, Timothy Dudley-Smith (for biographical details on whom see introduction to 'A song was heard at Christmas', No. 2) has written a poem to go on his family Christmas card. 'Child of the stable's secret birth' first appeared on the Dudley-Smiths' 1969 Christmas card, having been written as early as February that year in his study in the family home at Sevenoaks in Kent.

The text, which also appeared in *Crusade* magazine in 1969, was noticed by Christopher Dearnley, organist of St Paul's Cathedral, who set it to his arrangement of the old Cornish tune MORWENSTOW for the choir to sing. The words set to this tune were published in *English Praise* in 1975 and a recording was made in the same year by the St Paul's Choir. Dudley-Smith has confessed that had he known his verses were going to be sung, he might have tidied up the metrical consistency of the verses. As it is, 'Child of the stable's secret birth' has become one of his most popular carols, being included in *The New English Hymnal*, *Hymns for Today's Church*, where it is set to MORWENSTOW and a tune specially written for it by Norman Warren, SECRET BIRTH, and the Methodist collection, *Hymns and Psalms*, where it is set to MORWENSTOW and another specially composed tune, FOWE, written in 1981 by Valerie Ruddle (also of Sevenoaks) in an attempt to draw out the warmth and tenderness of the words.

Like 'A song was heard at Christmas', this carol has the merit of not just treating the theme of Incarnation but also introducing the Passion, victory and Judgement of Christ. The editors of the *Companion to Hymns and Psalms* have identified the following Biblical references in the text:

Verse 1, line 4: Matthew 27.29
Verse 2, lines 5-6: Revelation 20.11
Verse 3, line 3: Matthew 8.26–7
Verse 4, line 2: Luke 2.18–19
Verse 5, line 3: Mark 14.36

Timothy Dudley-Smith has written: 'My MS shows that verse 2 was written first, and indeed contains the original "vision" of the text. The words *drive, pierce, sink, thrust* were tried and discarded in favour of *strike* in verse 4.' The imagery in verse four is similar to that used later by Graham Kendrick in the third verse of 'From heaven you came, helpless babe' (No.22 in this collection).

'Child of the stable's secret birth' almost brought the 1987 Epiphany Carol Service at Walsingham Parish Church to a standstill. The vicar, John Barnes, who subsequently became a Roman Catholic priest, wrote to Timothy Dudley-Smith afterwards:

> The Choir sang 'Child of the stable's secret birth', which I had not heard before, and I found the words so moving that I was literally reduced to tears, and only pulled myself together in time to read the lesson allotted to me!

Child of the stable's secret birth,
The lord by right of the lords of earth;
Let angels sing of a king new-born –
The world is weaving a crown of thorn:
A crown of thorn for that infant head
Cradled soft in the manger bed.

2 Eyes that shine in the lantern's ray;
A face so small in its nest of hay –
Face of a child who is born to scan
The world he made, through the eyes of man:
And from that face in the final day
Earth and heaven shall flee away.

3 Voice that rang through the courts on high
Contracted now to a wordless cry,
A voice to master the wind and wave,
The human heart and hungry grave:
The voice of God through the cedar trees
Rolling forth as the sound of seas.

4 Infant hands in a mother's hand,
For none but Mary may understand
Whose are the hands and the fingers curled
But his who fashioned and made our world;
And through these hands in the hour of death
Nails shall strike to the wood beneath.

5 Child of the stable's secret birth,
The Father's gift to a wayward earth,
To drain the cup in a few short years
Of all our sorrows, our sins and tears –
Ours the prize for the road he trod
Risen with Christ; at peace with God.

16

CHRISTIANS, AWAKE! SALUTE THE HAPPY MORN

I am printing this fine Christmas morning hymn, which came fifteenth in the 2005 BBC *Songs of Praise* poll, not as it is found in hymn-books and carol sheets (i.e. in up to six stanzas of six lines each) but as it was originally written by John Byrom in 1749 as a Christmas present for his daughter (i.e. as a 52-line poem divided into three sections).

Despite, or perhaps because of his solidly bourgeois origins as the son of a Manchester merchant, John Byrom (1691–1763) was a romantic and eclectic figure with a mystical bent. Educated at Merchant Taylors' School and Trinity College, Cambridge, he studied medicine at Montpellier but never practised as a doctor and instead supported himself by teaching a system of shorthand of his own invention until a substantial legacy inherited by his wife enabled him to concentrate on a literary life.

Like John Wade, the author of *Adeste, fideles* (No. 5), Byrom had strong Jacobite sympathies and penned this jaunty and cryptic verse:

God bless the King, I mean the Faith's Defender;
God bless – no Harm in blessing – the Pretender;
But who pretender is, or who is king,
God bless us all – that's quite another thing.

Byrom's prolific poetic output includes another hymn which is still found in many hymn-books, 'My spirit longs for Thee'. He wrote 'Christians, awake' for his 11-year-old daughter, Dolly, who had told him that more than anything else she would like a poem for Christmas. Ah, to have been a parent in those far-off days before the advent of Barbie dolls and Power Rangers!

History does not record whether she received any additional present but we do know that when she came down to breakfast on Christmas Day 1749 there was a piece of paper on her plate with these verses on it, inscribed at the top 'Christmas Day – for Dolly'. The original manuscript is preserved in Cheetham's Library, Manchester.

Byrom's verses were set to music by John Wainwright (1723–68), organist of Manchester Parish Church. It is said that on Christmas Eve 1750 a group of singers led by Wainwright visited Stockport, where the Byroms lived, and at the stroke of midnight started up 'Christians, awake' outside the author's house. This seems to have been its first performance as a hymn. There is a further story that it was also sung later that morning at Stockport parish church. Wainwright's tune was first published around 1760 when it was set to a metrical version of Psalm 50 and given the name MORTRAM, probably a misprint for Mottram, a place near Stockport. In 1766 Wainwright printed it together with Byrom's words in his *Collection of Psalm Tunes, Anthems, Hymns and Chants*. When the tune re-appeared in Ralph Harrison's *Sacred Harmony* in 1784, it was given the appropriate name STOCKPORT although for some reason it later got changed to YORKSHIRE and appears under this title in several modern hymn-books. 'Christians awake' has, in fact, long had pride of place in the distinctive repertoire of carols sung in south Yorkshire villages and it is still sung there as Christmas Eve gives way to Christmas Day. A stirring rendering of the hymn, which is known locally as 'Old Christians', recorded at a festival of village carols held at Grenoside Community Centre near Sheffield in December 1994 is included on the compact disc 'A Festival of Village Carols' (VCF101, produced by Village Carols, Bridge House, Unstone, Sheffield, S18 5AF). In keeping with a tradition that may go back to Wainwright's time, the singers repeat the last line of each verse, a practice commended in several old tune books and still maintained in other parts of Yorkshire and Lancashire.

It is unclear how much of Byrom's original poem was sung by Wainwright and his waits at its first Stockport performance. The tune fits six line verses and some adjustment must have been made, either by dropping lines from the poem or repeating lines of the tune. Byrom himself made several alterations to the poem, possibly soon after the 1750 performance and a revised version appeared in a Manchester newspaper in December 1752. In his *Miscellaneous Poems*, published posthumously in 1773, it ran to only 48 lines and was printed in two sections to make a narrative and response, the division coming at the line 'Let us like these good Shepherds then employ'. This shortening was effected by excising the passage:

Joseph and Mary a distressed pair
Guard the sole object of the Almighty's Care;
To human eyes none present but they two
Where heaven was pointing its concentrated View.

Byrom also tidied up the poem by changing the last two lines of the first part of his original to read:

Wrapped up in swaddling clothes, the Babe divine
Lies in a manger; this shall be your sign.

The hymn first appeared in six-line verse form in the 1819 edition of Thomas Cotterill's *Selection of Psalms and Hymns for Public and Private Use* introduced at St Paul's and St James' churches, Sheffield, where he was incumbent. Cotterill was one of the first Church of England clergymen to include hymns in his services. He was supported by the radical Sheffield journalist, James Montgomery, whom we have already encountered as the author of 'Angels from the realms of glory' (No.7), and it was almost certainly he who turned Byrom's revised poem into the hymn that we now sing.

The first two stanzas of Montgomery's version of the hymn were simply lifted from the first twelve lines of the poem (with the second verse beginning 'Then to the watchful shepherds it was told'). The next four lines of the poem, beginning 'In David's city, shepherds, ye shall find' were dropped, despite

Byrom's revision of them, and the hymn's third verse was made up of the six lines beginning 'He spake; and straightway the celestial choir', which had formed the opening of the second part of the original poem. For the fourth verse Montgomery began by following Byrom's revision of the central part of his original second section:

> To Bethlehem straight the enlightened shepherds ran
> To see the wonder God had wrought for man,
> And found with Joseph and the blessed Maid,
> Her Son, the Saviour, in a manger laid;

He dropped the next two couplets ('Amazed, the wondrous story they proclaim,/The first Apostles of his Infant fame' and 'But Mary kept and pondered in her Heart/The heavenly vision which the swains impart') and ended his fourth verse with a revised version of the lines which had ended Byrom's narrative section:

> Then to their flocks, still praising God, return
> And their glad hearts with holy rapture burn.

More radical surgery was required to produce the last two verses of the hymn out of the sixteen lines that made up the original third section of the poem:

> O may we keep and ponder in our mind
> God's wondrous love in saving lost mankind;
> Trace we the Babe, who hath retrieved our loss,
> From his poor manger to his bitter Cross;
> Tread in his steps, assisted by his grace,
> Till man's first heavenly state again takes place.

> Then may we hope, the angelic hosts among,
> To sing, redeemed, a glad triumphal song:
> He that was born upon this joyful day
> Around us all his glory shall display;

Saved by his love, incessant we shall sing
Eternal praise to heaven's almighty King.

It is worth pointing out that Byrom himself had changed his original 'Follow we him who has our cause maintained/And man's first heavenly state shall be regained' to 'Treading His Steps, assisted by His grace,/Till man's first heavenly state again takes place' in his revision. The alteration of the last line of the poem from 'Of angels and of angel men the King' to the rather more pedestrian 'Eternal praise to heaven's almighty' was, however, Montgomery's work. In his book, *The Eighteenth Century Hymn in England* (1993), Donald Davie comments that despite producing a less arresting and memorable concluding line than Byrom had, Montgomery was right to make the change. He points out that the phrase 'angel men' reveals Byrom's adherence to the teachings of the German Lutheran mystic and theosophist, Jakob Boehme, and that 'Montgomery, faithful to his brief to change theological into devotional poetry, rightly eliminates what could impede the devotions of all but those very few who were Behmenist.'

Overall, not too much was lost in the process of turning Byrom's poem into a hymn, although it was undoubtedly a pity to lose (presumably because of their perceived Mariolatry) the lines

Like Mary let us ponder in our mind
God's wondrous Love in saving lost Mankind,
Artless and watchful as these favoured Swains,
While Virgin Meekness in the Heart remains.

The arrangement of the hymn in six verses of six lines each, which also appeared in Montgomery's *The Christian Psalmist* (1825) was adopted in the first edition of *Hymns Ancient and Modern* in 1861 and is the basis for all modern versions, although there have been minor variations and alterations of words and lines. I fear that I am not going to go into them here, feeling as I do, like the Lord Chancellor in Iolanthe, that the night has been long, ditto, ditto my song, and thank goodness they're both of them over. Readers who are desperate to know about minor modern variants are directed to the notes on this hymn in the excellent *Companion to Hymns and Psalms* (1988). The editors of the *New Oxford Book of Carols* have made a nine-verse hymn out of Byrom's poem by adding two lines of their own. It would have been much easier on hymnologists and editors if Dolly Byrom had asked just her Daddy for a Barbie doll, although we would have lost one of the treasures of Christmas hymnody.

Christmas Day – for Dolly

Christians, awake! salute the happy morn
Whereon the Saviour of the world was born;
Rise to adore the mystery of love,
Which hosts of angels changed from above:
With them the joyful tidings first begun
Of God incarnate and the Virgin's Son.
Then to the watchful shepherds it was told,
Who heard the angelic herald's voice, 'Behold,
I bring good tidings of a Saviour's birth
To you and all the nations upon earth:
This day hath God fulfilled his promised word,
This day is born a Saviour, Christ the Lord'.
In David's city, shepherds, ye shall find
The long foretold redeemer of mankind
Wrapped up in swaddling clothes, be this the sign,
A Cratch contains the holy Babe divine.

He spake; and straightway the celestial choir
In hymns of joy, unknown before, conspire;
The praises of redeeming love they sang,
And heaven's whole orb with Alleluias rang:
God's highest glory was their anthem still,
Peace upon earth, and mutual good will.
To Bethlehem straight the enlightened shepherds ran,
To see the wonder God had wrought for man,
They saw their Saviour as the angel said,
The swaddled Infant in the manger laid.
Joseph and Mary a distressed pair
Guard the sole object of the Almighty's Care;
To human eyes none present but they two
Where heaven was pointing its concentrated View.
Amazed, the wondrous story they proclaim,
The first Apostles of his Infant Fame.

But Mary kept and pondered in her Heart
The heavenly Vision which the Swains impart.
They to their flocks and praising God return,
With hearts no doubt that did within them burn.

Let us like those good shepherds then employ
Our grateful voices to proclaim the joy.
Like Mary let us ponder in our mind
God's wondrous love in saving lost mankind;
Artless and watchful as these favoured swains,
While Virgin meekness in the heart remains.
Trace we the Babe, who hath retrieved our loss,
From his poor manger to his bitter Cross;
Follow we him who has our cause maintained,
And man's first heavenly state shall be regained.
Then may we hope, the angelic thrones among,
To sing, redeemed, a glad triumphal song:
He that was born upon this joyful day
Around us all his glory shall display;
Saved by his love, incessant we shall sing
Of angels and of angel-men the King.

17

DECK THE HALL WITH BOUGHS OF HOLLY

If we take a carol to be a dance song with no specifically Christmas associations, then this is one of the few genuine examples of the species to be included in this book.

'Deck the hall' is a very free translation of a Welsh dance-carol traditionally sung at New Year's Eve. It belongs to the distinctive Welsh tradition of *canu penillion* in which merrymakers would dance in a ring around a harpist. Verses, either extemporized or remembered, would be thrown in by the dancers in turn with the harp playing the answering bars now made up with the 'fal, la la's'. Those who failed to come up with a new verse would fall out of the dance. '*Nos Galan*' is first found in *Musical and Poetical Relics of the Welsh Bards* published in 1784 by the harpist Edward Jones but the melody almost certainly goes back before that. Despite the fact that Jones heads the song 'Nos Galan' (New Year's Eve) the text in his version is a love song. In fact, the tune seems to have carried many different words before becoming specifically associated with New Year festivities. The standard Welsh text begins by describing the passing of the old year and the coming of the new.

Oer yw'r gwr sy'n methu caru
Hen fynyddoedd annwyl Cymru,
Iddo ef a'u car gynhesaf,
Gwyliau llawen flwyddyn nesaf.

The original Welsh New Year carol seems to have been turned into an English Christmas song in the latter part of the nineteenth century as part of the Victorian re-invention of Christmas. The first known appearance in print of 'Deck the hall' is in *The Franklin Square Song Collection* edited by J.P. McCaskey in 1881. The authorship of the English words, which, apart from the reference in the third verse to the passing of the old year and the coming of the new, bear no relation to the Welsh original, has never been established.

Numerous variations are found in all three verses. The third line of the first verse is sometimes rendered 'Fill the mead cup, drain the barrel' or 'Fill the beer up, drain the barrel'. In the second verse the first line is often 'See the flowing bowl before us' and the last 'While I sing of beauty's treasure'. Several versions of the song extol singers at the end of the first verse to 'Troll the ancient Christmas carol'. In the third verse, the third line is often rendered 'Laughing, quaffing, all together'.

Essentially this is a carol where the words don't really matter too much. The great thing is the tune and all those fa, la, las which according to the erudite editors of the *New Oxford Book of Carols* seem to have begun as substitutes in the original dance tune when no harp was present. It is not known what steps were danced to the original Welsh carol.

Nos Galan

Deck the halls with boughs of holly,
'Tis the season to be jolly,
Don we now our gay apparel,
Troll the ancient Yule-tide carol.

2 See the blazing Yule before us,
Strike the harp and join the chorus,
Follow me in merry measure,
While I tell of Yule-tide treasure.

3 Fast away the old year passes,
Hail the new, ye lads and lasses,
Sing we joyous all together,
Heedless of the wind and weather.

18

DING, DONG MERRILY ON HIGH

Here is another carol where the words perhaps do not matter all that much and which really needs the tune to do it justice. The great thing about this carol, as all good wassailers know, is to keep those glorias swinging, like the steeple bells, and if you are a bass or tenor, to get your entries right so you keep it going.

Although it has the feel of a traditional olde English carol dating back at least to Tudor times, if not the Middle Ages, 'Ding, dong merrily on high' belongs firmly to the twentieth century. It first appeared in 1924 in the *Cambridge Carol Book*.

The words are by George Ratcliffe Woodward (1848–1934). Born in Birkenhead and educated at Gonville and Caius College, Cambridge, he was ordained in 1874 and was successively curate of St Barnabas, Pimlico, vicar of Little Walsingham, Norfolk, and rector of Chelmondiston, Suffolk. He then returned to London for a second curacy at St Barnabas and ended his ministry as licentiate preacher in the diocese of London and curate of St Mark's, Marylebone.

Woodward was responsible for a number of important carol books which set new words to traditional European folk tunes. They included *Carols for Christmastide* (1892), *Carols for Easter and Ascensiontide* (1894), the *Cowley Carol Book* (first published in two sections in 1901 and 1902 and then in an enlarged edition in 1919), *Songs of Syon* (1904), the *Italian Carol Book* (1920) and the *Cambridge Carol Book*. He was particularly interested in rehabilitating tunes found in the sixteenth-century Finnish collection *Piae Cantiones* and providing them with words to bring them into the English carol repertoire. He produced another carol with a very similar opening line 'Ding dong ding' in order to rehabilitate the tune set in *Piae Cantiones* to a medieval song based on the opening of Psalm 133, '*O quam mudum, quam jocundum*'.

In many of these books, Woodward collaborated with Charles Wood, the Irish-born composer who was professor of harmony at the Royal College of Music and later lecturer in harmony and counterpoint at Cambridge University.

The tune for which Woodward wrote the words 'Ding, dong merrily on high' did not, in fact, come from *Piae Cantiones* and had no Christmas or religious associations. It is first found in a French book of dance tunes entitled *Orchésographie* and published in 1589. The editor of this collection, who was a canon of Langres, styled himself 'Thoinot Arbeau' but this was an anagram of his real name, Johan Tabourot (1519–93). The tune was written for a vigorous dance known as the *branle* which, according to the *Orchésographie*, is 'danced with little springs . . . by lackeys and serving wenches and sometimes by young men and maids of gentle birth masquerading as peasants and shepherds'. In the original rustic version of the dance, the men took the women by the waist and lifted them into the air but in the more gentrified version popularized by Tabourot this potentially taxing exercise was replaced by a simple kiss.

'Ding, dong merrily on high' is therefore a nice example of a carol in the original sense of the word (ie a wholly secular dance tune) transformed into a carol as it is understood in modern times (ie a song for Christmas).

Ding, dong merrily on high,
In heaven the bells are ringing
Ding dong, verily the sky
Is riv'n with angel-singing:
Gloria . . .. Hosanna in excelsis.

2 E'en so here below, below
Let steeple bells be swungen
And io, io, io
By priest and people sungen:
Gloria . . .. . . Hosanna in excelsis.

3 Pray you, dutifully prime
Your matin chime, ye ringers;
May you beautifully rhyme
Your evetime song, ye singers:
Gloria . . .. . . Hosanna in excelsis.

19

EVERY STAR SHALL SING A CAROL

This is the only Christmas carol I know which goes beyond the confines of this world, acknowledges the fact that there are billions of other planets and universes and raises the possibility that there may be other incarnations of God in far-off galaxies.

Its author, Sydney Carter, eloquently expressed his feelings that other planets may have other Christs in a note about his most popular song (which is also a carol), 'The Lord of the Dance':

> I see Christ as the incarnation of that piper who is calling us. He dances that shape and pattern which is at the heart of our reality. By Christ I mean not only Jesus; in other times and places, other planets, there may be other Lords of the Dance. But Jesus is the one I know of first and best.

A similar idea pervades 'Every star shall sing a carol' with its wonder about what other body Christ will hallow for his own and what other cradle may rock the King of Heaven on another Christmas Day.

Some Christians feel uneasy about the inter-faith implications of this carol with its line 'Come and praise the King of Heaven by whatever name you know', just as they are uneasy about aspects of Carter's 'Lord of the Dance' and 'One more step'. I have to say that I find its breadth and inclusiveness, as well as its questions, very exciting and challenging. It seems to me to have a real grasp of the cosmic dimension of Christ that is found in very few other carols.

Sydney Carter (1915-2004) was born in London and educated at Christ's Hospital and Balliol College, Oxford. He was a schoolmaster at Frensham Heights School and then served during the years of the Second World War with the Friends' Ambulance Unit in Greece and the Middle East. After the war, he taught and lectured for the British Council before turning to full-time writing and broadcasting. Songs and tunes came to him and shaped themselves while he was walking in the street or moving round the room. There is a strong rhythmical dance-like quality to much of his work - indeed many of his compositions could be categorized as carols.

'Every star shall sing a carol' , which was written in 1961, is accompanied, like most of Sydney Carter's work by his own tune composed specially for these words.

Every star shall sing a carol;
Every creature, high or low,
Come and praise the King of heaven
By whatever name you know.
God above, man below,
Holy is the name I know.

2 When the King of all creation
Had a cradle on the earth,
Holy was the human body,
Holy was the human birth.

3 Who can tell what other cradle
High above the milky way
Still may rock the King of heaven
On another Christmas Day?

4 Who can count how many crosses
Still to come or long ago
Crucify the King of heaven?
Holy is the name I know.

5 Who can tell what other body
He will hallow for his own?
I will praise the son of Mary,
Brother of my blood and bone.

6 Every star and every planet
Every creature high and low,
Come and praise the King of heaven
By whatever name you know.

20

FROM EAST TO WEST, FROM SHORE TO SHORE

This classic Christmas morning hymn is not sung as often now as it once was, although it is still found in several major hymnbooks which are in current use including the *New English Hymnal*, the Church of Ireland's *Church Hymnal*, the Methodists' *Hymns and Psalms* and the ecumenical Australian hymnal, *With One Voice*.

It is based on a Latin poem dating from the first half of the fifth century and entitled *Paean Alphabeticus de Christo* in which the life of Christ is described in 23 verses, each beginning with a successive letter of the alphabet. The first verse begins '*A solis ortus cardine*'. Little is known about the author, Caelius Sedulius, who is thought to have died around 450.

The poem, which survives in an eighth-century manuscript in the British Library, was widely taken up in the Western Church for liturgical use in the season from Christmas to Epiphany. The verses beginning A to G were chanted at Lauds during the Christmas period and those beginning H, I, L & N (beginning '*Hostis Herodes impie'*) were sung at Mattins and Vespers in the Epiphany season. In most old breviaries the text of '*A solis ortus cardine*' runs to 28 lines.

Both sets of verses were translated into English in the middle decades of the nineteenth century as part of the general Anglican attempt to recover the liturgical riches of the early church. Translations of '*A solis ortus cardine*' include Edward Caswall's 'From the far-blazing gate of morn' for his *Lyra Catholica* of 1849, J.M. Neale's 'From lands that see the sun arise' for the *Hymnal Noted* (1852) and R.F. Littledale's 'From where the sunshine hath its birth' for the *People's Hymnal* of 1867.

The translation which, in the words of Julian, 'is the most acceptable form of the hymn for congregational use' was made by John Ellerton (1826-93), one of the leading hymn-writers of the nineteenth century who was responsible for such gems as 'The day Thou gavest, Lord, has ended' and 'Saviour again to Thy dear name we raise'.

Educated at King William's College on the Isle of Man and Trinity College, Cambridge, where he came under the influence of F.D. Maurice and Christian socialism, Ellerton was ordained in 1850 and served as a curate first at Midhurst, Sussex, and then at Brighton. In 1860 he became vicar of Crewe Green in Cheshire and it was while there that he wrote 86 hymns, many of which were composed on his nightly walks to teach classes at the Mechanics' Institute patronized by the workers of the London and North Western Railway. He was subsequently rector of Hinstock in Shropshire, St Mary's, Barnes, and White Roding in Essex.

Ellerton produced his translation in two versions. The first in common metre (8686) appeared in *Church Hymns* in 1874 as a cento of five stanzas, the first four of which were based on verses one, two, six and seven of Sedulius' poem with the last being original. It can be found in the current Methodist hymnal, *Hymns and Psalms* and runs as follows:

From east to west, from shore to shore,
Let earth awake and sing
The holy Child whom Mary bore,
The Christ, the Lord, the King.

For lo! the world's Creator wears
The fashion of a slave;
Our human flesh the Godhead bears,
His creature, man, to save.

He shrank not from the oxen's stall,
Nor scorned the manger bed,
And he whose bounty feedeth all
At Mary's breast was fed.

To shepherds poor the Lord most high,

Great Shepherd, was revealed.
While the angel choirs sang joyously
Above the midnight field.

All glory be to God above,
And on the earth be peace
To all who long to taste his love,
Till time itself shall cease.

A second long metre (8888) version was published in Ellerton's *Hymns Original and Translated* in 1888 and was included, with some alterations, in both the 1889 supplement to and the 1950 revised edition of *Hymns Ancient and Modern*. Although dropped from the 1984 new standard edition of *Hymns Ancient and Modern,* it can still be found in the *New English Hymnal*. As well as having an extra two syllables in every second and fourth line, it also has two extra verses. It is that revised version which appears below.

Ellerton's translation of the second Epiphany part of Sedulius' poem, 'How vain the Herod's cruel fear', which originally appeared in the 1875 edition of *Hymns Ancient and Modern* was also once quite widely sung but has now almost entirely dropped out of use.

The tunes used for 'From east to west' vary depending on whether the common or long metre version is being sung. In those hymnals which favour the former it has been set to Gordon Slater's ST BOTOLPH and the old English carol melody THIS ENDRIS NYGHT. Long metre settings have included SEDULIUS, a German melody dating from the seventeenth century, J.B. Dykes' TRINITY COLLEGE, the German traditional carol melody PUER NOBIS NASCITUR and, in the case of the *English Hymnal*, a plainsong chant and a Rouen church melody harmonized by Ralph Vaughan Williams.

A solis ortus cardine

From east to west, from shore to shore,
Let every heart awake and sing
The holy Child whom Mary bore,
The Christ, the everlasting King.

2 Behold the world's Creator wears
The form and fashion of a slave;
Our very flesh our Maker shares,
His fallen creature, man, to save.

3 For this how wondrously he wrought!
A maiden, in her lowly place,
Became, in ways beyond all thought,
The chosen vessel of his grace.

4 She bowed her to the angel's word
Declaring what the Father willed,
And suddenly the promised Lord
That pure and hallowed temple filled.

5 He shrank not from the oxen's stall,
He lay within the manger bed,
And he whose bounty feedeth all
At Mary's breast himself was fed.

6 And while the angels in the sky
Sang praise above the silent field,
To shepherds poor the Lord most high,
The one great Shepherd, was revealed.

7 All glory for this blessed morn
To God the Father very be;
All praise to thee, O Virgin-Born,
All praise, O Holy Ghost, to thee.

21

FROM HEAVEN ABOVE

Like 'All my heart this night rejoices' (No. 6), this Christmas hymn comes from the Lutheran tradition. Indeed, the German original on which it is based was written by Martin Luther himself. He wrote '*Von Himmel hoch da komm ich*' in or around 1535 for his own family's Christmas Eve celebrations and specifically to teach the story of Jesus' birth to his children. He apparently decreed that the first five verses should be sung by a man dressed as an angel standing by the family crib, with the subsequent verses being sung by the children. The opening verse of his hymn was closely modelled on a popular folk song of the time which began:

Ich komm aus fremden Landen her,
Und bring euch viel der neuen Mähr,
Der neuen Mähr bring ich so viel,
Mehr dann ich euch hier sagen will.

The first verse of Luther's hymn runs:

Von Himmel hoch, da komm'ich her,
Ich bring' euch gute neue Mär,
Der guten Mär bring' ich so viel,
Davon ich sing'n und sagen will.

The subsequent verses of '*Von Himmel hoch*' depart from the model of the folk song and are entirely original. Luther's hymn first appeared in print in his native Wittenberg in 1535. In a publication of 1543 it was entitled 'A Children's Hymn for Christmas Eve on the child Jesus, taken from the Second Chapter of the Gospel of St.Luke'.

There have been numerous translations of Luther's hymn into

English. The earliest known, 'I come from hevin to tell' was made by the Wedderburn brothers of Dundee, who worked with Luther in Wittenberg in the late 1530s. It appeared in their compendium of *Gude and Godlie Ballads* (1565) and was later re-written by H.R. Bramley as 'From highest heaven I come to tell' for the collection of Christmas carols on which he collaborated with John Stainer in 1871. This version is used in the *New Oxford Book of Carols*. The *Moravian Hymn Book* of 1754 included a translation beginning 'I come from heaven to declare'. Nineteenth-century translations included 'I come, I come from yon celestial climes', 'From heaven high I wing my flight' and 'Good news from heaven the angels bring'.

As with so many other German hymns, the most successful and popular translation was made by Catherine Winkworth (on whom see notes to No.6). 'From heaven above to earth I come' first appeared in her *Lyra Germanica: Hymns for the Sundays and Chief Festivals of the Christian Year* published in 1855 with the note appended that the original hymn had been written by Luther 'for his little son Hans in 1540'. In fact, it is now thought to have been written around 1535 when Hans was nine and may have been equally aimed at Luther's other children, Elizabeth (eight), Magdalene (six), Martin (four), Paul (two) and Margaret (one).

The hymn appears here with all its fifteen verses, exactly as translated by Catherine Winkworth. Most hymnbooks not unreasonably print considerably shortened versions – some, indeed, begin the hymn at verse seven. The United Reformed Church's *Rejoice and Sing* divides the hymn, taking verses one, two and three as 'the Angel's Message' and verses 8, 10, 13, 14 & 15 as 'The Children's Welcome', and updating the language to remove 'thees' and 'thous'. Verses 13 & 14 were set to music by both Peter Warlock and Benjamin Britten to form the carol 'Balulalow'.

Luther seems originally to have intended his hymn to be sung to the tune of the song '*Ich komm aus fremden Landen her*' which had provided his inspiration and it was set to that tune when first published in 1535. It is a light dancing melody – the song involved boys dancing together for the reward of a crown presented by the girls and there may even have been an element of dancing in Luther's carol. When the hymn was next published in a Leipzig song book four years later it had a rather grander and more stately tune somewhat reminiscent of the melody of Luther's *Ein' feste Burg* which may well have been composed by the great reformer himself. The two tunes co-existed for some time, and both appeared with the hymn in a publication of 1544, but the later one gradually replaced the earlier one. It is favoured in almost all modern hymn-books where it is generally attributed to Luther and entitled VON HIMMEL HOCH. Bach used this tune in the closing chorale of the first part of his Christmas Oratorio.

Christmas Eve – a carol

From heaven above to earth I come
To bear good news to everyone;
Glad tidings of great joy I bring,
Of which I now will say and sing:

2 To you this night is born a child
Of Mary, chosen mother mild:
This new-born babe of lowly birth,
Shall be the joy of all the earth.

3 'Tis Christ our God who far on high
Has heard your sad and bitter cry;
Himself will your salvation be;
Himself from sin will make you free.

4 He brings those blessings, long ago
Prepared by God for all below;
Henceforth His kingdom open stands
To you, as to the angel bands.

5 These are the tokens ye shall mark,
The swaddling clothes and manger dark;
There shall ye find the young child laid,
By whom the heavens and earth were made.

6 Now let us all with gladsome cheer
Follow the shepherds, and draw near
To see this wondrous gift of God
Who hath His only Son bestowed.

7 Give heed, my heart, lift up thine eyes!
Who is it in yon manger lies?
Who is this child so young and fair?
The blessed Christ-child lieth there.

8 Welcome to earth, Thou noble guest,
Through whom e'en wicked men are blest!
Thou comest to share our misery;
What can we render, Lord, to Thee?

9 Ah, Lord, who hast created all,
How hast Thou made Thee weak and small,
That Thou must choose Thy infant bed
Where ass and ox but lately fed!

10 Were earth a thousand times as fair,
And set with gold and jewels rare,
She yet were far too poor to be
A narrow cradle, Lord, for Thee.

11 For velvets soft and silken stuff
Thou hast but hay and straw so rough,
Whereon Thou king, so rich and great,
As 'twere Thy heaven, art throned instate.

12 Thus hath it pleased Thee to make plain
The truth to us poor fools and vain
That this world's honour, wealth and might
Are nought and worthless in Thy sight.

13 Ah, dearest Jesus, holy child,
Make Thee a bed, soft, undefiled,
Within my heart, and it may be
A quiet chamber kept for Thee.

14 My heart for very joy doth leap;
My lips no more can silence keep;
I too must sing with joyful tongue
That sweetest ancient cradle song:

15 'Glory to God in highest heaven,
Who unto man his Son has given!'
While angels sing with pious mirth
A glad New Year to all the earth.

22

FROM HEAVEN YOU CAME, HELPLESS BABE

This may at first sight seem a strange item to find in a book devoted to Christmas hymns and carols. Does this enormously and deservedly popular contemporary hymn by Graham Kendrick have anything to do with Christmas? Certainly hymnal editors do not appear to think so, preferring to place it in sections devoted to discipleship (*Rejoice and Sing*) or renewed commitment (*Baptist Praise and Worship*).

Yet 'The Servant King', as this song is generally known, seems to me to be a hymn which could and should be sung at Christmas. Its starting point is very clearly the Incarnation. Indeed, its opening line is highly reminiscent of the first line of the hymn by Luther which precedes it in this collection. The fact it goes on to cover the sacrificial death of Jesus in 'the garden of tears' and to call on us to serve Christ does not diminish its appropriateness for this season. Too often the Christmas message stops at the Incarnation. 'The Servant King' takes us from the helpless babe to the man on the Cross, from Incarnation to Crucifixion and from Creator to Sacrificial Victim. In these days when many people attend church only once a year on Christmas Eve or Christmas Day, there is much to be said for getting across as much of the Christian story as possible in one go – atonement, resurrection as well as incarnation. I am not quite sure I would go as far as the vicar who regularly wishes his Christmas congregation a happy Easter because he knows that he won't see them again for twelve months but perhaps we should sing more hymns at Christmas which do point up the other episodes in Christ's life and work and don't just stop at his birth.

Born in 1950, the son of a Baptist minister, Graham Kendrick grew up in a succession of Baptist manses in Blisworth, Laindon and Putney. While at teacher training college, he underwent a profound religious experience in which he felt filled with the Holy Spirit. This set him off on his ministry as an itinerant musician, hymn writer and worship leader. After working in full-time evangelism, first with the touring team, In the Name of Jesus, and then for four years with Youth for Christ, he decided in 1984 to focus all his energies on congregational worship music.

Closely involved with the Ichthus fellowship, one of the largest and most dynamic of the new house churches which have come out of the charismatic revival, Kendrick has been particularly associated with the March for Jesus for which he has written such songs as 'Make way, make way for the king of kings'. He has also written songs for the annual Spring Harvest gatherings, including 'Shine, Jesus, shine'.

Graham Kendrick has written several songs specifically for Christmas, including 'Like a candle flame', written for a Christmas street musical, *The Gift,* and found in *Mission Praise Combined,* and 'Look to the skies, there's a celebration' which appears in *Carol Praise*, *Church Family Worship* and *Mission Praise Combined*. He has recorded two Christmas albums, *Rumours of Angels*, which features Advent and *The Gift – Make Way for Christmas*. He has a fascination with the Christingle service and was commissioned in 1997 to write a song for the annual Children's Society Christingle service.

The tune SERVANT KING is by Kendrick.

The Servant King

From heaven you came, helpless babe,
Entered our world, your glory veiled;
Not to be served but to serve,
And give your life that we might live.
This is our God, the Servant King,
He calls us now to follow him,
To bring our lives as a daily offering
Of worship to the Servant King.

2 There in the garden of tears,
My heavy load he chose to bear;
His heart with sorrow was torn,
'Yet now my will but yours,' he said.

3 Come see his hands and his feet,
The scars that speak of sacrifice,
Hands that flung stars into space
To cruel nailed surrendered.

4 So let us learn how to serve,
And in our lives enthrone him;
Each other's needs to prefer,
For it is Christ we're serving.

23

FUNNY KIND OF NIGHT

It is highly appropriate that this contemporary song should stand cheek by jowl with 'From heaven you came' in this collection. Its author, John Bell, ranks with Graham Kendrick as one of the outstanding hymn writers in contemporary Britain. The two men have very different theological perspectives but their work shares a firm Biblical basis and a strong emphasis on discipleship.

Born, like Kendrick, in 1950, John Bell hails from Kilmarnock in Ayrshire. Educated at Glasgow University, he was ordained into the ministry of the Church of Scotland in 1978 and served in the Scots Kirk in Amsterdam and as youth adviser to Glasgow Presbytery before beginning full-time work with the Iona Community in 1978.

As leader of the Iona Community's Wild Goose Worship Group, John Bell has almost single-handedly transformed the culture of worship and especially of church music in Scotland, introducing a range of new material, much of it his own but also the work of other contemporary writers and songs from the world church. He has convened the Church of Scotland's Panel on Worship and the committee preparing the next edition of the *Church Hymnary* (on which he and I have had many a tussle over Victorian hymns which he wants to scrap and I want to keep).

His influence has spread far beyond Presbyterian Scotland. Passionately ecumenical, he was the driving force behind *Common Ground*, a song book produced by representatives of all the main Scottish churches and published in 1998. He leads worship workshops throughout the UK, in the USA, Canada, Australia and Japan.

Like Kendrick, John Bell has written a large number of Christmas songs and carols, many of which can be found in his book, *Innkeepers and Light Sleepers*, published in 1992. 'Funny kind of night' first appeared in that collection and provided its title. Like much of Bell's work, it has a striking originality. Not many carols mention tax collectors and child inspectors who are, in their way, just as important to the Christmas story as shepherds and angels.

There is a marvellous topsy-turvy quality to this carol which conveys the wonder of Christmas in terms of its paradoxes and absurdity. It perhaps comes as close as anything in this book to Percy Dearmer's classic definition of carols as 'songs with a religious impulse that are simple, hilarious, popular and modern'. Bell himself has written to me about 'Funny kind of night':

> The text was intended to allude to the incarnation as an event which was unheralded in immediate history and took place amongst people who would be the last to expect that they might be the witnesses of God coming to earth. I have always been fascinated by the fact that God did not go to the place where the birth was expected, but crept in, as it were, among the insignificant people in order to redeem the world from below.

Like Kendrick, John Bell writes tunes for many of his songs although he is also much given to using traditional Scottish folksongs. Their musical styles are very dissimilar – Bell's more folky and less pop, written more for unaccompanied voices than for praise bands. For this song, he has written a tripping series of semi-quavers which he calls LESSER THINGS. The title, he says, 'is an allusion to how redemption begins among the insignificant people and places, rather than the trickle-down effect which suggests that grace distils from above via those whom the world considers to be important'.

Funny kind of night, funny kind of day,
Tax collectors, child inspectors, all in disarray;
Funny kind of day, funny kind of night,
Royal kings and lesser things align with dark and light.
To God in the highest be glory which never ends,
And on earth peace and goodwill to all God's friends.

2 Funny kind of night, funny kind of day,
Babies cry, traditions die and fear itself takes fright;
Country folk enquire what is right or wrong
While above, in tongues of love, the sense is veiled in song:

3 Funny kind of night, funny kind of day,
First begotten, half forgotten treasure lies in hay;
Wise men on the move wonder what to bring,
While innkeepers and light sleepers hear poor shepherds sing:

24

GIRLS AND BOYS, LEAVE YOUR TOYS

The much-loved English conductor, Sir Malcolm Sargent (1895–1967) probably has two main claims to popular memory. He was principal conductor of the Proms from 1944 until his death and he presided over the Christmas concerts of the Royal Choral Society held, like the Proms, in the Royal Albert Hall.

In this carol, unusually, Sargent was responsible for both words and music. He wrote 'Girls and boys, leave your toys' in 1958 to accompany a Czech folk tune. Entitled the Zither Carol, presumably because it is particularly suited to accompaniment by that instrument, it appeared in the first (1961) edition of *Carols for Choirs* and in the *Malcolm Sargent Carol Book* of 1970.

The words may not represent the highest poetry nor the deepest theology but they have a certain charm and take us back to more traditional Christmas imagery after 'Funny kind of night'. The emphasis in this carol is on the ethereal rather than the earthy and the remoteness of the Nativity ('on that day far away') rather than its nearness. There is also some very Victorian moralizing ('Oh, that we all might be good as he') reminiscent of Mrs Alexander's 'Christian children all should be mild, obedient, good as he' in 'Once in Royal David's city'.

One of the most marked and attractive features of this carol, which I fear does not come out in the words-only version printed below, is the accompaniment provided by the altos, tenors and basses to the melody line sung by the sopranos. This consists of a series of 'zings' and 'zms'. A note indicates that zing is pronounced tzing and zsm pronounced tzoomm, making one think of the chorus of peers in *Iolanthe* who sing 'Tantantara, tzing boom, tzing boom'. Gilbert and Sullivan lover though he was, however, Sargent does not seek to emulate what might be called 'the Savoy sound'. The effect which he creates is reminiscent rather of the student song 'The Spanish Guitar'. The Czech folk tune is in exuberant waltz time and not surprisingly the carol has been included in many children's hymnbooks including *Junior Praise* and *Praise God Together*.

Several books leave out verse four. *Church Family Worship* (1986) prints just the first three verses, changing the third line of verse one to 'For this shrine, Child divine, is the sign' and changing 'thy' to 'your' in verses two and three.

It is not recorded whether Sargent hit on the idea for the opening line of this carol when, trying to persuade exuberant Promenaders to give up waving their banners, honking their hooters and unleashing streamers and balloons, he ordered 'Now give your toys back to Nanny!'.

Girls and boys, leave your toys, make no noise,
Kneel at his crib and worship him.
At thy Shrine, Child divine, we are thine,
Our Saviour's here.
'Hallelujah' the church bells ring,
'Hallelujah' the angels sing,
'Hallelujah' from everything,
All must draw near.

2 On that day, far away, Jesus lay,
Angels were watching round his head,
Holy Child, Mother mild, undefiled,
We sing thy praise.
'Hallelujah' etc.
Our hearts we raise

3 Shepherds came at the fame of thy name,
Angels their guide to Bethlehem;
In that place saw thy face, filled with grace,
Stood at thy door.
'Hallelujah' etc.
Love evermore.

4 Wise men too haste to do homage new,
Gold, myrrh and frankincense they bring,
As 'twas said, starlight led, to thy bed,
Bending their knee.
'Hallelujah' etc.
Him we see.

5 Oh, that we all might be as good as he
Spotless with God in Unity!
Saviour dear, ever near, with us here
Since life began.
'Hallelujah' etc.
Godhead made Man.

6 Cherubim, Seraphim worship him,
Sun, moon, and stars proclaim his power,
Every day, on our way, we shall say –
Hallelujah!
'Hallelujah', etc.
Hallelujah.

25

GO, TELL IT ON THE MOUNTAIN

This African-American spiritual is found in a bewildering number of different versions. Just about all that is common to them is the chorus.

The song seems to have originated among negro slaves in the American south in the nineteenth century and has similar roots to spirituals such as 'Go down, Moses', 'Swing low, sweet chariot' and 'Let my people go'.

It achieved popularity when it was taken up at the end of the nineteenth century by the Fisk Jubilee Singers, a celebrated black choir whose members were all students at Fisk University, Nashville, Tennessee, which was established by the American Missionary Association in the 1860s for freed slaves. The choir was regularly shut out of hotels, railway waiting rooms and ships' cabins and excluded from some churches because of its members' colour. On a highly successful visit to England in 1873, they sang before Queen Victoria, W.E. Gladstone and Edward, Prince of Wales, who apparently asked them to sing 'No more auction-block for me'. At D.L. Moody's Crusade Meetings they sang 'Steal away to Jesus' and at Spurgeon's Tabernacle 'O brothers, don't stay away, for my Lord says there's room enough in the heavens for you'.

'Go, tell it on the mountain' seems to have been added to the Fisk Jubilee Singers' repertoire by John Wesley Work II (1872–1925), who conducted the choir in the early years of the twentieth century. He was certainly responsible for arranging the tune and may well have written the verses which appear below. Work was born, lived and died in Nashville, taught Latin and Greek at the university there and devoted his spare time to collecting and arranging black spirituals.

Work's version of the song, which dates from 1907, is, as far as I can establish, the earliest extant and certainly the most regularly sung in modern America. It appears (without verse three) in the current hymnal of the Presbyterian Church of the USA, and in *Voices United*, the hymn and worship book of the United Church of Canada. In Britain this version can be found in *Rejoice and Sing*,

'Go, tell it on the mountain' also exists in numerous other versions. A number of books dispense with the first verse, beginning the song 'While shepherds kept their watching' or, as *Carols for Today* has it, 'While shepherds sat a-watching'. The *New Oxford Book of Carols* favours a version first published in Thomas Fenner's *Religious Songs of the Negro as Sung on the Plantations* (1909):

In the time of David,
Some call him a king,
And if a child is true-born,
Lord Jesus will hear him sing:

When I was a seeker
I sought both night and day;
I ask the Lord to help me,
And he showed me the way.

He made me a watchman
Upon a city wall,
And if I am a Christian
I am the least of all.

Geoffrey Marshall Taylor produced wholly new verses for the book *Come and Praise*, which was first published by the BBC in 1978 for use at primary school assemblies and has subsequently been through numerous editions. His version began:

He possessed no riches,
No home to lay his head,
He saw the needs of others
And cared for them instead

Taylor's version, which has no specifically Christmas connotations and describes rather the life, death, resurrection and continuing presence of Jesus in five verses, has been taken up in several current British hymnals, including the Methodists' *Hymns and Psalms* and *Baptist Praise and Worship,* but with the second two lines of the first verse changed to 'He fasted in the desert,/He gave to others bread'. Other versions noted in the invaluable *Hymn Quest dictionary of hymnody* begin 'As Mary used to feed him', 'When I was a sinner' and 'Man began in summer'.

All the various versions are at least sung to the same tune, GO TELL IT ON THE MOUNTAIN. John Rutter made a fine arrangement of it for *A Little Carol Book* in 1981. Also popular in Britain is an arrangement by Martin How published in 1982 by the Royal School of Church Music, while in the USA much use is made of a harmonization by Melva Wilson Costen.

Go, tell it on the mountain,
Over the hills and ev'rywhere:
Go tell it on the mountain
That Jesus Christ is born.

While shepherds kept their watching
O'er silent flocks by night,
Behold, throughout the heavens
There shone a holy light:

2 The shepherds feared and trembled
When, lo, above the earth
Rang out the angel chorus
That hailed our Saviour's birth:

3 And lo! When they had seen it
They all bowed down and prayed;
They travelled on together
To where the babe was laid.

4 Down in a lonely manger
The humble Christ was born;
And God sent us salvation
That blessed Christmas morn:

26

GOD REST YOU MERRY, GENTLEMEN

Commas are very important in hymns. Much of the criticism directed at the infamous verse in Mrs Alexander's 'All things bright and beautiful' beginning 'The rich man in his castle, the poor man at his gate' arises from a misconception that the next line reads 'God made them high or lowly' rather than 'God made them, high or lowly' which is what the author actually wrote.

The comma is important in the opening line of this hymn. It is not, as so often thought, addressed to merry gentlemen but rather to those who may be anxious. Indeed, its message of God's reassuring love is specifically directed at the shepherds who are frightened by the sudden appearance of an angel in their midst.

The fact that the opening line is addressed to shepherds also explains its gender specific language. I fear, however, that this will cut little ice with the growing ranks of the politically correct who wish to de-sex it. Other carols such as 'Good Christian men, rejoice' are easier to make inclusive – 'God rest you merry, gentlefolk' sounds even more quaint than the original.

I am afraid that once you start examining the language of this carol, there is much to take exception to. Those of us considering Christmas material for the fourth edition of the *Church Hymnary*, the Church of Scotland hymnbook, were treated to a detailed exegesis of 'God rest you merry' by John Bell which revealed three examples of exclusive language ('gentlemen' in verse one, 'Heavenly Father' in verse three and 'brotherhood' in verse seven), two statements for which there is no Biblical evidence ('their flocks a-feeding in tempest, storm and wind' and Mary kneeling), several archaisms and at least one piece of dubious theology (the notion in the closing couplet that Christmas defaces all other holy tides). I fear that as a result it did not find its way into the new edition of the Hymnary published in 2005.

This is, of course, what happens when the rough-hewn products of folk tradition are subjected to critical theological and literary analysis. The fact is that this hymn is not the work of a liturgical scholar but has rather grown out of folk tradition, probably coming from the west of England and originating in the eighteenth or early nineteeenth century. Despite its archaism and political incorrectness, it remains very popular, standing at sixteenth place in the 2005 BBC *Songs of Praise* poll.

The version which I print here is that found in William Sandys' *Christmas Carols, Ancient and Modern* (1833). It has become the standard text, with the second line of the refrain amended to repeat the words 'Comfort and joy'. The second and fourth verses are usually omitted. Although Sandys gives 'friends of Satan' in the last line of verse four, it seems that this line was generally sung as 'fiends'.

Another version found in an early nineteenth-century broadside follows the spirit of Sandys with slight variations but omits verse two and has an extra verse between verses six and seven:

With sudden joy and gladness,
The shepherds were beguiled,
To see the Babe of Israel,
Before his mother mild,
On them with joy and cheerfulness,
Rejoice each Mother's Child.

The broadside version also includes an additional eighth verse:

God bless the ruler of this house,
And send him long to reign,
And many a merry Christmas
May live to see again.
Among your friends and kindred,
That live both far and near,
And God send you a happy new year.

'God rest you merry' has been the victim of a number of

parodies. In 1820 William Hone, a radical journalist, produced 'A Political Christmas Carol to be chanted or sung throughout the United Kingdom and the Dominions Beyond the Seas by all persons thereunto especially moved'. It was directed at Lord Castlereagh, the leader of the House of Commons who was identified with the repressive measures enacted in the aftermath of the Napoleonic Wars. It began (with the comma in the wrong place!):

God rest you, merry Gentlemen,
Let nothing you dismay;
Remember we were left alive
Upon last Christmas day,
With both our lips at liberty
To praise Lord C———h,
With his 'practical' comfort and joy!

In his book *The Folk-Carol of England*, Douglas Brice quotes a parody of this carol which he says G.K. Chesterton was moved to write when an un-named Chief Constable appealed to the public to refrain from carol singing on the grounds that it was morally and physically injurious. I have not been able to find any reference to this poem, which Brice entitles 'The Puritan', in any book on Chesterton and it does not appear in his collected poems but here is the first verse:

God rest you merry gentlemen,
Let nothing you dismay;
The Herald Angels cannot sing,
The cops arrest them on the wing,
And warn them of the docketing
Of anything they say.

'God rest you merry' has been sung to a number of different tunes, especially in the west country. The *New Oxford Book of Carols* publishes one which is said to have been especially popular in Cornwall and another described as the usual west country tune and printed by Sandys. It is, however, another melody to which the carol is nearly always sung today. Known as the 'London tune', it was collected in the London area by E.F. Rimbault, first printed in 1846 and given its present form in Bramley and Stainer's *Christmas Carols New and Old* in 1871.

The London tune was used for other Christmas songs, including 'Here we come a wassailing', 'While shepherds watched their flocks by night', 'Wassail and wassail all over the town', 'God's dear Son without beginning', 'Come all you worthy gentlemen' and the Advent Images Carol. In Nova Scotia it was set to a twelve-verse version of 'The Joys of Mary'. In the mid-eighteenth century the tune was used for a patriotic song 'Awake, awake sweet England' apparently written in the aftermath of the 1745 Jacobite rebellion. It may well have an even longer pedigree. A.L. Lloyd, the great folk music collector, traced its use back to a ballad on the London earthquake of 1580, also entitled 'Awake, awake, sweet England', and described it as 'England's most persistent *quete* (luck-visit) tune'. He pointed to its close affinity with *quete* tunes from Hungary, Sweden, Bulgaria and France and believed that it travelled to England from the Continent.

God rest you merry, gentlemen,
Let nothing you dismay,
For Jesus Christ our Saviour
Was born upon this day,
To save us all from Satan's power
When we were gone astray:
O tidings of comfort and joy,
For Jesus Christ our Saviour was born on
Christmas Day!

2 In Bethlehem in Jewry
This blessed babe was born,
And laid within a manger
Upon this blessed morn;
The which his mother Mary
Nothing did take in scorn.

3 From God our Heavenly Father
A blessed angel came,
And unto certain shepherds
Brought tidings of the same,
How that in Bethlehem was born
The Son of God by name:

4 Fear not, then said the Angel
Let nothing you affright,
This day is born a Saviour
Of virtue, power and might;
So frequently to vanquish all
The friends of Satan quite

5 The shepherds at those tidings
Rejoiced much in mind,
And left their flocks a-feeding
In tempest, storm and wind,
And went to Bethlehem straightway
This blessed Babe to find:

6 But when to Bethlehem they came,
Whereat this Infant lay,
They found him in a manger
Where oxen feed on hay;
His mother Mary kneeling
Unto the Lord did pray:

7 Now to the Lord sing praises,
All you within this place,
And with true love and brotherhood
Each other now embrace;
This holy tide of Christmas
All others doth deface.

27
GOING THROUGH THE HILLS

John Rutter is undoubtedly one of the most talented and prolific writers of contemporary Christmas music. Like John Bell, Graham Kendrick and Sydney Carter, he writes both words and tunes although his main work is as a composer.

Born in 1945, he was educated at Highgate School and Clare College, Cambridge, where he read music. It was in 1966 while in his fourth year of studies there that he wrote both the words and music of this carol, which he entitled 'The Shepherd's Pipe Carol'. In a letter to me he describes how he came to write it:

I was putting together an album of carols for a record company who had expressed interest in my work: the performers were my friends and fellow-students. Most of the album consisted of arrangements of traditional carols, but I thought it would be nice to include one or two original carols. Given that the project was for a recording, not for church performance, I felt free to write something a bit jollier than might have been appropriate, say, in King's College Chapel, and the idea for the Shepherd's Pipe carol sprang out of the bright woodwind piping and the verbal (and musical) phrase 'on the way to Bethlehem'. The rest grew from there. I don't, incidentally, think of myself as a great wordsmith, but I have frequently had to write my own texts in the absence of an existing one that fits the music, and, over the years, I have increasingly enjoyed the challenge of writing words for music, both original texts and translations for singing. On the subject of rhyme, you may have noted that, as with Oscar Hammerstein's lyric for 'Some enchanted evening', the text of the Shepherd's Pipe carol has only one rhymed couplet and is otherwise unrhymed!

'The Shepherd's Pipe Carol' was recorded by the Clare College choir conducted by David Willcocks on an LP entitled 'In Dulci Jubilo'. Willcocks sent a copy of the record and the carol to the music editor at Oxford University Press who responded enthusiastically: 'We think this carol will be very popular in schools and ladies choirs.' In December 1967 Willcocks featured it in the Bach Choir's Christmas carol concert at the Royal Albert Hall.

This carol has proved remarkably popular. Oxford University Press asked Rutter to arrange it for unison and solo singing as well as for SSAA and SATB choirs. The popular Geordie bass-baritone, Owen Brannigan, was greatly taken with it and wrote to the publishers asking for it to be transposed down a minor third to the key of C. His letter, now in the OUP archives, dated 31 January 1969, asks for this to be done as soon as possible: 'As you know, they soon start wanting programmes – its really funny that "carol people" begin shouting for items from me from the Boxing Day before!'.

Frequently broadcast and recorded, including by Rutter's own Cambridge Singers, 'The Shepherd's Pipe Carol' with its delightfully fresh and infectiously bouncy melody will surely remain in the classic carol repertoire for many years to come.

The Shepherd's Pipe Carol

Going through the hills on a night so starry
  On the way to Bethlehem,
Far away I heard a shepherd boy piping
  On the way to Bethlehem.

Angels in the sky
Brought this message nigh:
'Dance and sing for joy
That Christ the new-born King
Is come to bring us peace on earth,
And he's lying cradled there at Bethlehem.'

2 'Tell me, shepherd boy piping tunes so merrily
  On the way to Bethlehem,
Who will hear your tunes on these hills so lonely
  On the way to Bethlehem?'

3 'None may hear my pipes on these hills so lonely
  On the way to Bethlehem
But a King will hear me play sweet lullabies
  When I get to Bethlchem.'

Angels in the sky
Came down from on high,
Hovered o'er the manger where the babe was lying
Cradled in the arms of his mother Mary,
Sleeping now in Bethlehem.

4 'Where is the new King, shepherd boy piping merrily,
  Is here there at Bethlehem?
I will find him soon by the star shining brightly
  In the sky o'er Bethlehem.'

5 'May I come with you, shepherd boy piping merrily,
Come with you to Bethlehem?
Pay my homage too at the new King's cradle,
Is it far from Bethlehem?'

Angels in the sky
Brought this message nigh:
'Dance and sing for joy
That Christ the infant King
Is born this night in lowly stable yonder,
Born for you at Bethlehem.'

28

GOOD CHRISTIAN MEN, REJOICE

This is another carol that has had to be purged of its gender specific language. In North America the preferred opening is now 'Good Christian friends, rejoice', as in *Voices United*, the hymn and worship book of the United Church of Canada, and the *Presbyterian Hymnal*, while in Britain it is 'Good Christians all, rejoice', as in *Rejoice and Sing*, *Baptist Hymns and Worship* and *Hymns and Psalms*. There is less certainty about what should replace the dreaded 'man' in the sixth line of verse two – *Hymns and Psalms* has 'mankind', *Rejoice and Sing* 'you', *the Presbyterian Hymnal* 'we' and *Baptist Hymns and Worship* 'all'.

'*Good Christian men, rejoice*' was one of several carols written by J.M. Neale (on whom see notes to No.1) to fit tunes found in a sixteenth-century Finnish song book which was rediscovered in the mid-nineteenth century. *Piae Cantiones*, a collection of 73 Latin hymns and carols edited by Theodoric Petri of Abo was first published in Finland in 1582. A copy of this rare work, which seems previously to have been unknown in Britain, was acquired by G.J.R. Gordon, Her Majesty's Envoy and Minister at Stockholm. Gordon presented the book in 1853 to Neale, who had already made his name as a translator and writer of hymns. Neale wrote 'Good Christian men, rejoice' to fit the tune of the old German carol, *In dulci jubilo* (No.37). Among other carols written to fit tunes found in *Piae Cantiones* were 'Good King Wenceslas' (No. 29) and 'Of the father's love begotten' (No. 57).

Neale's original text included a short fourth line in each verse – 'News! News!' in verse one, 'Joy! Joy!' in verse two and 'Peace! Peace!' in verse three. This was to fit the note values of the tune as transcribed by Thomas Helmore, master of the choristers of the Chapel Royal and Neale's associate in preparing *Carols for*

Christmas-tide (1853) in which 'Good Christian men rejoice' first appeared.

In fact, Helmore made a rare lapse in transcribing the melody of '*In dulci jubilo*' from *Piae Cantiones*. He mistakenly took the two quavers needed to cover the Finnish word *ligger* (lies) to be double breves. It was to provide suitably weighty words for these long notes that Neale provided his words after the third line. When other older versions of the tune of '*In dulci jubilo*' were examined, the mistake was revealed and it became evident that the two weighty words were not needed after the third line of each verse. They remained in several twentieth-century hymn-books, notably the 1916 *Congregational Hymnary* and the 1933 *Methodist Hymn Book* but have disappeared in all modern publications which have brought the hymn in line with the more accurate version of the tune for which it was written.

The secularization of Christmas has inspired, or provoked, this parody by Christ Fabry in his *Away with the Manger:*

Good secular men, rejoice
With heart and soul and voice.
Give ye heed to what we say,
Don't sing your Christmas song today
Sing of reindeers and of Claus,
Just don't say 'Jesus' now because
We'll be sued today,
We'll be sued today.

Good Christian men, rejoice
With heart and soul and voice;
Give ye heed to what we say,
Jesus Christ is born today:
Ox and ass before him bow,
And he is in the manger now.
  Christ is born today!
  Christ is born today!

2 Good Christian men, rejoice
With heart and soul and voice;
Now ye hear of endless bliss,
Jesus Christ was born for this:
He hath oped the heavenly door,
And man is blessed evermore.
  Christ was born for this!
  Christ was born for this!

3 Good Christian men, rejoice
With heart and soul and voice;
Now ye need not fear the grave,
Jesus Christ was born to save,
Calls you one, and calls you all,
To gain his everlasting hall.
  Christ was born to save!
  Christ was born to save!

29

GOOD KING WENCESLAS

This remains one of the most popular carols in Britain although there is some evidence that its appeal may be waning. While a Gallup Poll in 1996 placed it fourth equal along with 'O little town of Bethlehem' and 'Once in Royal David's city', it only just scraped into the 2005 BBC *Songs of Praise* poll in twentieth place. It has not had a good press, having been described as 'doggerel' and 'poor and commonplace to the last degree'. The editors of the *Oxford Book of Carols*, who deplored its 'rather confused narrative' and described it as one of Neale's 'less happy pieces', felt obliged to include it in their 1928 collection while expressing the hope that 'with the present wealth of carols for Christmas, "Good King Wenceslas" may gradually pass into disuse'. This seems unlikely. As Erik Routley commented, it 'contains snow and philanthropy in just the proportions calculated to make it a favourite'.

Like 'Good Christian men, rejoice', 'Good King Wenceslas' was written by J.M. Neale (on whose life see notes to No.1) to fit a tune in the recently discovered sixteenth-century Finnish carol book, *Piae Cantiones*. His rather charming but almost entirely fanciful story of the tenth-century Bohemian prince, described by Routley as 'one of the earliest examples of the modern synthetic carol', first appeared as a Boxing Day carol in *Carols for Christmastide* (1853–4), a collaboration between Neale and the musician Thomas Helmore.

The original Wenceslas, or Vaclav, to give him his native name, was born around 907 near Prague at the time when Bohemia was emerging from paganism. His Christian father, Duke Vratislav, died when he was still a child and he was separated from his pagan mother, Dragomira, and brought up by his Christian grandmother, Ludmilla. Around 925 Vaclav succeeded to his father's Dukedom, possibly thanks to support from the German emperor, and instituted an energetic programme of Christianization and reform in Bohemia. His rule was short – in 929 he was murdered on the orders of his pagan elder brother, Boleslav, in a church where he had been given sanctuary. Miracles were reported at his tomb and possibly on account of them, or as a result of a punitive expedition from the Emperor to avenge his vassal's murder, Boleslav became a Christian, repented of his dastardly deed and had Vaclav's remains translated to a shrine in Prague. Officially canonized by Detmar, the first bishop of Prague, Vaclav became patron saint of Bohemia. His bones still lie in St Vitus' Cathedral in Prague, where his skull is ceremonioiusly crowned with a golden diadem on special occasions and the new Czech Republic has adopted him as its patron saint.

Neale's account of Wenceslas' philanthropic activities is largely fictitious and contains a number of inaccuracies. Wenceslas was never a king – there were several Bohemian monarchs with that name in the later Middle Ages but none of them could be described as good. The original Duke Vaclav is known to have been philanthropic and a friend of the people. Medieval wall paintings in St Vitus' Cathedral apparently depict him distributing goods to the poor and there are stories of him working in the fields with the peasants to harvest corn and grapes to make bread and wine for the Mass. The reference to the page boy may have had a grain of truth. Vaclav does seem to have had a faithful servant, Podivin, who was a close adviser drawn from the ranks of the peasantry and who slew one of his master's murderers, an act for which he was hanged on the orders of Boleslav. The place of his death, in the middle of woods, is marked by a chapel.

There are strange touches to Neale's account. It is not clear, for example, why Wenceslas and his page had to drag pine logs a long distance when the object of their philanthropy lived 'right against the forest fence'. Then there is the heated footprint miracle, described by the late George Hill in an article in *The Times* as 'faintly reminiscent of Baked Alaska'. Neale was clearly wanting to find an improving moral tale about charitable deeds for St Stephen's Day, the day after Christmas Day which was traditionally associated with good works. Boxing Day may well be so called because of this association, either because alms boxes kept in churches throughout the Christmas season were opened on that day and their contents distributed to the poor, or because it was when 'boxes' or gifts were distributed to tradespeople and those providing a public service, such as lamplighters and parish watchmen.

There is a story that Neale wrote this carol, rather as John Byrom produced 'Christians, awake', as a gift for his daughter, Agnes, which may possibly explain the reference to St Agnes Fountain. She later related that her father was approached by a teetotal vegetarian who asked if he might change the line 'bring me flesh and bring me wine' to 'bring me milk and bring me bread', with a consequent change in the third line to 'Thou and I will see him fed'. Neale, who had written a ballad criticizing teetotallers, chose to ignore the request.

The tune for which Neale wrote 'Good King Wenceslas', and to which it is always sung, was set in *Piae Cantiones* to an Easter carol '*Tempus adest floridum*'. Neale turned another Spring carol from the *Piae Cantiones*, '*In vernali tempore*' into a Christmas one, 'O'er the hill and o'er the vale'. In a vain bid to have the tune to 'Good King Wenceslas' restored to Spring rather than Christmas use, the editors of the *Oxford Book of Carols* provided a translation of the original Latin beginning 'Spring has now unwrapped the flowers' but it has signally failed to catch on. King Wenceslas, however, shows no sign of retreating and still marches on making those strange warmed footprints in the snow. Long may he continue to do so.

Good King Wenceslas looked out
On the feast of Stephen,
When the snow lay round about,
Deep and crisp and even;
Brightly shone the moon that night,
Though the frost was cruel,
When a poor man came in sight,
Gathering winter fuel.

2 'Hither, page, and stand by me,
If thou knowst it, telling,
Yonder peasant, who is he?
Where and what his dwelling?'
'Sire, he lives a good league hence,
Underneath the mountain,
Right against the forest fence,
By St. Agnes' fountain.'

3 'Bring me flesh and bring me wine,
Bring me pine logs hither,
Thou and I will see him dine,
When we bear them thither.'
Page and monarch forth they went,
Forth they went together,
Through the rude wind's wild lament
And the bitter weather.

4 'Sire, the night is darker now
And the wind grows stronger;
Fails my heart I know not how;
I can go no longer.'
'Mark my footsteps, good my page;
Tread thou in them boldly;
Thou shalt find the winter's rage
Freeze thy blood less coldly.

5 In his master's steps he trod
Where the snow lay dinted;
Heat was in the very sod
Which the saint had printed,
Therefore Christian men be sure,
Wealth or rank possessing,
Ye who now will bless the poor.
Shall yourselves find blessing.

30

HARK, HARK, WHAT NEWS

This carol, which is not in any current hymn-book, was once extremely popular in England and appeared in the collections of both Davies Gilbert and William Sandys. It probably originated in the seventeenth or eighteenth century and seems to have been especially popular in Dorset and Somerset. One of its first known appearances in print was in the 1775 edition of *Church Harmony Sacred to Devotion* by Joseph Stephenson, who was parish clerk in Poole, Dorset.

The version which I have chosen to print in full here is that found in Sandys' collection and is the longest that I have come across. I particularly like the phrase 'Stupendous Babe!' at the beginning of verse ten and the injunction in verse five 'Arise my soul, and then, my voice/In hymns of praise early rejoice'. There is a good gutsy enthusiasm to this carol which one can imagine being bellowed out by west gallery choirs and blasted by village bands.

Davies Gilbert prints a much shorter version, consisting of verses one, two, six, eleven and twelve of those recorded by Sandys. There are numerous other versions of the carol. Several use Sandys' first, second, sixth (with 'as' changed to 'if' in the first line) and seventh (with 'Sweet' substituted for 'Dear' at the start of the first line) together with this extra last verse:

May we contemplate and admire,
And join with the celestial choir,
Extend your voice above the sky,
'All glory be to God on high'.

'Hark! hark what news' remains a favourite item with the village carollers of South Yorkshire who go round pubs at

Christmas singing traditional versions of carols that have largely disappeared in most other parts of the country. Sung to 'Good News', a tune by a Sheffield blacksmith, John Hall, who died in 1794, it was, in fact, the most popular item in the Yorkshire carollers' repertoire when a survey was taken in 1970. The CD *A Festival of Village Carols*, recorded at Grenoside Community Centre near Sheffield in December 1994 and issued in 1995, includes a version which begins:

Hark! Hark, what news the angels bring
Glad tidings of a new born King,
Born of a maid, a virgin pure,
Born without sin, from guilt secure.

Hail mighty prince, eternal King!
Let heaven and earth rejoice and sing!
Angels and men with one accord
Break forth in songs: 'O praise the Lord!'

Behold! he comes, and leaves the skies:
Awake, ye slumbering mortals, rise!
Awake to joy, and hail the morn
The Saviour of this world was born!

Other versions of the carol, similar to the Yorkshire one quoted above in respect of the first two verses but very different thereafter, are found in manuscript books of carols from Leighland, Odcombe and Long Burton, Dorset. Some have a refrain of repeated 'Hallelujahs', while others have a longer refrain:

Let heaven and earth their praises bring,
Angels and men rejoice and sing!

'Hark, hark' has been set to numerous tunes, several of which are in the fuguing style so popular in the west gallery tradition. The *New Oxford Book of Carols* prints three, the first of which, from Benjamin Smith's *Harmonious Companion* of 1732, has an extensive fuguing 'Hallelujah' refrain. The second is from Stephenson's *Church Harmony Sacred to Devotion* and the third was taken down in 1919 by H.E.D. Hammond from the singing of the Walton waits in Buckinghamshire and bound into a copy of Sandys in the Vaughan Williams Memorial Library in London. The *University Carol Book* includes a Leicestershire melody as well as an eighteenth-century tune taken up by Sandys.

The Old Hark

Hark, hark, what news the angels bring:
Glad tidings of a newborn King
Who is the Saviour of mankind
In whom we shall salvation find.

2 This the day; this blessed morn
The Saviour of mankind was born;
Born of a maid, a virgin pure,
Born without sin, from guilt secure.

3 Hail, blessed Virgin, full of grace!
Blessed above all mortal race,
Whose blessed womb brought forth in one,
A God, a Saviour, and a Son.

4 A perfect God, a perfect man,
A mystery which no man can
Attain to, though he's e'er so wise,
Till he ascend above the skies.

5 Arise, my soul, and then, my voice,
In hymns of praise early rejoice,
His fame extol and magnify,
Upon these errands Angels fly.

6 As angels sung at Jesus' birth,
Sure we have greater cause for mirth;
For why? It was for our sake
Christ did our human nature take.

7 Dear Christ, Thou didst Thyself debase,
Thus to descend to human race,
And leave Thy Father's throne above,
Lord, what could move Thee to this love.

8 Man that was made out of the dust,
He found a paradise at first;
But see the God of Heaven and earth
Laid in a manger at his birth.

9 Surely the manger where he lies
Doth figure out his sacrifice,
And by his birth all men may see
A pattern of humility.

10 Stupendous Babe! my God and King,
Thy praises I will ever sing,
In joyful accents raise my voice,
And in my praise of God rejoice.

11 My soul, learn by thy Saviour's birth
For to debase thyself on earth,
That I may be exalted high,
To live with him eternally.

12 I am resolved whilst here I live,
As I'm in duty bound, to give
All glory to the Deity,
One God alone, in persons three.

31

HARK, HOW ALL THE WELKIN RINGS

This is the original version of 'Hark, the herald angels sing'. As with '*Adeste, fideles*' and 'O come, all ye faithful', I am using separate entries for the original hymn and the more modern version sung nowadays since there are sufficient variations between them to make virtually two different hymns.

'Hark, how all the welkin rings' was written by Charles Wesley (for biographical details, see notes to No. 44) and first published as a 'Hymn for Christmas Day' in his *Hymns and Sacred Poems* in 1739.

Like all Wesley's work, the text of this hymn is packed with Biblical imagery. As well as the obvious New Testament influences in the first four verses, there are many Old Testament allusions. The images in the fifth verse are taken from Isaiah 9.6: 'His name shall be called ... The Prince of Peace' and Malachi 4.2: 'But for you who fear my name the sun of rightenousness shall rise, with healing in its wings'. Verse seven takes its cue from Haggai 2.7: 'The desire of all nations shall come' and then explores the complex imagery of Genesis 4.15 where God tells the serpent: 'I will put emnity between thee and the woman, and between thy seed and her seed; it shall bruise thy head and thou shalt bruise its heel.'

'Hark, how all the welkin rings' is doctrinally as well as Biblically rich. In addition to the Incarnation, it explores the Virgin birth (verse three), the kenosis, or self-emptying, of Christ (verse six with its echoes of Philippians 2.7), and a second Adam Christology (verse nine). Perhaps the most original theme put forward is that of Christ's cosmic powers of redemption. The attribution of the statement 'Christ the Lord is born today' to Universal nature in verse two and the description of his mission as being the restoration of 'ruined nature' in verse eight give a cosmic rather than a narrowly human dimension to Christ's saving power. Here, indeed, is ecotheology, with the proclamation of a Christ who is concerned with redeeming the whole environment and not just the human part of creation. This theme is lost in the much revised version of the hymn that we sing today.

Wesley's original hymn underwent a complex series of alterations. I will concentrate in these notes on the early alterations which preserved the hymn in its original four-line verse form and survey later changes which re-cast it in its modern eight-line form in the notes to the next hymn (No.32).

The first significant alterations to 'Hark, how all the welkin rings' were made by George Whitefield (1714–70), another leading figure in the Evangelical Revival but an arch-theological opponent of the Wesleys, being a Calvinist rather than an Arminian and so having a much more limited doctrine of atonement. He included Wesley's Christmas Day hymn in his *Collection* published in 1753, changing the first two lines to 'Hark the herald angels sing, Glory to the new-born King'. It is not clear what objection he had to the word 'welkin' which was certainly not archaic then as it is now. Of Middle English origin, it means cloud, or apparent arch or vault of heaven overhead and so came to mean the sky or firmament. The phrase 'make the welkin ring' came into general use to indicate the making of a great noise – as in by Surtees 'Making the welkin ring with the music of their deep-toned notes'. Davies Gilbert's 1823 collection included a West of England carol which begins:

Hark! all around the welkin rings
Bright seraphs hail the morn
That ushers in the King of Kings,
That sees a Saviour born.

Whitefield omitted verses eight and ten of Wesley's original hymn. There may well have been a theological reason for this. He was probably unhappy about the cosmic and mystical dimensions of verse eight and would almost certainly have been uneasy with the implications of 'O! to all Thyself impart,/

Formed in each believing heart'. He may well also not have liked the phrase 'Heavenly Man', feeling that it smacked somewhat of Arianism and could have been taken to suggest that Jesus did not have a true earthly existence and was fully human. For similar reasons, he also changed the opening line of verse five from 'heavenly' to 'heaven-born'.

Whitefield's version was taken up in numerous later eighteenth and nineteenth century hymn-books. Although it effectively supplanted Wesley's original version from the mid-nineteenth century, various attempts were made to go back to 'Hark, how all the welkin rings'. The editors of the 1904 edition of *Hymns Ancient and Modern* restored the original opening, bringing down a barrage of criticism led by the *Daily Express* and the *Evening Star* which complained that 'since the late Mr Bowdler rewrote the plays of Shakespeare we have had no more pitiful exhibition'. The first edition of the *English Hymnal* (1906) also went back to Wesley's original hymn, omitting only its ninth and tenth verses, but this provoked a further chorus of protest and the editors were forced to insert a printed slip into all copies with the familiar amended opening.

Meanwhile, other changes had been made. When Martin Madan included the hymn in his *Collection of Psalms and Hymns extracted from various authors* (1760), he removed the reference to universal nature in the second verse and substituted the lines: 'With th'angelic host proclaim,/Christ is born in Bethlehem'. This change caught on in many hymn-books, although not all. Other changes did not have the same impact, for example that made by Thomas Cotterill who in the various editions of his *Selections* which appeared between 1810 and 1820 altered the first verse to:

Hark! the herald angels sing,
Glory to the new-born King;
Glory in the highest heaven,
Peace on earth and man forgiven.

In some late eighteenth- and early nineteenth-century hymn-books the hymn was split into two with verses seven to nine of the original (beginning 'Come, desire of nations, come') being printed as a separate hymn.

The use of the hymn's opening couplet as a refrain first occurred when the hymn was given semi-official authorization in the Church of England by being added to the Supplement of the 1782 edition of Tate and Brady's *New Version of the Psalms*. The Supplement, which was bound in with the *Book of Common Prayer*, consisted of 16 hymns, with 'Hark, the herald angels sing' joining 'While shepherds watched' as the only Christmas hymns authorized to be sung in Anglican church services. The repetition of the opening couplets of hymns as a refrain was not uncommon – the same thing happened with 'Christians, awake! Salute the happy morn' (No. 16).

The 1782 Supplement changed the phrase 'man with men' in the third line of verse four to 'man with man'. In his *Select Portions of Psalms* (1810) John Kempthorne made a more substantial alteration to this verse to make it 'Pleased as man with man to dwell,/Jesus, our Emmanuel'. This change was taken up by the editors of *Hymns Ancient and Modern* in 1861.

Although settings of Wesley's hymn which treated it as though it were in eight-line stanzas can be traced back as far as 1769, it continued to be sung in its original four-line form for much of the nineteenth century. Indeed, its standard singing until 1860 would have been as a four line, six to eight verse hymn, often with the opening couplet repeated as a refrain. This is how it appears, for example, in Sandys' collection where verses one, two, three, five and six are used to make a five-verse hymn with refrain.

Its enormous popularity meant that numerous tunes were associated with it – Routley speculates that Wesley himself may have had in mind SAVANAH which his brother had recently brought over from the Moravians at Herrnhut. DENT DALE, to which the hymn was set in the *English Hymnal,* was undoubtedly used. Perhaps the most popular tune to which the hymn was sung in the eighteenth century was EASTER HYMN (the tune we now associate with 'Jesus Christ is risen today') with 'Allelujah' being sung at the end of each verse. I have myself used this tune with the original Wesley words to great effect.

Hark, how all the welkin rings!
'Glory to the King of Kings,
Peace on earth and mercy mild,
God and sinners reconciled'.

2 Joyful, all ye nations rise,
Join the triumph of the skies;
Universal nature say
'Christ the Lord is born to-day'.

3 Christ, by highest heaven adored,
Christ, the everlasting Lord,
Late in time behold him come
Offspring of the Virgin's womb.

4 Veiled in flesh, the Godhead see!
Hail the incarnate Deity!
Pleased as man with men to appear,
Jesus, our Emmanuel here!

5 Hail the heavenly Prince of Peace!
Hail the Sun of Righteousness!
Light and life to all he brings,
Risen with healing in his wings.

6 Mild he lays his glory by,
Born that man no more may die,
Born to raise the sons of earth,
Born to give them second birth!

7 Come, Desire of Nations, come,
Fix in us thy humble home;
Rise, the woman's conquering seed,
Bruise in us the serpent's head.

8 Now display thy saving power,
Ruined nature now restore,
Now in mystic union join
Thine to ours, and ours to thine.

9 Adam's likeness, Lord, efface;
Stamp thine image in its place;
Second Adam from above,
Reinstate us in thy love.

10 Let us Thee, tho' lost, regain
Thee, the Life, the Heavenly Man.
O! to all Thyself impart,
Formed in each believing heart.

32

HARK! THE HERALD ANGELS SING

Readers who have patiently waded through the rather circuitous notes that accompanied the last item in this collection will know that this one is the result of an unusual amount of tweaking and altering by several hands.

The version of 'Hark! the herald angels' printed here, which is substantially that now sung in English-speaking churches across the world, is, as we have seen, a composite based on an original hymn by Charles Wesley but also involving the input of George Whitefield, Martin Madan, John Kempthorne and others.

What Wesley thought of the alterations, several of which were carried out in his own lifetime, we do not know. We do know what his brother John thought about the alteration of hymn texts, thanks to a comment that he made in the preface to the 1779 edition of *A Collection of Hymns for the use of the people called Methodists*:

> Many Gentlemen have done my Brother and me (though not without naming us) the honour to reprint many of our hymns. Now they are perfectly welcome to do so, provided they print them just as they are. But I desire they would not attempt to mend them – for they really are not able.

John Wesley went on to suggest that where editors cannot resist the temptation to amend and alter, they should at least print the original texts in the margin 'that we may no longer be held responsible either for the nonsense or the doggerel of other men'. It has to be said that he himself was not above altering other people's hymns and changed the opening of Isaac Watts' great paraphrase of Psalm 90 from 'Our God and help in ages past' to 'O God, our help in ages past'.

As promised, these notes will concentrate primarily on the process whereby the original ten four-line verses of this hymn were turned into three eight-line verses. The first setting in this latter form is found as early as 1769 in Martin Madan's *Lock Collection* of 1769 where a version of the hymn for high voices and organs treats it in eight-line stanzas while retaining the original four-line numbering. The composer of this setting, which is reproduced in the *New Oxford Book of Carols*, may have been the historian and organist, Charles Burney.

There may have been other settings from the later eighteenth and early nineteenth century which treated the hymn in a similar way but, as we have seen, it was most commonly sung throughout this period in four-line stanzas, sometimes with a refrain repeating the opening couplet. By the middle of the nineteenth century, however, it seems increasingly to have been sung as a three or four verse eight-line hymn to a chorale-like tune. Mercer's *Church Psalter and Hymn Book*, for example, sets it to the German chorale tune SALZBURG.

What really established 'Hark, the herald angels sing' in the eight-line form that we now sing it (again, with a refrain taking up the opening couplet) was its marriage to the tune by Felix Mendelssohn Bartholdy (1809–47) from which it is now inseparable. As the editors of the *New Oxford Book of Carols* remark, until the mid-nineteenth century Wesley's hymn was 'a poem in search of a melody. Mendelssohn's music, on the other hand, was a melody in search of a poem'. The process that brought them together is one of those happy accidents that bestride the history of hymnody.

In the early 1850s W.H. Cummings, the youthful organist of Waltham Abbey parish church in Essex, who had sung under Mendelssohn's baton in 1847 at the first London performance of 'Elijah', was leafing through the score of a four-movement *Festgesang* for male chorus and brass which the great German composer had written for the Gutenberg Festival held in Leipzig in 1840 to celebrate the 400th anniversary of the invention of printing. The melody of a chorus which formed the second movement, and was repeated in the fourth, struck him as being perfect for 'Hark! the herald angels sing' and he set about adapting it.

Mendelssohn himself had, in fact, toyed with the idea of adapting the tune for more widespread use and wrote to his English publishers:

I think there ought to be other words to No. 2. If the right ones are hit at, I am sure the piece will be liked very much by the singers and the hearers, but it will never do to sacred words. There must be a national and merry subject found out, something to which the soldier-like and buxom motion of the piece has some relation, and the words must express something gay and popular as the music tries to do it.

Cummings, unaware of those strictures, proceeded to set 'Hark! the herald angels sing' to an adaptation of Mendelssohn's melody. His setting was published in 1856 and taken up by Richard Chope in his *Congregational Hymn and Tune Book* (1857) where the tune was called ST VINCENT and in the Wesleyan Sunday School Tune Book of 1858 where it was called BERLIN. W.H. Monk took it up for the first edition of *Hymns Ancient and Modern* (1861), a book which sealed so many marriages between words and tunes, although he hedged his bets by providing a second and much inferior tune especially written for the hymn by Chappell Batchelor, organist of Southwall Minster. Since then, MENDELSSOHN, as it was then called, has been the inseparable companion.

The text that its original author would probably have considered a travesty and the tune that its composer said should never do for sacred words have combined to produce one of the most popular hymns in the English language which came third in the 2005 BBC *Songs of Praise* poll of the nation's favourite carols. Virtually no midnight service or carol concert is complete without it. It has also achieved the accolade of being much parodied. During the Abdication Crisis of 1937 a version circulated which began 'Hark the heralds angels sing,/Mrs Simpson's pinched our king'. It has also been taken up as an advertising jingle:

Hark! the herald angels sing,
Beecham's pills are quite the thing,
Two for a woman, one for a child,
Peace on earth and mercy mild.

Even in the twentieth century, however, the shape of this hymn has not been entirely settled and constant. The version printed on page 144, formed by coupling together verses one and two, three and four and five and six of the original in their amended form, is probably the most commonly sung but by no means universal. The 1933 *Methodist Hymn Book*, for example, reversed the order in the third verse, so that 'Mild he lays his glory by' comes before 'Hail the heaven-born Prince of Peace'. In common with *Congregational Praise* and the revised edition of *Hymns Ancient and Modern*, it also preserves the phrase 'man with men' in the seventh line of verse two. That little bit of gender specificity has not escaped the attentions of more recent and more politically correct hymn-book editors – *Hymns for Today's Church* renders it as 'man for us' and also changes the end of the third verse to

Born that we may no more die;
Born to raise us from the earth,
Born to give us second birth.

The United Reformed Church's *Rejoice and Sing* has 'man with us' in verse two and has similar changes in verse three, while re-introducing something of Wesley's original conception of the cosmic Christ with the line 'Born to raise the things of earth'.

Hark! the herald angels sing

Hark! the herald angels sing
Glory to the new-born King,
Peace on earth and mercy mild,
God and sinners reconciled.
Joyful all ye nations rise,
Join the triumph of the skies;
With th'angelic host proclaim:
'Christ is born in Bethlehem.'
Hark! the herald angels sing
Glory to the new-born King.

2 Christ, by highest Heav'n adored,
Christ, the Everlasting Lord,
Late in time behold him come,
Offspring of a virgin's womb.
Veiled in flesh the Godhead see,
Hail the incarnate Deity!
Pleased as Man with man to dwell,
Jesus, our Emmanuel.
Hark! the herald angels sing
Glory to the new-born King.

3 Hail, the heaven-born Prince of Peace!
Hail, the Sun of Righteousness!
Light and life to all he brings,
Risen with healing in his wing.
Mild he lays his glory by,
Born that man no more may die,
Born to raise the sons of earth,
Born to give them second birth.
Hark! the herald angels sing
Glory to the new-born King.

33

HERE WE COME A WASSAILING

Here is a traditional English carol which makes no mention of the birth of Jesus. God's blessing is invoked in the refrain and in the seventh verse but otherwise this is a jolly and wholly secular ditty full of Christmas and New Year cheer and merry making.

The tradition of wassailers going from door to door singing carols and drinking the health of those they visit goes back to medieval times. The word 'wassail' derives from the Old English 'Waes hael' (be whole or well) and was originally a phrase of welcome – 'hael' is the origin of the greetings 'hail' and 'hallo'. Strutt's *Sports and Pastimes of the People of England* gives a good description of the practice and the drink that lay at its heart:

> Wassail, or rather the wassail bowl, which was a bowl of spiced ale, formerly carried about by young women on New-year's eve, who went from door to door in their several parishes singing a few couplets of homely verses composed for the purpose, and presented the liquor to the inhabitants of the house where they called, expecting a small gratuity in return.

The wassail cup was a potent brew. A recipe in Nicholas Culpepper's *Herbal* (c.1600) lists the ingredients as two cinnamon sticks, four cloves, two blades of mace, one ginger root, four apples, a teaspoonful of nutmeg, four ounces of sugar, and half a pint each of brown ale and cider.

This song brings together the key elements in the wassailing tradition – the progress round the village singing and wishing people the compliments of the season, the alcoholic refreshment and request for money and victuals (even if it is just mouldy cheese) and the general air of revelry and merry making. The editors of the *Oxford Book of Carols* point out that the second and fourth verses 'are not suitable when the carol is sung in church, but they give a vivid picture of the Waits of old times'. The name 'waits' was increasingly given to wassailers in the nineteenth century. It derived from the watchmen of earlier times who had sounded their horns or played a tune to mark the passing hours of the night but came to be applied to parties of singers and musicians who performed outside people's houses at Christmastide.

This text comes from William Husk's *Songs of the Nativity* published in 1864. Husk (1814–87) was a leading Victorian musicologist who followed Gilbert and Sandys in collecting, publishing and popularizing traditional English folk carols. He found 'Here we come a wassailing' in a broadside printed in Bradford, Yorkshire, around 1850 and noted that 'its appearance so recently seems to furnish presumptive evidence of the custom of Wassailing, or, at least, some remains of it, being still in existence in the West Riding of the great northern county'. Husk also surmised that the carol was popular on the other side of the Pennines, having discovered it, under the title 'Wessel Cup Hymn' in a chap-book printed in Manchester and in a recently published volume of *The Ballads and Songs of Lancashire*.

Other evidence points to the northern English origins of this carol. Martin Shaw included in the *Oxford Book of Carols*, of which he was music editor, a tune to which his father, James Shaw, remembered the carol being sung in the streets of Leeds in the 1850s. Very similar in its first eight bars to the 'London' tune of 'God rest you merry, gentlemen', it was still being sung in the West Riding in the 1910s. In their *Christmas Carols, New and Old* (1871), Bramley and Stainer used another tune also from Yorkshire.

Husk may well have been right in asserting that 'the carol in the main be of no great antiquity'. Its penultimate verse, however, is identical with the the opening of a short carol printed in Ritson's *Ancient Songs and Ballads* which seems to have gone back at least to the beginning of the seventeenth century:

God bless the master of this house
Likewise the mistress too,
And all the little children
That round the table go.
And all you kin and kinsfolk,
That dwell both far and near;
I wish you a Merry Christmas,
And a happy New Year.

The editors of the *Oxford Book of Carols* speculate that 'Shakespeare may well have heard them sung outside his house on Christmas night.'

Wassailers' Carol

Here we come a wassailing
Among the leaves so green;
Here we come a wandering
So fair to be seen.

Love and joy come to you,
And to you your wassail too,
And God bless you, and send you a happy
new year,
And God send you a happy new year.

2 Our wassail cup is made
Of the rosemary tree,
And so is your beer
Of the best barley.

3 We are not daily beggars
That beg from door to door,
But we are neighbours children
Whom you have seen before.

4 Call up the butler of this house
Put on his golden ring;
Let him bring us up a glass of beer,
And better shall we sing.

5 We have got a little purse
Of stretching leather skin;
We want a little of your money
To line it well within.

6 Bring us out a table
And spread it with a cloth
Bring us out some mouldy cheese,
And some of your Christmas loaf.

7 God bless the master of this house
Likewise the mistress too,
And all the little children
That round the table go.

8 Good master and good mistress
While you're sitting by the fire,
Pray think of us poor children
Who are wandering in the mire.

34

HOW BRIGHTLY SHINES THE MORNING STAR

Like 'All my heart this night rejoices' and 'From heaven above' (Nos. 6 & 21), this hymn comes from the German Lutheran tradition. The original German text of which it is a translation, '*Wie schön leuchtet der Morgenstern*', was the work of Philip Nicolai (1556–1608) and was a companion piece to his great Advent hymn '*Wachet auf, ruft uns die Stimme*' (*Daily Telegraph Book of Hymns* No. 142). Both hymns commemorated the young Count of Waldech, to whom Nicolai had been tutor and who died at the age of 15 in a plague that swept through Westphalia in 1598, and first appeared in print in 1599. Nicolai, who was ordained into the Lutheran priesthood at the age of 20, served as pastor in a number of German towns and ended his ministry as chief pastor of St Katherine's Church in Hamburg.

'*Wie schön leuchtet der Morgenstern*' ran to seven stanzas of ten lines each. The initial letters of the verses spelled out the first letters of the count's name (*W*ilhelm *E*rnst, Graf *u*nd *H*err *z*u *W*aldech). The hymn was entitled 'A spiritual bridal song of the believing soul concerning Jesus Christ, her heavenly Bridegroom, founded on the 45th Psalm of the prophet David'. It is arguable that it has no specifically Christmas connotations. The editors of the *New Oxford Book of Carols*, who provide their own free translation of all seven verses, beginning 'How brightly shines the pointed star', point out that for a long time the chorale was sung not at Christmas but rather at weddings and deathbeds. They further note that 'the Morning Star of the opening has nothing to do with the star of the magi: this is Christ the "dayspring from on high" (Luke 1.78) and the "Sun of righteousness"' (Micah 4.2).

There is no doubt, however, that '*Wie schön leuchtet der Morgenstern*' came to be sung in German churches at Christmas and it can clearly be read as having a strong incarnational focus. Its reference to Jesus as coming from David's line links it with other Christmas hymns, notably, of course, 'Once in Royal David's city'. Nicolai's original first verse also spoke of Jesus springing from the branch of Jesse, picking up references in Isaiah 11:1 and Romans 15.12 which feature in several Advent hymns, notably 'O come, O come Emmanuel' (*Daily Telegraph Book of Hymns*, No. 42).

Numerous translations of Nicolai's hymn into English were made in the nineteenth century. They include J.C. Jacobi's 'How bright appears the Morning Star!', Catherine Winkworth's 'O Morning Star! how fair and bright', A.T. Russell's 'How graciously does shine afar', H. Harbaugh's 'How lovely shines the Morning Star' and M.W. Stryker's 'How brightly glows the morning star'. The one that I have chosen was made by William Mercer (1811–73) and appears in the *New English Hymnal*. It has the clearest Incarnational focus and very definitely does belong in the Christmas hymns section.

Mercer, who was born at Barnard Castle, Durham, and educated at Trinity College, Cambridge, spent the greater part of his adult life as incumbent of St George's Church in Sheffield. He translated several German and Latin hymns for *The Church Psalter and Hymn Book*, on which he collaborated with the organist John Goss. For several years after its publication in 1854, this was one of the most widely used hymnbooks in the Church of England, only gradually being supplanted by *Hymns Ancient and Modern*.

Several current hymnbooks have Mercer's version of this hymn, including the *New English Hymnal*, *Hymns for Church and School*, the *Popular Carol Book* and the *New Catholic Hymnal*. Other books include translations of a later re-working of Nicolai's hymn by Adolf Schlegel (1721–93), '*Wie herrlich strahlt der Morgenstern*' which was published in 1766, also with seven stanzas of ten lines, under the title 'Longing after union with Jesus'. Born in Meissen, Saxony, Schlegel studied at the University of Lepizig and after periods teaching and writing, served as pastor at Zerbst and Hanover.

Several English translations of '*Wie herrlich strahlt der Morgenstern*', which is often attributed jointly to Nicolai and Schlegel, were made in the nineteenth century. The best is almost certainly 'How brightly beams the morning star!' by the redoubtable Catherine Winkworth, published in her *Chorale Book for England* in 1863. Hymnal editors are somewhat doubtful about whether to regard it as a Christmas hymn. The *Oxford Book of Carols* classifies it as 'general: Epiphany: Easter', *Songs of Praise* considers it most suitable for 'Epiphany and the Sundays after' and the *BBC Hymn Book* places it in the section on 'The Lord Jesus Christ – his presence and power'. The Church of Ireland's *Church Hymnal* avoids the issue by consigning it to the section labelled 'Chiefly for the Use of Choirs'. Although it has no specifically incarnational focus, its arresting first verse, which gives a marvellous invocation of the morning star filling darkened souls with light, has echoes of the prologue of St John's Gospel read at so many Christmas morning services, as well of the star that guided the wise men. This comes over strongly in Catherine Winkworth's translation:

How brightly beams the morning star!
What sudden radiance from afar
Doth glad us with its shining?
Brightness of God, that breaks our night
And fills the darkened souls with light
Who long for truth were pining!
Thy word, Jesus, inly feeds us,
Rightly leads us,
Life bestowing,
Praise, oh praise such love o'erflowing!

A very free translation of '*Wie schön leuchtet der Morgenstern*' by H.N. Bate has been incorporated into the hymn 'Three kings from Persian lands afar' (No. 89)

Translations of both Nicolai's '*Wie schön leuchtet der Morgenstern*' and Schlegel's '*Wie herrlich strahlt der Morgenstern*' are generally set to the tune which accompanied the first appearance of Nicolai's hymn in 1599. It may well have been composed by Nicolai himself and was possibly suggested by the tune of '*Resonent in Laudibus*'. WIE SCHÖN LEUCHTET was harmonized both by J.S. Bach in his Cantata No.1, and Felix Mendelssohn in his 1847 oratorio, *Christus*. Both these harmonizations are in regular use – they can be found side by side in the *Oxford Book of Carols* and *Hymns for Church and School*. The tune was played from numerous church towers and remains a favourite for carillons in Germany and the Low Countries.

'Wie schön leuchtet der Morgenstern'

How brightly shines the Morning Star!
The nations see and hail afar
The Light in Judah shining.
Thou David's son of Jacob's race,
The Bridegroom, and the King of grace,
For thee our hearts are pining!
Lowly, holy,
Great and glorious, thou victorious
Prince of graces,
Filling all the heavenly places!

Though circled by the hosts on high,
He deigns to cast a pitying eye
Upon his helpless creature;
The whole creation's Head and Lord,
By highest seraphim adored,
Assumes our very nature.
Jesu, grant us,
Through thy merit, to inherit
Thy salvation;
Hear, o hear our supplication.

Rejoice, ye heav'ns; thou earth, reply;
With praise, ye sinners, fill the sky,
For this his Incarnation.
Incarnate God, put forth thy power,
Ride on, ride on, great Conqueror,
Till all know thy salvation.
Amen, Amen!
Alleluya, Alleluya!
Praise be given
Evermore by earth and heaven.

35

I SAW THREE SHIPS COME SAILING IN

This extraordinary and fascinating carol raises numerous questions. Why were three ships needed to transport Christ and his lady, and, come to that, who is she – his mother, Mary Magdalen or someone else? Surely one vessel would have sufficed? How on earth could the ships have sailed into Bethlehem – in the words of *The Times* arts editor, Richard Morrison, after a visit to that town, 'It is on the top of a hill, surrounded by land of an indisputably dry disposition. Where do ships sail in? It is hard enough just to get a taxi' – and how does the notion of Christ and his lady arriving in this way at Bethlehem on Christmas Day tie in with the Biblical story that Mary and Joseph came to the city on a donkey?

The truth is that the original on which this carol and many others like it are based had nothing to do with Jesus' nativity but rather described the journey of the relics of the wise men, or Magi, who were the first Gentiles to visit the infant Christ.

The Gospel accounts are decidedly uninformative as to the number, status and exact provenance of the Magi who visit Bethlehem after following the star. Their identity was gradually filled in, or invented, by the early church. Tertullian, the late second-century North African apologist, first called them kings and Origen, the Greek theologian, was the first Christian writer to say that they were three in number, presumably deducing this from the fact that they brought three gifts. Later the names Casper, Melchior and Balthazar came to be attached to them.

During the Middle Ages stories about the three kings became increasingly elaborate. The tradition grew that 250 years or so after their deaths their bodies had been brought to Byzantium by the Empress Helena, mother of the Emperor Constantine who re-named the city Constantinople. They were later supposedly transferred by St Eustatius to Milan and from there in 1162 the Emperor Frederick Barbarossa brought their skulls to Cologne where they are said still to be preserved as relics in the cathedral.

Some versions of this song tell the story of the bringing of the three skulls, or crawns, of the Magi from Milan to Cologne by ship – either through the Mediterranean and then through the Bay of Biscay, the English Channel and the North Sea, or perhaps more likely by river and canal up the Rhine. This latter route is suggested by a version of the carol collected from a boatman on the River Humber in 1895, the verses of which begin with the lines 'I saw three ships come sailing by', 'I asked them what they'd got on board', 'They said they'd got three crawns', 'I asked them where they was taken to', 'They said they was ganging to Coln upon Rhine', 'I asked them where they came frae' and 'They said they came from Bethlehem'.

It may well be that the earliest versions of this song came from Germany where there was also a strong tradition of 'ship carols' in which Jesus' coming is compared in a mystical way to the arrival of a ship. One of the finest, '*Es kommt ein Schiff geladen*' ('A ship there comes, a-laden'), which dates from the fourteenth century and may be associated with the mystic Johannes Tauler (1300–61), is quoted in full in the *New Oxford Book of Carols* whose editors suggest that English carols like 'I saw three ships' may represent a fusion of the legends of the voyage to Cologne and the quite different tradition of ships symbolizing the Nativity.

In his book *The English Carol* Erik Routley offers an alternative explanation and speculates that 'I saw three ships' may be bound up with 'a deep-rooted psychological instinct in the imagination which associates the sea with the Great Division between heaven and earth, and a sea journey successfully completed with a major gesture against the powers of darkness'.

Whatever their ultimate provenance and deeper meaning, there is no doubt that there were early carols in the British Isles using ship imagery to portray Jesus' arrival in and ministry on earth. One thought to originate in Scotland in the mid-sixteenth century pictures just one ship:

There comes a ship for sailing then,
St Michael was the steres-man,
St John sat in the horn (stern):
Our Lord harped, Our Lady sang
And all the bells of heaven they rang
On Christ's Sunday at morn.

Numerous other versions of this carol describe two rather than three ships. One taken down on the Kent-Sussex border in 1905 has the following first lines:

1) As I sat under a holly tree
2) I saw two ships come sailing in
3) Who d'you think were in those two ships?
4) Joseph and Mary was in those two ships?
5) Where d'you think they were going to?
6) They were going to Bethlehem
7) What d'you think they were going for?
8) They were going to pay their tax.

A version found in Kent in the mid-nineteenth century has three ships bearing Mary and her son to Bethlehem:

As I sat under a sycamore tree,
I looked me out upon the sea,
I looked me out upon the sea
On Christmas Day in the morning.

I saw three ships a-sailing there,
The Virgin Mary and Christ they bare;
The Virgin Mary and Christ they bare;
On Christmas Day in the morning.

He did whistle and She did sing,
And all the bells on earth did ring;
And all the bells on earth did ring;
On Christmas Day in the morning.

And now we hope to taste your cheer
And wish you all a happy new year;
And wish you all a happy new year;
On Christmas Day in the morning.

A popular version of the carol, similar to the above, said to have originated in Warwickshire or Staffordshire but found in the nineteenth century throughout north and west England, began 'As I sat on a sunny bank,/On Christmas day in the morning'. Another version, collected on Tyneside in the 1830s by Sir Cuthbert Sharpe, who was Collector of Customs at Sunderland and Newcastle, has the three ships sailing in on New Year's Day and bringing three pretty girls:

One could whistle, and one could sing,
And one could play on the violin;
Such joy there was at my wedding,
On new Year's Day in the morning.

This secular version appears in Iona and Peter Opie's *Oxford Dictionary of Nursery Rhymes* and is almost certainly a children's parody of the original. It also appears, with 'Christmas Day' substituted for 'New Year's Day' in the *Faber Book of Carols* where it is described as 'An old English Nursery Rhyme'. Most other modern carol books opt for the more spiritual version which I print in full on page 160. It is this version of the carol that Sandys included in his 1833 collection and Husk in his *Songs of the Nativity*. It is also this version which appears in the *New Oxford Book of Carols* and its predecessor, the *Oxford Book of Carols*, which records that 'a unique version introducing the Passion ('As I sat by my old cottage door') was taken down by Cecil Sharp in Worcestershire'. That one, I fear, we will pass over. I suspect that long-suffering readers who have struggled thus far have had quite enough of this particular and rather troublesome ditty. There is just one other version worth mentioning – Jubilate Hymns' *Carols For Today* (1986) contains an up-dated version which has been taken up in several collections, including *Church Family Worship*:

When God from heaven to earth came down,
On Christmas Day, on Christmas Day,
The songs rang out in Bethlehem town
On Christmas Day in the morning.

About the tune there is mercifully much less to say. It goes under that marvellously vague and catch-all label 'English traditional'. Sandys noted its similarity to one of the old Shakespearian tunes, 'There lived a man in Babylon' sung by Sir Toby Belch in *Twelfth Night*.

I saw three ships come sailing in,
On Christmas Day, on Christmas Day,
I saw three ships come sailing in,
On Christmas Day in the morning.

2 And what was in those ships all three?
On Christmas Day, on Christmas Day,
And what was in those ships all three?
On Christmas Day in the morning.

3 Our Saviour Christ and his lady,
On Christmas Day, on Christmas Day,
Our Saviour Christ and his lady,
On Christmas Day in the morning.

4 Pray, whither sailed those ships all three?
On Christmas Day, on Christmas Day,
Pray, whither sailed those ships all three?
On Christmas Day in the morning.

5 O they sailed into Bethlehem,
On Christmas Day, on Christmas Day,
O they sailed into Bethlehem,
On Christmas Day in the morning.

6 And all the bells on earth shall ring,
On Christmas Day, on Christmas Day,
And all the bells on earth shall ring,
On Christmas Day in the morning.

7 And all the angels in heaven shall sing,
On Christmas Day, on Christmas Day,
And all the angels in heaven shall sing,
On Christmas Day in the morning.

8 And all the souls on earth shall sing,
On Christmas Day, on Christmas Day,
And all the souls on earth shall sing,
On Christmas Day in the morning.

9 Then let us all rejoice again!
On Christmas Day, on Christmas Day,
Then let us all rejoice again!
On Christmas Day in the morning.

36

I WONDER AS I WANDER

After the pages required to do justice to the last carol, this one can be explained in a few paragraphs. It was collected in Murphy, Cherokee County, North Carolina, in 1933 by John Jacob Niles and almost certainly comes from the Appalachian mountains.

Niles (1892–1980) was a leading American folksong collector. Among other carols he collected were 'Lullay, thou tiny little child' a version of the traditional English 'Lully, lulla, thou little tiny child' (No.49) which he came across in Gatlinburg, Tennessee.

He published 'I wonder as I wander' in his *Songs of the Hill-Folk* (1934). It is difficult to establish how old it is and there are some scholars who maintain that it does not go back before the twentieth century.

This is a carol which really needs its tune to do it justice. The clean, haunting melody to which Niles heard it being sung in the mountains, and which has since been its faithful companion, maintains the open-air atmosphere and the sense of wistful wandering conjured up in the first line. It has appealed to a number of arrangers, including John Rutter who has recorded his simple but effective arrangement with the Cambridge Singers.

I wonder as I wander, out under the sky,
How Jesus the Saviour did come for to die
For poor or'n'ry people like you and like I;
I wonder as I wander, out under the sky.

2 When Mary birthed Jesus, 'twas in a cow's stall
With wise men and farmers and shepherds and all.
But high from God's heaven a star's light did fall,
And the promise of ages it did then recall.

3 If Jesus had wanted for any wee thing,
A star in the sky, or a bird on the wing,
Or all of God's angels in heaven for to sing,
He surely could have it, 'cause He was the King.

4 I wonder as I wander, out under the sky,
How Jesus the Saviour did come for to die
For poor or'n'ry people like you and like I;
I wonder as I wander, out under the sky.

37

IN DULCI JUBILO

This carol, which has long been a favourite choir item in the annual Christmas eve service at King's College, Cambridge and occupies nineteenth place in the 2005 BBC *Songs of Praise* poll, belongs to a distinctive genre where Latin phrases are interspersed with lines in the vernacular and which is technically known as the macaronic style.

In its original form, 'In dulci jubilo' was a mixture of Latin and medieval German:

In dulci jubilo,
Nun singet und seid froh!
Unsers Herzen Wonne leit
In praesipio,
Und leuchtet als die Sonne
Matris in gremio.
Alpha es et O!

'In dulci jubilo' is said to have been taught by angels to the German mystic Heinrich Suso (1295–1366). A Dominican monk, Suso was a pupil of Meister Eckhart and a friend of Johannes Tauler. He acted as spiritual director to a number of women's convents. His autobiography, written in 1328, gives a graphic account of how a group of angels, led by 'a heavenly musician', sang a 'joyous song about the infant Jesus' and drew him by the hand into a dance.

The leader of the song knew right well how to guide them, and he sang first, and they sang after him in the jubilee of their hearts. Thrice the leader repeated the burden of the song, 'Ergo meritis', etc. This dance was not of the kind that are danced on earth, but it was a heavenly movement, swelling up and falling back again into the wild abyss of God's hiddenness.

Suso's description of a leader, repeated refrain and round-dance establishes 'In dulci jubilo' as standing firmly in the classic carol tradition. It is almost certainly the oldest of the German macaronic carols. The earliest source, a manuscript in Leipzig University dating from around 1400, contains the first verse only without the '*Ergo meritis*' refrain referred to by Suso. Later fifteenth-century manuscripts give four verses, again without the refrain, with the vernacular lines in a variety of Low German and Dutch dialects. The final verse, beginning '*Mater et filia*' fell foul of Protestant unease about Mariology and was omitted when the song was printed in a Lutheran collection in 1533. However, a Lutheran songbook published in Leipzig twelve years later reinstated it.

There have been numerous English translations of this catchy carol. The earliest, 'In dulci jubilo, now let us sing with mirth and joy', appeared in the *Gude and Godly Ballads* in 1568. The *Lyra Davidica* of 1708 contained an all-English version which began 'Let Jubill trumpets blow, and hearts in rapture flow'. Nineteenth-century translations included Sir John Bowring's 'In dulci jubilo – to the house of God we'll go', Catherine Winkworth's 'In dulci jubilo, sing and shout all below' and the version that appears on page 167, 'In dulci jubilo, let us our homage show' which was made by Robert Lucas de Pearsall in 1837.

Pearsall's translation, which appeared first in the *Musical Times* and then in Novello's *Part Song Book* in 1887, is probably the most widely taken up. It is in the *Oxford Book of Carols*, the *Faber Book of Carols* and the *University Carol Book*. The *New Oxford Book* has a new translation made by the editors. For some reason, the editors of the *Oxford Book of Carols* substituted 'Right poor art thou today' for Pearsall's 'My heart is sore for thee' in verse two.

Pearsall was born in Clifton in 1795. After studying law and briefly practising at the bar, he went to the Continent to study music. He spent the last thirty years of his life in Germany, first at Carlsruhe and then at Wartensee Castle overlooking Lake Constance in Switzerland where he dabbled in archaeology and wrote and composed madrigals and part-songs. He added the 'de' to his name when he converted to Roman Catholicism. He died at Wartensee in 1856. He made his translation from a version of the carol printed in a 1570 service book for the Protestant congregations of Zweibuken and Neuburg. He noted:

> Even there it is called 'a very ancient song for Christmas-eve' so there can be no doubt that it is one of those very old Roman Catholic melodies that Luther, on account of their beauty, retained in the Protestant service. It was formerly sung in the processions that took place on Christmas-eve, and is so still in those remote parts of Germany where people yet retain old customs. The words are rather remarkable, being written half in Latin and half in the upper German dialect. I have translated them to fit the music, and endeavoured to preserve, as much as I could, the simplicity of the original. Of the melody there can be but one opinion; namely, that which in spite of religious animosity, secured it the approbation of the Protestant reformers, and that of the German people during many centuries.

The tune is found with the words in the 1400 Leipzig manuscript and in all subsequent sources. Arranged and harmonized by Praetorius and Bach, it also provides the tune for 'Good Christian men, rejoice' (No. 28), J.M. Neale's very free adaptation of 'In dulci jubilo'. Unlike Pearsall, Neale was working not from a German version of the carol but from a Swedish text in the recently rediscovered Finnish collection *Piae Cantiones* (1582). As has already been explained, Thomas Helmore, music editor for Neale's *Carols for Christmas-tide,* misread the value of two notes, causing Neale to add the extra line 'News, news'. The words of Pearsall's translation exactly follow the metre of the original.

In dulci jubilo
Let us our homage show:
Our heart's joy reclineth
In praesepio;
And like a bright star shineth
Matris in gremio.
Alpha es et O!

2 *O Jesu parvule,*
My heart is sore for Thee!
Hear me, I beseech Thee,
O puer optime;
My praying let it reach Thee!
O princeps gloriae.
Trahe me post te.

3 *O Patris caritas!*
O Nati lenitas!
Deeply were we stained
Per nostra crimina:
But Thou for us hast gained
Coelorum guadia.
Qualis gloria!

4 *Ubi sunt gaudia,*
If that they be not there?
There are Angels singing
Nova cantica;
And there the bells are ringing
In Regis curia.
O that we were there!

38

IN THE BLEAK MID-WINTER

According to the 2005 BBC *Songs of Praise* poll, this beautiful poem is Britain's favourite Christmas carol, supplanting even 'Silent Night'. It has probably done as much as anything to give generations of children the impression that the birth of Jesus took place in the snow. Winter was a favourite theme for the author, Christina Rossetti – among her other poems are 'Winter, my secret' and 'Winter rain'.

There is, of course, no Biblical warrant for associating the Nativity with mid-winter. The reason we celebrate it on 25 December is that this date was fixed on by the early fourth-century church largely to take over and Christianize the various pagan festivals associated with the mid-winter solstice. Christina Rossetti was not the first to suggest Christ's birth took place in a snowy landscape. Milton's poem 'On the morning of Christ's Nativity', which began 'It was the Winter Wilde' made an even more explicit association and suggested that snow fell at Christ's birth to cover the fallen world with a pure whiteness.

There are other decidely unscriptural touches in this poem. The ox, ass and camel do not appear in the Synoptic Gospel accounts of Jesus' birth. Nor is the theology quite clear. Is it right to say that heaven cannot hold God, nor the earth sustain, and what about heaven and earth fleeing away when he comes to reign – earth perhaps, but is heaven going to flee at the second coming?

The fact is, of course, that this is not the sort of text that bears or warrants detailed exegesis and analysis. It is a mystical offering by a Victorian poet justly famous for her devotional verse. One can forgive a lot to have that lovely last stanza calling for a personal response from us to Jesus, reminiscent in many ways of

'The wise may bring their learning' (No.83). The image of God as the one that heaven cannot hold can, in fact, be read as a bold and original attempt to express the mysterious paradox at the heart of the Christian doctrine of the Incarnation.

Christina Rossetti (1830–94) was born in London, whither her father, Gabrieli Rossetti, a poet and revolutionary, had fled to escape the authoritarian regime in his native Naples. He later became a professor at King's College, London. The youngest of four children, Christina followed her father and her brother, the pre-Raphaelite painter, Dante Gabriel Rossetti, in writing poems. Her sister, Maria, became an Anglican nun. Described as 'strikingly beautiful', Christina sat as a model for her brother and his friends John Millais and William Holman Hunt. She was strongly influenced by her English mother's Anglo-Catholicism and developed a serious religious bent which led her to refuse the proposals of marriage from two men on the grounds that they were not spiritual enough for her. She lived quietly with her mother and devoted herself to writing devotional poetry. She was described as 'timid, nun-like, bowed down by suffering and humility . . . a great saint and a great poet'.

'In the bleak mid-winter' appeared in the author's posthumous *Poetical Works*, edited by her brother, Michael and published in 1904. It is there described as having been written before 1872. Although originally entitled 'A Christmas carol', it was not written as a hymn and has a free rhythm and irregular metre which makes it somewhat tricky to sing. It was first used as a hymn in the *English Hymnal* of 1906 and has since been taken up by most of the major denominational hymnbooks in the English-speaking world. Verse three is omitted in a number of non-Anglican books, including *Hymns and Psalms* and *Baptist Praise and Worship*. The editors of the *New Oxford Book of Carols* seem to suggest that this is because of unease over the phrase 'a breastful of milk' but I am not really sure that this is the reason. It has been restored in the fourth edition of the *Church Hymnary*.

Much of the popularity of this hymn must be put down to the tune specially composed for its appearance in the *English Hymnal* by Gustav Holst. It takes its name CRANHAM from the

Cotswold village near Cheltenham where the composer's mother's family came from. It has been adapted in various ways to fit the irregular metre of the words – in several books the penultimate bar is printed to give the first word of each final line (notably, of course 'long' in verse one) three beats.

Another tune by Harold Darke, which varies from verse to verse, was made in 1909 when the composer was just 21 and a student at the Royal College of Music. It covers the first three verses only. Darke (1888–1976) was organist of St Michael, Cornhill, in the City of London, from 1916 to 1966.

In the bleak mid-winter

In the bleak mid-winter
Frosty wind made moan;
Earth stood hard as iron,
Water like a stone;
Snow had fallen, snow on snow,
Snow on snow,
In the bleak mid-winter,
Long ago.

2 Our God, heaven cannot hold him
Nor earth sustain;
Heaven and earth shall flee away
When he comes to reign:
In the bleak mid-winter
A stable-place sufficed
The Lord God almighty,
Jesus Christ.

3 Enough for him whom cherubim
Worship night and day,
A breastful of milk
And a mangerful of hay;
Enough for him, whom angels
Fall down before,
The ox and ass and camel
Which adore.

4 Angels and archangels
May have gathered there,
Cherubim and seraphim
Thronged in the air:
But only his mother
In her maiden bliss
Worshipped the Beloved
With a kiss.

5 What can I give him,
Poor as I am!
If I were a shepherd
I would bring a lamb;
If I were a wise man
I would do my part
Yet what I can I give him –
Give my heart.

39

INFANT HOLY

This beautifully simple carol comes originally from Poland. Its date is uncertain but it may well go back to the Middle Ages. The full Polish text, which begins '*Wzlobie lezy,Któz pobiezy*', can be found in the *New Oxford Book of Carols*.

This translation, which has rightly become so popular throughout the English-speaking world, was made by Edith Margaret Gellibrand Reed (1885–1933). Born in Islington, she devoted her life to the cause of promoting music among young people. She contributed to the *Kingsway Carol Book*, *Sunday School Praise* and *The School Assembly*.

It was first published in the December 1921 issue of *Music and Youth*, a magazine which Edith Reed founded and edited to promote musical education, and included with the tune in *School Worship* in 1926.

The tune, which is that used for the original Polish carol, first appeared in England in the 1877 edition of *The Hymnal Companion to the Book of Common Prayer* where it was set in straight common time to 'Angels from the realms of glory'. Since the appearance of Edith Reed's translation, it has been inseparably wedded to 'Infant holy'. It is a perfect marriage. Her text perfectly fits the unusual metre of the tune and provides especially suitable words for the descending phrases in bars nine to twelve.

Infant holy,
Infant lowly,
For his bed a cattle stall;
Oxen lowing,
Little knowing,
Christ the babe is Lord of all.
Swift are winging,
Angels singing,
Nowells ringing,
Tidings bringing,
  Christ the babe is Lord of all,
  Christ the babe is Lord of all.

2 Flocks were sleeping,
Shepherds keeping
Vigil till the morning new
Saw the glory.
Heard the story,
Tidings of a gospel true,
Thus rejoicing
Free from sorrow,
Praises voicing,
Greet the morrow,
  Christ the babe was born for you!
  Christ the babe was born for you!

40

IT CAME UPON THE MIDNIGHT CLEAR

Like 'Away in a manger' and 'O little town of Bethlehem', this popular Christmas hymn, which came sixth in the 2005 BBC *Songs of Praise* poll, comes from nineteenth-century America. Its author, Edmund Hamilton Sears, was a Unitarian minister in Massachusetts.

Born in Sandisfield, Massachusetts, in 1810, Sears claimed descent from one of the original Pilgrim Fathers. As a child he developed a love of poetry and was particularly fond of chanting Pope's *Iliad*. He was educated at Union College, Schenectady, New York, and the Divinity School at Harvard. He then served as a pastor in his native state until ill-health forced a premature retirement in the 1850s. He devoted the rest of his life to writing and died in Weston, Massachusetts in 1876.

The birth of Christ might at first sight seem an unlikely topic for a Unitarian to write about. In fact, Sears wrote another Christmas hymn, 'Calm on the listening ear of night' which is still sung in the United States, and proclaimed his own belief in the divinity of Jesus. 'It came upon the midnight clear' does not contain any explicitly Christological references and could be sung with a clear conscience by those of a Unitarian disposition. Erik Routley notes that 'as we sing it, in its original form, the hymn is little more than an ethical song extolling the worth and splendour of peace among men'.

The hymn was written in 1849 during Sears' time as pastor of the First Church at Wayland, Massachusetts, and published in Boston in the *Christian Register* on 29 December that year. It subsequently appeared in Sears' *Sermons and Songs of the Christian Life* (1875). It is sometimes asserted that the reference to the 'men of strife' in the third verse was inspired either by the disorder in Europe in 1848, the year of revolutions, or by the violence of the recent war between America and Mexico. These events may well have been in Sears' mind but I suspect that he was making a more general comment on the aggressiveness of human nature.

The hymn first appeared in Britain in 1870 when Edward Bickersteth included it in his *Hymnal Companion to the Book of Common Prayer*, the evangelical counterpart to the moderately high church *Hymns Ancient and Modern*. Significantly, Bickersteth put it in the section headed 'The Church Triumphant' rather than alongside other Christmas hymns, omitted the third verse and recast the fifth to eliminate the decidedly unbiblical reference to a coming 'age of gold' (which some commentators, surely rather fancifully, have taken to be a reference to the gold rush in mid-nineteenth-century America) and give it a more Christo-centric focus:

For lo, the days are hastening on,
By prophets seen of old,
When with the ever-circling years
Shall come the time foretold,
When the new heaven and earth shall own
The Prince of Peace their King,
And the whole world send back the song
Which now the angels sing.

Subsequent British hymnbook editors have played around with Sears' words to give them a more orthodox Christian spin. In *Church Hymns* (1874), for example, the fifth verse was omitted and the fourth recast as follows:

O Prince of Peace, thou knowest well
This weary world below;
Thou seest how men climb the way
With painful steps and slow.
O still the jarring sounds of earth
That round the pathway ring,
And bid the toilers rest awhile
To hear the angels sing!

For his *University Carol Book* (1961) Erik Routley provided another re-writing of the final verse, 'being of the opinion that in its original form it was sufficiently misleading theologically to mar an otherwise excellent hymn':

For lo, the days have hastened on,
By prophets seen of old,
And with the ever-circling years
Came round the day foretold,
When men, surprised by joy, adored
The prince of peace, their King;
Come all who hear! Join in the song
Which men and angels sing.

The editors of most current hymnals, while dropping verse four, have been content to leave verse five as Sears wrote it, complete with its 'prophet-bards', 'coming age of gold' and somewhat naïve and unChristian optimism. It is perhaps no bad thing to have some broadly humanist carols. At least this one has lots of angels – again, one might think, a strange obsession for a Unitarian – and there is a wonderful sense of reciprocity in the closing couplet with humankind returning to the angels the song which they sing in Luke 2.14.

By far the most common tune for 'It came upon the midnight clear', in the British Isles at least, is NOEL, a re-working by Arthur Sullivan of a traditional carol tune apparently sent to him by a friend. It has been identified as a Herefordshire tune called EARDISLEY and apparently used for the carol 'Dives and Lazarus' although it also bears a strong resemblance to the melody of 'The Sussex Mummers Carol'. Sullivan extended the tune to fit this hymn for *Church Hymns* in 1874 and it was published there with the attribution 'Traditional Air rearranged'. I have written at length elsewhere about Sullivan's particular sensitivity in setting religious lyrics to music despite his own apparent agnosticism. Sears' humanist Unitarian ethic probably appealed strongly to the composer and chimed in with his own outlook on life. It is fitting that a collection of Sullivan's sacred music (which includes his original arrangement of NOEL) was recently issued on compact disc under the title 'That Glorious Song of Old'.

Before NOEL, 'It came upon the midnight clear' was sung in England to a melody derived from a tune by Ludwig Spohr (ironically, one of the German composers whose 'masses and fugues and ops' were prescribed as a punishment for music-hall singers by the Mikado) and to an adaptation of one of Mendelssohn's *Songs Without Words*.

In the United States Sears' hymn has more often been sung to a tune originally written for the organ by Richard Storrs Willis (1819–1900) and re-arranged as a hymn tune by the magnificently named Uzziah Christopher Burnap (1834–1900).

It came upon the midnight clear,
That glorious song of old,
From angels bending near the earth
To touch their harps of gold:
'Peace on the earth, good will to men,
From heaven's all-gracious King!'
The world in solemn stillness lay
To hear the angels sing.

2 Still through the cloven skies they come,
With peaceful wings unfurled;
And still their heavenly music floats
O'er all the weary world:
Above its sad and lowly plains
They bend on hovering wing;
And ever o'er its Babel-sounds
The blessed angels sing.

3 Yet with the woes of sin and strife
The world has suffered long;
Beneath the angel-strain have rolled
Two thousand years of wrong;
And man, at war with man, hears not
The love-song which they bring:
O hush the noise, ye men of strife,
And hear the angels sing.

4 And ye, beneath life's crushing load,
Whose forms are bending low,
Who toil along the climbing way
With painful steps and slow,
Look, now! for glad and golden hours
Come swiftly on the wing;
O rest beside the weary road
And hear the angels sing.

5 For lo, the days are hastening on,
By prophet-bards foretold,
When, with the ever-circling years,
Comes round the age of gold;
When peace shall over all the earth
Its ancient splendours fling,
And the whole world give back the song
Which now the angels sing.

41

IT'S ROUNDED LIKE AN ORANGE

One of the most popular recent innovations in worship in the Christmas season has been the Christingle service. Usually held on one of the Sundays in Advent, although perhaps liturgically more appropriate for Epiphany, it involves children, and often also adult members of the congregation, being given an orange which they decorate with four sticks or feathers, a candle and a red ribbon. The orange symbolizes the earth, the four sticks the corners of the world over which Jesus is king, the candle represents his light and the ribbon his death for the world. Sometimes sweets and raisins are speared on the sticks to show that God is the provider of all good things in the world and supply something to chew on during the subsequent sermon.

The Christingle service comes originally from the Moravian Church which was born in eighteenth-century Saxony out of the old Bohemian Brethren who had largely died out following the Thirty Years War. Also known as the Church of the United Brethren and *Unitas Fratrum*, the Moravians, who were essentially a missionary movement, spread to North America and Asia. In the early Moravian Christingle services, which may go back to late eighteenth-century Saxony, there were no oranges, sticks or sweets and children simply received lighted candles (Christingles) tied round with red ribbons which they carried from church to church.

This hymn was written for a Christingle Service held at the United Reformed Church in Stamford, Lincolnshire in December 1985. Its author, Basil Bridge, who was minister of the church at the time, spoke at the service about the origins of Christingle, using material which he had obtained from the London headquarters of the Moravian Church in Great Britain and Ireland.

Basil Bridge was born in 1927 in Norwich and trained for the Congregational ministry at Cheshunt College. Ordained in 1951, he served in pastorates in Warwickshire, Leicestershire, Lincolnshire and Bedfordshire until his retirement in 1994. He has written a number of hymns, the most popular of which, 'The Son of God Proclaim', is found in more than two dozen collections in the UK, USA, Australia and Canada.

'It's rounded like an orange', which was written to be sung to the tune of 'The Holly and the Ivy' (No. 78), was published in *New Songs of Praise 5* in 1990 and *Junior Praise Book 2* in 1992. It has also been included in the recent *BBC Songs of Praise* hymnbook (1997).

This is not the only Christingle hymn in existence, although I think it is the best. Fred Pratt Green, the distinguished Methodist hymnwriter (1903–2000) wrote one which can be found in the *Galliard Book of Carols*. It begins:

O round as the world is the orange you give us!
And happy are they who to Jesus belong:
So let the world know, as we join in Christingle,
That Jesus, the Hope of the World, is our song.

It’s rounded like an orange,
This earth on which we stand
And we praise the God who holds it
In the hollow of his hand.
So Father, we would thank you
For all that you have done,
And for all that you have given us
Through the coming of your Son.

2 A candle, burning brightly,
Can cheer the darkest night
And these candles tell how jesus
Came to bring a dark world light.

3 The ribbon round the orange
Reminds us of the cost;
How the Shepherd, strong and gentle,
Gave his life to save the lost.

4 Four seasons with their harvest
Supply the food we need,
And the Spirit gives a harvest
That can make us rich indeed.

5 We come with our Christingles
To tell of Jesus’ birth
And we praise the God who blessed us
By his coming to this earth.

From *New Songs of Praise 5*

42

JOSEPH WAS AN OLD MAN

This delightful carol which transports Mary and Joseph from the Holy Land to an English cherry orchard is of considerable antiquity and is found in early printed broadsides from many different parts of the country. No two versions are the same but the essential theme of what for obvious reasons has become known as the Cherry Tree Carol is unmistakeable.

There are several theories about the origins of the symbolism in this carol. Some folklorists point to the widespread use in folklore of the gift of a cherry, or similar fruit carrying its own seed, as a divine authentication of human fertility. Sabine Baring-Gould, the Victorian clergyman and folklore collector, compared it to a story in the final canto of the ancient Finnish epic, *Kalewala,* where a beautiful virgin, Mariatta, tries to reach a scarlet berry on a tree. She manages to knock it off, using a stick. The berry dances on her lap and then leaps into her mouth. She swallows it and later gives birth to *Ilmori* (the air), on whose birth the old gods sing their last song and ride away into the sky. Baring-Gould also suggested links with the story of Eve being tempted to eat the fruit of the forbidden tree in the Garden of Eden:

> The legend of the Cherry Tree is the lingering on of a very curious, mysterious tradition, common to the whole race of man, that the eating of the fruit in Eden was the cause of the descendant of Eve becoming the mother of Him who was to wipe away that old transgression. In the carol this tradition is strangely altered, but its presence cannot fail to be detected.

Others maintain that the origins of the story told in this carol go back to the apocryphal Gospel of Pseudo-Matthew which recounts how during their flight into Egypt, Mary, Joseph and the infant Jesus rest under the shade of a palm tree. Mary asks Joseph to pick her some of the fruit, only to be met with the tetchy response that there are more important things to attend to. At this point, Jesus speaks and immediately the tree bows down to enable Mary to gather fruit from its branches. Joseph is filled with remorse and asks Mary's forgiveness. The Cherry Tree carol may also draw on another apocryphal gospel, the *Protoevangelium of James* which describes Joseph's doubts about the paternity of Jesus and recounts a walk that he takes, while Mary is in labour in a cave outside Bethlehem, during which he encounters an angel. The *Protoevangelium* makes much of Joseph's age and has him saying, 'I am an old man, but she is a girl.' This point is also taken up in some other carols (see notes to No. 74, 'The angel Gabriel from heaven came').

The depiction of Christ's birth in the cycle of mystery plays performed in Coventry on the feast of Corpus Christi, which date from the fifteenth century or earlier, began with a scene where Mary and Joseph are on their way to Bethlehem. Mary sees a tree laden with cherries and asks Joseph to pick some fruit for her. He refuses and she offers a prayer to God whereupon the tree bows down to her. Seeing this miracle, Joseph repents of his callousness and begs to be forgiven.

Versions of the Cherry Tree Carol are found in virtually all the major collections made of traditional English carols in the nineteenth century, including Sandys' *Christmas Carols, Ancient and Modern* (1833), Rimbault's *Collection of Old Christmas Carols* (1861), Husk's *Songs of the Nativity* (1864), Bramley and Stainer's *Christmas Carols Old and New* (1871) and A.H. Bullen's *Carols and Poems from the fifteenth century to the present time* (1886). The longest and the earliest text in a printed book is in William Hone's *Ancient Mysteries Described* (1822). The eighteen-verse version I give here, which follows that in the *Oxford Book of Carols* and is also the one printed in W.J. Phillips' *Carols: Their Origin, Music, and Connection with Mystery Plays* (1921), is the longest known and is made by putting material together from several different sources. The carol is not often found in this full form but usually in shortened versions. Verses 11 to 15 (beginning 'As Joseph was a walking') were often split off to form a separate carol entitled 'Joseph and the Angel' and the last three verses became a Passiontide carol sung in Lent. Although strictly speaking not appropriate for Christmas, they represent perhaps the most profound verses in the carol. Douglas Brice in his *The Folk Carol of England* has described them as 'surely the most poignant and the saddest in the whole of English literature'.

To list all the variations found in different versions of this carol would occupy several pages. In some, Mary and Joseph walk through a garden rather than an orchard, perhaps reflecting more closely the garden of Eden motif. The text quoted by Husk has Mary as 'Queen of Galilee' in line one and has an additional second verse which sets the scene:

When Joseph was married,
And Mary home had brought,
Mary proved with child,
And Joseph knew it not.

Cecil Sharp collected eight different versions of the Cherry Tree carol. One which he took down in 1917 from the singing of a settler in the southern Appalachian mountains portrayed Joseph as a young man walking with Mary through apple and cherry trees. The last two verses of this version had an unusual twist:

And Joseph took Mary
All on his left knee.
Pray tell me little baby
When your birthday will be?

On the fifth day of January
My birthday will be,
When the stars and the elements
Doth tremble with fear.

The Cherry Tree carol was clearly very popular in country

districts of England well into the twentieth century. A version collected in Cornwall in 1916 seems to mix in verses from 'The Holly and the Ivy' with a refrain:

Then sing O the holy holy
And sing O the holly
And of all the trees that are in the wood
It is the holly.

In his classic autobiographical novel *Cider with Rosie* (1959), Laurie Lee described taking part as a boy in a carol singing party round his native Cotswold village of Slad in the 1920s where the verses beginning 'As Joseph was a walking' were sung to a farmer called Joseph who lived high up on the hill. He noted: 'We always felt that singing it added a spicy cheek to the night.'

The Cherry Tree Carol has had almost as many tunes as variant words. Different tunes are given by Sandys, Husk and Bramley and Stainer. When as a young curate in the West riding of Yorkshire in 1864, Sabine Baring-Gould attempted to teach the carol to local mill girls to a tune collected by the prolific Victorian composer, Henry Gauntlett, they retorted 'Nay! we know one a great deal better than yond' and proceeded to sing ' to a curious old strain':

Saint Joseph was an old man,
And an old man was he;
He married sweet Mary
And a virgin was she.

The *New Oxford Book of Carols* follows its predecessor in giving three different tunes for the three parts of the carol. The first, covering verses 1–10, is a traditional English folk melody which is found set to the carol in an early nineteenth-century manuscript collection of Cornish carols and in Husk's *Songs of the Nativity*. The tune suggested for the second part (verses 11–15) is another traditional tune apparently first set to the Cherry Tree carol in R.R. Terry's *Old Christmas Carols* (1923). An alternative, possibly older tune for this part, is printed in Fyfe's *Christmas, its Customs and Carols* (1860) and included in the *Oxford Book of Carols*. For the third Easter part of the carol, the editors of the *New Oxford Book* suggest a tune collected in 1910 by Cecil Sharp in Buckinghamshire which is virtually identical to a tune given as traditional in Bramley and Stainer's carol book.

It is perhaps worth briefly mentioning here another 'fruity' carol which I nearly included as a separate item in this collection but is probably brief enough to include at the end of this rather lengthy note. 'The Apple Tree' was discovered by Joshua Smith in New Hampshire in 1784 and almost certainly reflects a much earlier English folk poem which draws its imagery from the English countryside. Set to a melody by Elizabeth Poston, it was sung by the choir of King's College, Cambridge in their 1965 Christmas Eve service of lessons and carols. Other modern tunes have been written for it and it is popular with choirs on both sides of the Atlantic. In contrast to the Cherry Tree carol, it is delightfully brief:

This beauty doth all things excel,
By faith I know but ne'er can tell,
The glory which I now can see,
In Jesus Christ the apple tree.

The Cherry Tree Carol

Joseph was an old man,
And an old man was he,
When he wedded Mary
In the land of Galilee.

2 Joseph and Mary walked
Through an orchard good,
Where were cherries and berries
So red as any blood.

3 Joseph and Mary walked
Through an orchard green,
Where was berries and cherries
As thick as might be seen.

4 O then bespoke Mary,
With words so meek and mild,
'Pluck me one cherry, Joseph,
For I am with child.'

5 O then bespoke Joseph,
With answer most unkind,
'Let him pluck thee a cherry
That brought thee now with child.'

6 O then bespoke the baby
Within his mother's womb-
'Bow down then the tallest tree
For my mother to have some.'

7 Then bowed down the highest tree,
Unto his mother's hand.
Then she cried, 'See, Joseph,
I have cherries at command.'

8 O then bespake Joseph–
'I have done Mary wrong;
But now cheer up, my dearest,
And do not be cast down.

9 'O eat your cherries, Mary,
O eat your cherries now,
'O eat your cherries, Mary,
That grow upon the bough.'

10 Then Mary plucked a cherry,
As red as any blood;
Then Mary she went homewards
All with her heavy load.

11 As Joseph was a walking,
He heard an angel sing:
'This night there shall be born
On earth our heavenly King.'

12 He neither shall be born
In house nor in hall,
Nor in the place of Paradise,
But in an ox's stall.

13 He neither shall be clothed
In purple nor in pall,
But all in the fair white linen,
As wear the babies all.

14 He neither shall be rocked
In silver nor in gold,
But in a wooden cradle
That rocks upon the mould.

15 He neither shall be christened
In white wine nor red,
But with fair spring water
As we were christened.

16 Then Mary took her young son,
And set him on her knee:
Saying, 'My dear son, tell me,
Tell me how this world shall be.'

17 'O I shall be as dead, mother,
As stones are in the wall;
O the stones in the streets, mother,
Shall sorrow for me all.

18 On Easter-day dear mother,
My rising up shall be;
O the sun and the moon, mother,
Shall both arise with me.'

43
JOY TO THE WORLD

This exuberant piece, which came eighteenth in the 2005 BBC *Songs of Praise* poll of Britain's favourite carols, is the work of the man often described as the father of English hymnody. Isaac Watts broke the stranglehold of metrical psalmody and provided 'hymns of human composure' for British congregations to sing.

Watts was born in Southampton in 1674, the son of an elder in an Independent (i.e. Congregational) Church, the denomination to which he was to remain loyal throughout his life. Educated in the local grammar school at the Dissenting Academy at Stoke Newington, he served as private tutor to the son of an eminent Puritan, Sir John Hartopp, and as pastor of Mark Lane Chapel in London. Ill-health forced him to spend the last 36 years of his life as a semi-invalid in the home of Sir Thomas Abney, first in Hertfordshire and then in Stoke Newington. He died in 1748.

Many of Watts' hymns were Christianized versions of the psalms and this one is a case in point. 'Joy to the World', which first appeared in 1719 in Watts' *Psalms of David* exactly as it is printed here, is based on the second part of Psalm 98 (verses 4–9):

Make a joyful noise unto the Lord, all the earth:
Make a loud noise, and rejoice, and sing praise.
Sing unto the Lord with a harp, and the voice of a psalm.
With trumpets and sound of cornet
Make a joyful noise before the Lord, the King.
Let the sea roar, and the fullness thereof;
The world, and they that dwell therein.
Let the floods clap their hands:
Let the hills be joyful together
Before the Lord; for he cometh to judge the earth:

With righteousness he shall judge the world,
And the people with equity.

'Joy to the World' has been sung in several different versions which diverge markedly from Watts' original. Thomas Cotterill, a Sheffield vicar who was one of the first clergymen to attempt to introduce hymn singing into the Church of England, published a much altered version in a hymn-book which he produced for his congregation in 1810. It provides the basis for the three stanza version still sung in South Yorkshire villages where the last line of the first verse is rendered 'And all creation sing' and the subsequent verses more closely follow the original psalm:

Ye saints rejoice, the Saviour reigns.
In praise your tongues employ,
Clouds clap your hands, exalt ye plains,
And shout ye hills for joy.
Behold, He comes, He comes to bless
Their nations as their God;
To show the world his righteousness
And send his truth abroad.

In his *Songs of the Nativity* William Husk printed a version which he described as being popular in Devon and Cornwall:

Joy to the world, the Lord is come,
Let earth receive her King;
Let every tongue with sacred mirth
His loud applauses sing.
Hark, hark, what news, what joyful news,
To all the nations round;
Today rejoice, a King is born,
Who is with glory crowned.
Behold! He comes, the tidings spread!
A Saviour full of grace:
He comes, in mercy, to restore
A sinful, fallen race.

In his classic book, *The English Carol*, Erik Routley brackets 'Joy to the World' with 'O come, O come, Emmanuel' as 'Advent hymns which have almost carol-like status among modern churchgoers'. Curiously, Watts' hymn is much better known in North America than in Britain where it was for long neglected. However, most recent denominational hymn-books have included it, generally with minor variations. The third verse proves rather too strong meat for several editors. *Hymns and Psalms* omits it, *Baptist Praise and Worship* substitutes 'sin's curse' for 'the curse' in the last line and *Rejoice and Sing* provides a toned-down version:

No more let thorns infest the ground,
Or sins and sorrows grow;
Wherever pain and death are found
He makes his blessings flow.

In the interests of inclusive language, both *Hymns and Psalms* and *Rejoice and Sing* change the second line of verse two to 'Let all their songs employ'.

ANTIOCH, the vigorous tune with its repeating entries to which 'Joy to the World' is usually sung, seems to derive from a melody entitled COMFORT first published in 1833 in a collection of tunes compiled for Methodists by Thomas Hawkes of Watchet, Somerset. It was there recommended for use with Charles Wesley's 'O joyful sound of gospel grace' and 'How large the promise, how divine'. The following year a slightly different version of the tune was printed in a book of melodies collected by William Holford, conductor of the choir of St Clement's Church, Manchester, who attributed it to Handel and set it to Watts' 'O the delights, the heavenly joys'. Handel was also credited as the composer by Lowell Mason whose *Occasional Psalm and Hymn Tunes* (1836) introduced the tune in America and first gave it the name ANTIOCH, perhaps because St Ignatius is said to have introduced antiphonal singing in that city. The tune certainly has Handelian echoes with several of its phrases recalling extracts from the *Messiah* choruses 'Lift up your heads' and 'Glory to God'. It was only set to 'Joy to the World' in Britain in the 1955 *Redemption Hymnal* but has rapidly caught on and become a deservedly popular item with choirs and congregations alike. In the South Yorkshire village carolling tradition, 'Joy to the World' is sung to a number of different tunes, of which the most popular is probably MOUNT OF OLIVES.

Joy to the world

Joy to the world! the Lord is come:
Let earth receive her King!
Let ev'ry heart prepare him room,
And heav'n and nature sing!
And heav'n and nature sing!
And heav'n and heav'n and nature sing!

2 Joy to the earth! the Saviour reigns:
Let men their songs employ,
While fields and floods, rocks, hills and plains
Repeat the sounding joy.
Repeat the sounding joy.
Repeat, repeat the sounding joy.

3 No more let sins and sorrows grow,
Nor thorns infest the ground:
He comes to make his blessings flow
Far as the curse is found.
Far as the curse is found.
Far as, far as the curse is found.

4 He rules the world with truth and grace,
And makes the nations prove
The glories of his righteousness
And wonders of his love.
And wonders of his love.
And wonders and wonders of his love.

44

LET EARTH AND HEAVEN COMBINE

This is very much a hymn rather than a carol but it belongs unmistakably to the Christmas season and provides a profound theological treatment of the Christian doctrine of the Incarnation.

It is the work of Charles Wesley, whom we have already encountered as the author of 'Hark, how all the welkin rings' (No.31). Born in 1707 at Epworth, Lincolnshire, where his father was rector, he was educated at Westminster School and Christ Church Oxford, where he was instrumental in founding the Holy Club, the group from which the origins of Methodism are often traced. Ordained in 1735, Charles and his elder brother, John, travelled to Georgia where they were much influenced by Moravian missionaries. After returning to England, Charles underwent a conversion experience in 1738 which inspired his great hymn 'And can it be'. While remaining loyal to the Church of England, he provided the growing Methodist movement with its incomparable stock of hymns. Altogether it has been estimated that the man justly described as the prince of English hymn writers produced more than 6,500 hymn texts. He died in 1788.

'Let earth and heaven combine' first appeared in Wesley's *Hymns for the Nativity of our Lord* (1744). It is based on the account of Jesus' birth in Luke 2:8–20 and also draws on the commentary on it in 1 John 1:1–4 and 1 John 4:7–11 as well as on numerous other Scriptural references. The striking couplet at the end of the first verse, which so superbly sums up the mystery of the Incarnation, draws on imagery first found in a poem entitled 'The Pulley' by the seventeenth-century Anglican divine, George Herbert:

When God at first made man,
Having a glass of blessings standing by;
Let us (said he) poure on him all we can:
Let the worlds riches, which dispersed lie,
Contract into a span.

Here, of course, 'contract into a span' is used in terms of God's creation of man rather than his revelation of himself in Christ. The phrase was also used in Jeremy Taylor's *Holy Living and Holy Dying* and in a 'Hymn to God the Son' by Charles' father, Samuel Wesley.

The final line of the first stanza of 'Let earth and heaven combine' could only come from the pen of Charles Wesley, who gets away with using words of a length and complexity that no other hymn writer would dare ask people to sing. At least 'incomprehensibly made man' is not quite such a tongue-twister as the line 'With inextinguishable blaze' in 'O thou who camest from above'.

The striking phrase in verse two, 'the latent Godhead', almost certainly derives from the opening line of a Latin hymn attributed to St Thomas Aquinas, *Adoro te devote latens deitas*. The concluding couplet of the third verse has distinct echoes of lines in 'And can it be':

'Tis mercy all! let earth adore,
Let angel minds inquire no more.

The fifth verse, with its confident assertion that the clothing of God in flesh will 'make us all divine' indicates Wesley's adherence to the doctrine of deification found in the Greek spiritual tradition. The opening couplet of the final verse proclaims another favourite and distinctive Wesleyan theme, the doctrine of sanctification so beautifully expressed in the phrase 'changed from glory into glory' in the hymn 'Love divine, all loves excelling'. The image of the departed human soul being 'lost in God' anticipates the powerful picture in George Matheson's 'O love that wilt not let me go' of the 'restless soul' being given back to flow in God's 'ocean depths'.

It is not surprising given the weight and richness of imagery and allusion which it contains that Erik Routley described this as 'Charles Wesley's incomparable hymn on the Incarnation, without which no hymnbook can really be called complete.' In fact, it is found in remarkably few hymnbooks and those which do include it, which tend to be of Methodist provenance, generally omit the third verse.

The favoured tune for this hymn, at least in Methodist circles, is ST JOHN, also known as ADORATION, which first appeared anonymously in the monthly journal of the Society for Promoting Church Music, *The Parish Choir*, in 1851. It was first set to 'Let earth and heaven combine' in the *Methodist Hymn Book* of 1904, an association continued in the *Methodist Hymn Book* of 1933 and in *Hymns and Psalms in 1988.*

Let earth and heaven combine,
And joyfully agree,
To praise in songs divine
The incarnate Deity,
Our God, contracted to a span,
Incomprehensibly made man.

2 He laid his glory by
He wrapped his in our clay;
Unmarked by human eye,
The latent Godhead lay;
Infant of days he here became,
And bore the mild Immanuel's name.

3 See in the Infant's face
The depths of Deity,
And labour while ye gaze
To sound the mystery:
In vain; ye angels, gaze no more,
But fall, and silently adore.

4 Unsearchable the love
That has the Saviour brought;
The grace is far above
The power of human thought:
Suffice for us that God, we know,
Our God, is manifest below.

5 He deigns in flesh to appear,
Widest extremes to join;
To bring our baseness near,
And make us all divine:
And we the life of God shall know,
For God is manifest below.

6 Made perfect first in love,
And sanctified by grace,
We shall from earth remove,
And see his glorious face:
His love shall then be fully showed,
And we shall all be lost in God.

45

LITTLE JESUS, SWEETLY SLEEP

This delightful little carol is Czech in origin. Collected and transcribed in the early 1920s by a Miss Jacubickova, '*Hajej, nynjej*' was translated by Percy Dearmer for the *Oxford Book of Carols* and first appeared in its familiar English form in that volume in 1928.

Dearmer played a significant role in bringing hitherto unknown Continental European carols to the attention of the English-speaking world. His work on *The Oxford Book of Carols* also rescued many hitherto neglected English carols, including many appropriate for seasons other than Christmas. Born in London in 1867 and educated at Christ Church, Oxford, he took Holy Orders and became vicar of St Mary's, Primrose Hill. He served in the First World War as a Red Cross chaplain and worker with the YMCA and in 1918 was appointed Professor of Ecclesiastical Art at King's College, London. He became a canon of Westminster Abbey in 1931 and died in 1936. An active Christian socialist, he was keen to get contemporary concerns and expressions of the social gospel included in the church's hymnody and the contents of *Songs of Praise*, the collection that he edited (1925 and 1931), bear witness to this aim. He was also editor of the *English Hymnal*.

There is one unfortunate feature of Dearmer's translation of this carol. In Erik Routley's words, 'it has a dreadfully embarrassing final line'. Various attempts have been made to provide a slightly less cringe-making alternative. When the carol was sung in the service of nine lessons and carols at King's College in 1928 the line appeared in the printed programme as 'Little Jesus, God and Man'. In 1949, Geoffrey Bush applied for, and was refused, permission to alter it in his *Christmas Cantata* to 'Gentle Jesus, God made man'.

The Galliard Book of Carols (1980) prints another translation of this carol by Margaret Tausky which begins:

Sleep now, Jesus, Baby King,
We will sing,
And a coat of fur we'll bring.
We will rock you, rock you, rock you,
Safe and warm in sleep we'll lock you,
Serve and love you all we can,
Son of God and Son of Man.

The tune for the Rocking Carol, as it has come to be known for obvious reasons, bears a very close resemblance to that of 'Twinkle, twinkle, little star' and clearly belongs to a traditional nursery rhyme found across Europe.

Another Czech carol, '*Zezulka z lesa vylitla kuku*', taken down in Christmas 1921 from the singing of a peasant girl in the hills between Bohemia and Moravia, was also translated by Percy Dearmer and included in the *Oxford Book of Carols*. Although it has not achieved the popularity of 'Little Jesus, sweetly sleep' it deserves to be better known and I am happy to reproduce it in full here as an additional item in this collection:

From out of a wood did a cuckoo fly,
Cuckoo,
He came to a manger with joyful cry,
Cuckoo;
He hopped, he curtsied, round he flew,
And loud his jubilation grew,
Cuckoo, cuckoo, cuckoo.

A pigeon flew over to Galilee,
Vrercroo,
He strutted and cooed, and was full of glee,
Vrercroo,
And showed with jewelled wings unfurled,
His joy that Christ was in the world,
Vrercroo, vrercroo, vrercroo.

A dove settled down upon Nazareth,
Tsucroo,
And tenderly chanted with all his breath,
Tsucroo:
'O you' he cooed, 'so good and true,
My beauty do I give to you -
Tsucroo, tsucroo, tsucroo'.

The Rocking Carol

Little Jesus, sweetly sleep, do not stir;
We will lend a coat of fur,
  We will rock you, rock you, rock you,
  We will rock you, rock you, rock you:
See the fur to keep you warm
Snugly round your tiny form.

2 Mary's little baby, sleep, sweetly sleep,
Sleep in comfort, slumber deep,
  We will rock you, rock you, rock you,
  We will rock you, rock you, rock you,
We will serve you all we can,
Darling, darling little man.

From the *Oxford Book of Carols*.

46

LO! HOW A ROSE, E'ER BLOOMING

The picture of the infant Jesus as a rose blooming from a tender stem, so beautifully expressed in this translation from a German carol, is one found in a number of hymns and carols across the centuries. It derives from the statement in Isaiah 11.1 'And there shall come forth a rod out of the stem of Jesse; and a branch shall grow out of his roots'. In medieval iconography, the tree of Jesse was often depicted as a rose plant.

Several medieval English carols picked up this image. One, well known because of its inclusion in Benjamin Britten's Ceremony of Carols, begins:

There is no rose of such virtue
As is the rose that bare Jesu.
Alleluia.
For in this rose contained was
Heaven and earth in little space;
Res miranda.

In the mid-nineteenth century Matthew Bridges took up the image in the second verse of his great hymn 'Crown him with many crowns' (*Daily Telegraph Book of Hymns* No.30):

Fruit of the mystic Rose,
As of that Rose the Stem;
The Root whence mercy ever flows,
The Babe of Bethlehem.

Perhaps the finest and best-known treatment of this theme is in the fifteenth-century German hymn '*Es ist ein' Ros entsprungen*':

Es ist ein' Ros entsprungen
Aus einer Wurzel zart,
Als uns die Alten sungen;
Aus Jesse kam die Art;
Und hat ein Blumlein bracht,
Mitten im kalten Winter,
Wohl zu der halben Nacht.

The reference to 'kalten Winter' makes this one of the earliest known hymns to give a wintry setting to the Nativity story and shows that it was not just the Victorians who scattered snow on the Christmas scene.

'*Es ist ein' Ros*' is thought to have originated in the diocese of Trier in the fifteenth or early sixteenth century as a Christmas or Twelfth Night folk carol. The text is found in various forms in late sixteenth-century sources, including a 19-stanza version in the *Gebetbüchlein des Fater Conradus* (Father Conrad's Little Prayer Book) of 1582/8, a 23-stanza version in the *Alte Catholische Geistliche Kirchengesänge* of 1599 and a six-stanza one in the *Catholische Geistliche Gensänge* published in Cologne in 1608. This last source also has a Latin version beginning '*De stirpe David nata*'.

Several English translations have been made of *Es ist ein' Ros entsprungen*. They include Catherine Winkworth's 'A spotless Rose is blowing' (1869) and G.R. Woodward's 'The noble stem of Jesse'. Herbert Howells set another translation beginning 'A spotless rose' as a carol anthem. A more recent translation by Gracia Grindal (born in 1943), ' Lo, how a rose is growing,/ A bloom of finest grace', appears in *Rejoice and Sing* (1991), the only major contemporary British hymnbook to include the hymn.

The translation given on page 209, which is particularly popular in North America where it is found in several hymnals, is by two hands. The first and second verses are by Theodore Baker (1851–1934) and the third by Harriet Spaeth (1845–1925).

The tune for *Es ist ein' Ros* is the one which accompanied it in the *Alte Catholische Geistliche Kirchengesänge* published in Cologne in 1599 and almost certainly dates, like the words, from the fifteenth century. The setting generally used is that made by Michael Praetorius in his *Musae Sioniae* in 1609. The tune was used by the editors of the *English Hymnal* for their adaptation of Neale's 'A great and mighty wonder' which is found in more hymnbooks and probably sung more often in Britain, although not perhaps in North America, than are translations of the original German text (see notes to No.1).

Es ist ein' Ros entsprungen

Lo! how a Rose, e'er blooming,
From tender stem hath sprung,
Of Jesse's lineage coming
As seers of old have sung:
It came, a blossom bright,
Amid the cold of winter
When half-spent was the night.

2 Isaiah 'twas foretold it,
The Rose I have in mind;
With Mary we behold it,
The Virgin Mother kind:
To show God's love aright
She bore to us a Saviour
When half-spent was the night.

3 O Flower, whose fragrance tender
With sweetness fills the air,
Dispel in glorious splendour
The darkness everywhere;
True man, yet very God,
From sin and death now save us
And share our every load.

47

LONG TIME AGO IN BETHLEHEM

Standing at No.11 in the 2005 BBC *Songs of Praise* poll, this is, as far as I am aware, the only carol that has made it to No.1 in the Hit Parade. Recorded by Harry Belafonte under the title 'Mary's Boy Child', it was the best-selling record during the run-up to Christmas 1957.

Belafonte, born in New York in 1927, was an appropriate singer to record this carol which is of traditional Caribbean origin. He spent five years of his youth in Jamaica and went on to specialize in Caribbean songs, of which the best remembered are probably 'Jamaica Farewell' and 'Banana Boat Song' (also known as 'Day-O'). His album, *Calypso*, was No.1 in the USA album chart for 31 weeks and in 1959 became the first long-playing record to sell a million copies. As well as being recorded as a single, 'Mary's Boy Child' was also included on his LP, *An Evening with Belafonte*. Harry Belafonte was active in the American civil rights movement in the 1960s and a director of the Southern Christian Leadership Conference.

Because of its traditional folk origins, this song is found in a number of different versions. Many books print only the first four verses with the first verse repeated at the end. The *Galliard Book of Carols*, which prints all six verses, ends with a coda: 'Joy to the world! Born on Chris-a-mus Day!' apparently taken from Watts' hymn (no. 41) which was popular throughout the Caribbean. It also has a completely different chorus:

Mary had a boy-child, Jeesa Chrise,
He's a-born on Chris-a-mus Day (My,my,my,my!)
Mary had a boy-child, Jeesa Chrise,
He's a-born on Chris-a-mus Day!

Mary's Boy Child

Long time ago in Bethlehem,
So the Holy Bible say
Mary's boy child Jesus Christ
Was born on Christmas Day.

Hark now hear the angels sing – a new king born today
And man will live for ever more because of Christmas Day
Trumpets sound and angels sing –
Listen to what they say
That man will live for ever more because of Christmas Day

2 While shepherds watched their flocks by night
Them see a bright new shining star;
Them hear a choir of angels sing –
The music seems to come from afar.

3 Now Joseph and his wife Mary
Come to Bethlehem that night;
Them find no place for to born the child
Not a single room was in sight

4 By and by they find a little nook,
In a stable all forlorn,
And in a manger cold and dark
Mary's little boy was born.

5 The three wise men tell old King Herod
We hear a new King born today,
We bring he frankincense and myrrh,
We come from far, far away.

6 When old King Herod he learned this news,
Him mad as him can be,
He tell de wise men find this child,
So that I may worship he!

48

LOVE CAME DOWN AT CHRISTMAS

Like 'In the bleak mid-winter' (No. 38), this carol started life as a poem by Christina Rossetti. It was first published in 1885 in her *Time Flies: a Reading Diary* which provided short meditations and poems for the Christian year, following the usage of the *Book of Common Prayer*. 'Love came down at Christmas' appeared as the entry for December 29 under the heading 'Christmastide'. It was first turned into a hymn in 1908 by the editors of the *Oxford Hymn Book*.

In the original poem, the fourth line of the first verse began 'Stars' rather than 'Star'. It was changed in the complete edition of Christina Rossetti's *Poetical Works* published posthumously in 1904, presumably to bring the poem more in line with the Biblical evidence which suggests that it was one particular star that gave the sign of Jesus' birth. The final line of the poem was originally 'Love the universal sign'. This was altered to 'Love for plea and gift and sign' when the poems from *Time Flies* were reprinted in 1893, the year before the poet's death, to form the section 'Songs for Strangers and Pilgrims' in Christina Rossetti's *Verses*. The hymn is printed here in its amended state which is how it has appeared in virtually all the hymnbooks which have used it.

Erik Routley has commented that 'seldom has so much theological insight been packed into sixty-three words'. Richard Watson in his recent book, *The English Hymn*, notes that apart from the brief reference to the star and the angels, 'the poem treats the Incarnation as a theological, almost abstract, affair. The reader has to supply the manger, the Virgin and Joseph, the ox and the ass . . . The last line contains a whole systematic theology, and the little poem is so packed with meaning that there is no time to admire the beauty of the Christmas scene'. It provides a marvellous poetic evocation of the complex incarnational theology of love begetting love expressed in 1 John 4:7-11:

> Beloved, let us love one another: for love is of God; and every one that loveth is born of God, and knoweth God. He that loveth not knoweth not God; for God is love. In this was manifested the love of God toward us, because that God sent his only begotten Son into the world, that we might live through him. Herein is love, not that we loved God, but that he loved us, and sent his Son to be the propitiation of our sins. Beloved, if God so loved us, we ought also to love one another.

Politically correct hymnal editors bothered by exclusive language have not generally felt the need to change the third line of verse three but in *Hymns and Psalms* it becomes 'Love to God and all the world'.

A variety of tunes have been used for this hymn. HERMITAGE, composed by R.O. Morris for the hymn's appearance in *Songs of Praise* (1925) is favoured by *Rejoice and Sing, Hymns and Psalms* and by the third edition of the *Church Hymnary* which gives as an alternative choice GARTAN, a traditional Irish melody named after Lough Gartan in Donegal, the supposed birthplace of St Columba, and supplied by a clergyman in County Kilkenny to C.V. Stanford for a collection of Irish melodies published in 1907. GARTAN also appears bracketed with HERMITAGE in the new *BBC Songs of Praise* (1998) and in *Baptist Praise and Worship* where it is paired with LOVE INCARNATE, a tune by Edgar Pettman to which the hymn was set in the *BBC Hymn Book* of 1951 and the *University Carol Book* of 1961. LOVE INCARNATE also appears as an alternative in *Hymns and Psalms* and is the first choice of the Church of Ireland's *Church Hymnal* (the second being GARTAN).

Christmastide

Love came down at Christmas
Love all lovely, Love divine,
Love was born at Christmas,
Star and angels gave the sign.

2 Worship we the Godhead
Love incarnate, Love divine,
Worship we our Jesus:
But wherewith for sacred sign?

3 Love shall be our token
Love be yours and love be mine,
Love to God and all men,
Love for plea and gift and sign.

49

LULLY, LULLA, THOU LITTLE TINY CHILD

This is one of the earliest extant carols in the English language. It comes from the Pageant of the Shearman and the Tailors, part of the cycle of mystery plays performed in the streets of Coventry during the Middle Ages on the feast of Corpus Christi.

The first known reference to the Coventry mystery plays is in 1392 but the earliest manuscript source for this carol is nearly 200 years later and we cannot be certain that it was included in the pageant from the beginning. It probably dates from the fifteenth century, as does another carol found in the same manuscript and also belonging to the Pageant of the Shearman and the Tailors which begins 'As I rode out this enderes night' and has come to be known as the Coventry Shepherds' Carol. These two carols are the only vernacular songs from the medieval mystery plays to have survived with both text and music intact. In the version printed below, the spelling has been modernized.

The Pageant of the Shearman and the Tailors is introduced by the prophet Isaiah and has two parts separated by a dialogue between two prophets. The first part tells the story of the Annunciation, the Nativity and the Angels' appearance to the shepherds, the second covers the adoration of the three kings, the flight into Egypt and the massacre of the innocents. 'Lully, lulla' comes from the depiction of this last episode towards the end of the pageant and is sung by the mothers of Bethlehem in order to put their children to sleep lest their crying alert Herod's men to their presence and cause them to be killed. In fact, Herod's soldiers do burst in on the scene and slay the children. The pageant ends with a brief scene in which the soldiers report back to Herod.

The song would probably have been sung in the pageant by a boy and two men standing on the pageant cart on which the mystery plays were performed. It was usual in medieval mystery plays for men or boys to play the part of women. The reference in the second verse to Herod raging echoes a stage direction earlier in the pageant – 'Here Herod rages in the pageant and in the street also'.

The tune of the Coventry Carol, as it has become known, is the one which seems to have been used in the pageant and was reproduced, rather inaccurately, in Thomas Sharp's *Dissertations on the Pageants or Dramatic Mysteries, anciently performed in Coventry* (1825). The carol is given an entirely different tune and an extra verse in a version collected by John Niles in Gatlinburg, Tennessee, in 1934. The 'old lady with the grey hat' from whose singing Niles took down the carol added this stanza to the original:

And when the stars ingather do,
In their far venture stay,
Then smile as dreaming, little one,
Bye-bye, lulle, lullay.

It will be noticed that no specific mention is made in this carol of the infant Jesus. The focus rather is on the children threatened with death by Herod. Another early lullaby carol, first found in a collection of 'psalms, sonnets and songs of sadness and piety' printed in 1587 with music by William Byrd, also takes the Massacre of the Innocents as its theme but has a slightly more Christological focus:

Lulla, la lulla, lulla lullaby,
My sweet little baby, what meanest thou to cry?
Be still, my blessed babe, though cause thou hast to mourn,
Whose blood most innocent to shed the cruel king hath sworn:
And lo, alas, behold what slaughter he doth make,
Shedding the blood of infants all, sweet Saviour, for Thy sake,
A King is born, they say, which King this king would kill;
Oh wo, and woful heavy day, when wretches have their will.

There are other lullaby carols which have Jesus much more specifically as their subject. In his scholarly work *The Early English Carols* R.L. Greene quoted fourteen examples of the genre. The outstanding one is surely 'This endrys night' which is found in several versions, including one from a manuscript in the Bodleian Library dated between 1460 and 1490 which begins:

This endris night
I saw a sight,
A star as bright as day;
And ever among
A maiden sung,
'Lullay, by, by, lullay.'

This lovely lady sat and sung
And to her child did say:
'My son, my brother, father, dear,
Why liest thou thus in hay?
My sweetest bird, thus 'tis required,
Though thou be king verray;
But nevertheless I will not cease
To sing, by, by, lullay.'

The child then spake in his talking,
And to his mother said:
'Yea, I am known as heaven-king,
In crib though I be laid;
For angels bright down to me light:
Thou knowest 'tis no nay;
And for that sight thou may'st delight
To sing, by, by, lullay.'

The rest of this delightful dialogue between Jesus and his mother can be followed in the *Oxford Book of Carols* (No. 39) and its successor, *The New Oxford Book of Carols* (No. 39).

The Coventry Carol

Lully, lulla, thou little tiny child,
By by, lully, lullay, thou little tiny child,
By by lully, lullay

O sisters too, how may we do
For to preserve this day
This poor youngling for whom we do sing,
By by, lully lullay?

2 Herod the king, in his raging,
Charged he hath this day
His men of might, in his own sight,
All young children to slay.

3 That woe is me, poor child for thee!
And ever mourn and say,
For thy parting neither say nor sing
By by, lully, lullay.

50

MARY, BLESSED TEENAGE MOTHER

At first sight this almost aggressively modern carol seems a world away from the gentle medieval lullaby which precedes it in this collection. Yet both focus on the vulnerability of motherhood and perhaps they are closer in spirit than first impressions might suggest. A number of writers in the late twentieth century have sought to re-tell the Christmas story in the language and idiom of our own times. Albert Bayly was one of the first with his 'If Christ were born in Burnley'. Carols by John Bell and Michael Ewlett seeking to refresh the traditional Christmas story with up-to-date images can be found elsewhere in this book (Nos. 23, 97 & 100). This one goes rather further in its modernity than most. With its identification of Mary as a black, single teenage mother, it might be described as the very model of the modern politically correct carol.

The author, Michael Forster, was born in 1946, the son of an Anglican priest. After working as a music teacher, he felt the call to enter the Baptist ministry and was ordained in 1986 after training at Regent's Park College, Oxford. Following a period as pastor of a Baptist Church in Leicester, he now combines chaplaincy in Leicestershire Mental Health Services with writing. He has written over 400 hymn texts as well as children's songs, two religious musicals, a nativity pantomime entitled 'A Lad in a Manger' and a considerable amount of material for worship in church, home and school.

'Mary, blessed teenage mother' first appeared in *Thirty New Hymns* published by Kevin Mayhew in 1992. It has subsequently appeared in *Fasts and Festivals: Worship Resources for the Liturgical Year* (1994) and *Hymns Old and New, New Anglican Edition* (1996). It is worth quoting in full what Forster himself has written about this hymn:

This was the first Marian hymn I wrote. Part of its purpose was to attempt to offer an alternative to the romanticised and quite unrealistic image often presented. Mary is an immensely powerful figure in Christian tradition, and it is a tragedy that the very figure who should have been a liberating influence for women has been used to manipulate and enslave them.

All around the world, in this and other countries, women labour against incredible odds to bring hope to birth, and become signs of the presence and the grace of God. The references to South Africa and to the Middle East have not become any less relevant in the years since the text was written. Indeed, if anything South Africa's need to be kept in the world's eye is even greater.

To identify Mary with single teenage mothers is understandably offensive to many people who point out that the doctrine of the virginal conception gives her quite a different place in history. However, much as scholars and others may argue about that doctrine, we must surely recognise that for all of Mary's family, friends, neighbours and associates to have believed it would have been improbable in the extreme. So whatever the reality behind the pregnancy, she would certainly have been exposed to humiliation and shame. To that extent, at the very least, she stands with all who are judged and condemned by a society which often seems to regard sex as intrinsically evil.

It is hardly surprising that this hymn has already provoked strong criticism. Susan Elkin, an English teacher and journalist who wages a campaign for traditional hymnody, first alerted me to its existence in an article in the *Daily Telegraph* in December 1996, 'In praise of proper carols', in which she castigated it as 'a dreary ditty on half a dozen predictable notes' and commented on the 'black madonna' reference:

> Since the young will most likely connect the word 'madonna' only with a pop singer, this 'lyric' is unlikely to communicate anything much of value. This miserable example of what happens when you allow the 'relevance' cult to run riot can be found in the 1996 edition of *Hymns Old and New*, a book now used in most Anglican churches. How can such vapidity ever carry the same weight and majesty as, say, the 18th century words to *Hark the Herald Angels Sing*, which soars through the consciousness to Mendelssohn's superb melody?

Susan Elkin returned to the attack in an article a year later in the *Sunday Times*, 'Requiem for the traditional Christmas carol' in which she asked 'Is the dreary dirge on half a dozen notes which begins "Mary blessed teenage mother" and continues "out of wedlock pregnant found" really what children and adults want to sing in celebration of the profound and magical message of Christmas?'

Michael Forster is doubtless unperturbed by such criticism. He comments that when one member of a congregation objected that the lines concluding verse one were crude and shocking, 'I was very pleased to hear it since the point had obviously been conveyed.'

I myself find much to applaud in this hymn. I do not think it is necessarily a bad thing that it sets out to shock and it certainly seems to have succeeded in that aim. Perhaps too many Christmas hymns are bland and comforting.

The tune to which this hymn is sung, BLACK MADONNA, was written specially for it by Alan Ridout, born in 1934. It is rather anodyne for such strong words but perhaps the contrast is deliberate.

Mary, blessed teenage mother,
With what holy joy you sing!
Humble, yet above all other,
From your womb shall healing spring.
Out of wedlock pregnant found,
Full of grace with blessing crowned.

2 Mother of the homeless stranger
Only outcasts recognise,
Point us to the modern manger;
Not a sight for gentle eyes!
O the joyful news we tell:
'Even here, Immanuel!'

3 Now, throughout the townships ringing,
Hear the black madonna cry,
Songs of hope and freedom singing,
Poor and humble lifted high.
Here the Spirit finds a womb
For the breaker of the tomb!

4 Holy mother, for the nations
Bring to birth the child divine:
Israel's strength and consolation,
And the hope of Palestine!
All creation reconciled
In the crying of a child!

51

MASTERS IN THIS HALL

This is one of two carols in this collection (the other is No. 61) written by William Morris, the polymath and pioneer socialist probably best remembered now for his wallpaper and fabric designs.

He wrote these verses in the late 1850s to fit an old French carol tune at the request of Edmund Sedding, an amateur carol collector who published books of both Christmas and Easter carols. Morris and Sedding were working at the time in the same architect's office. 'Masters in this hall' was published in Sedding's 1860 collection, *Ancient Christmas Carols*.

Born in 1834 in Walthamstow, East London, Morris came of solidly bourgeois stock and was educated at Marlborough College and Exeter College, Oxford. Deeply affected by the Oxford Movement, he seriously considered taking Holy Orders but decided instead to devote himself to art. A passionate Medievalist, he embarked first on an architectural training and in 1856 became apprenticed to G.E. Street, who was later to design the Law Courts in the Strand. It was while working in Street's Oxford offices that he met Sedding. Morris did not stick to architecture for long. Falling under the spell of the Pre-Raphaelites, he moved to London where he shared lodgings with Edward Burne-Jones and devoted himself to drawing, painting and designing wallpaper and fabrics. Later Morris branched out into furniture design and became a pioneer in the Arts and Crafts movement which sought to restore the standards and simplicity of medieval craftsmanship in an era of mass production. He wrote poems and novels and founded the Socialist League. He died in 1896 at Kelmscott House in Hammersmith, his London home.

'Masters in this hall' provides a lively dialogue between narrator and shepherds, couched in a pleasant but wholly sham medieval style and presented as though it is taking place in a baronial hall. It is all very Victorian. The *Oxford Book of Carols*, which includes the carol in its entirety, suggests that verses 2,3,4,5,6,7,11 & 12 can all easily be omitted while advising that 'a long carol is useful sometimes for processions, both in and out of church. This one should be popular with children. The characters can be distinguished in the singing, and the chorus sung by all'.

The reference in verse 11 to the ox and ass knowing Jesus and kneeling on his knee is an allusion to the statement in Isaiah 1.3 that 'the ox knoweth its owner and the ass his master's crib: but Israel does not know, my people doth not consider'. The notion that oxen in particular have a special affinity with Jesus and an almost instinctive knowledge of the time of his Nativity was taken up by a number of Victorian poets and hymn writers. It is perhaps most famously and beautifully expressed in Thomas Hardy's poem *The Oxen*:

Christmas Eve, and twelve of the clock,
'Now they are all on their knees,'
An elder said as we sat in a flock
By the embers in hearthside ease.
We pictured the meek mild creatures where
They dwelt in their strawy pen,
Nor did it occur to one of us there
To doubt they were kneeling then.

There is a French carol, first published in 1876, which takes this theme as its starting point. It begins '*Entre le boeuf et l'ane gris,/ Dors, dors, dors le petit Fils*' (Between the ox and the ass sleeps the little Son).

The vigorous tune which inspired 'Masters in the hall' had been obtained by Sedding from the organist of Chartres Cathedral and is sometimes known as CHARTRES. It was reharmonised by Gustav Holst for the *Oxford Book of Carols*.

Masters in this Hall,
Hear ye news today
Brought from overseas
And ever you I pray.

Nowell! Nowell! Nowell!
Nowell sing we clear:
Holpen are all folk on earth,
Born is God's son so dear:
Nowell! Nowell! Nowell!
Nowell sing we loud:
God today hath poor folk raised
And cast a down the proud

2 Going o'er the hills,
Through the milk-white snow,
Heard I ewes bleat
While the wind did blow.

3 Shepherds many an one
Sat among the sheep,
No man spake more word
Than they had asleep:

4 Quoth I, 'Fellows mine,
Why this guise sit ye?
Making but dull cheer,
Shepherds though ye be?'

5 'Shepherds should of right
Leap and dance and sing,
Thus to see ye sit,
Is a right strange thing'.

6 Quoth these fellows then,
'To Bethlehem town we go,
To see a mighty lord
Lie in a manger low'.

7 'How name ye this lord,
Shepherds?' then said I,
'Very God,' they said,
'Come from Heaven high'.

8 Then to Beth'lem Town
We went two by two
And in a sorry place
Heard the oxen low.

9 Therein did we see
A sweet and goodly may
And a fair old man,
Upon the straw she lay.

10 And a little child
On her arm had she,
'Wot ye who this is?'
Said the hinds to me.

11 Ox and ass him know,
Kneeling on their knee,
Wondrous joy had I
This little Babe to see.

12 This is Christ the Lord,
Masters be ye glad,
Christmas is come in,
And no folk should be sad.

52

NO USE KNOCKING AT THE WINDOW

Although the manger figures prominently in many carols, relatively few make much of St Luke's explanation that Mary had to give birth to her baby in this location 'because there was no room for them in the inn'. Sydney Carter's 'No use knocking at the window' takes this statement not just as its starting point but as its entire theme, using the image of the man standing in the rain and knocking at the window as a parable of social exclusion and contrasting it with the comfortable complacency of Christians safely installed in the warmth and privacy of their homes.

Sydney Carter (for whose biographical details see the notes to No. 19) wrote 'No use knocking at the window' in 1963. It is tempting to categorize it as a classic product of the 1960s, standing alongside other Carter songs like 'When I needed a neighbour' which express the social gospel and call on Christians to examine their prejudices and put down their defences. In fact, it is not as simple as that. This is what the author wrote about it in his book *Green Print for Song*:

'With whom do you identify yourself?' somebody asked. 'With the man (or woman) who is singing, or the one who is knocking at the window?'

With both. I do not want to be like the Christian who has just been woken up, but I often am. I am not so frank or so unsophisticated. I am not, perhaps, so honest. I do not want to stand out in the rain either; I do not want to beg for anything. But I find myself in that position too.

With whom do you think Jesus would identify? Think twice before you answer. How much do you really know about the man outside? Could he be an impostor?

The easy way to sing this song is to caricature the singer. But try, for a change, to see it from his point of view. Try to convince the listeners that you (he) are right. Do not say: 'I am a villain! Boo me!' Try to get inside the character. It may hurt a bit, but try.

So this carol is not all it seems. It has rightly found its way into a large number of collections, including the New Standard edition of *Hymns Ancient and Modern* and the BBC's highly popular series of books for school assemblies, *Come and Praise*. Its disturbing and challenging message deserves to go on being heard at Christmas time.

The tune STANDING IN THE RAIN is also by Sydney Carter.

Standing in the Rain

No use knocking on the window,
There is nothing we can do, sir.
All the beds are booked already,
There is nothing left for you, sir.
Standing in the rain,
Knocking on the window,
Knocking on the window,
On a Christmas Day.
There he is again
Knocking on the window,
Knocking on the window
In the same old way.

2 No use knocking on the window,
Some are lucky, some are not, sir.
We are Christian men and women,
But we're keeping what we've got, sir.

3 No, we haven't got a manger,
No we haven't got a stable,
We are Christian men and women,
Ever willing, ever able.

4 Christ the Lord has gone to heaven,
One day He'll be coming back, sir.
In this house He will be welcome,
But we hope he won't be black, sir.

5 Wishing you a Merry Christmas,
We will now go back to bed, sir.
'Til you woke us with your knocking
We were sleeping like the dead, sir.

53

O COME, ALL YE FAITHFUL

Here, coming in at just over the half way point in this collection is the one you have all been waiting for, the English version of *Adeste, fideles* (No. 4) which has established itself as one of the most popular of all Christmas hymns and came in fifth place in the 2005 BBC *Songs of Praise* poll. Particularly suited for processional use, it has been given an added boost by the popularity of late-night Christmas Eve services in which it is often the final hymn, enabling its last verse to be sung out with special conviction and feeling in the early moments of Christmas morning.

In his monumental *Dictionary of Hymnology*, John Julian lists no fewer than 38 English translations of *Adeste, fideles*, and there have doubtless been some more since it was published in 1892. The earliest known, which dates from 1789, begins 'Come, faithful all, rejoice and sing'. Other renderings of the opening line include 'Be present, ye faithful', 'Approach, all ye faithful', 'Assemble, ye faithful', 'Draw nigh, all ye faithful' and, in the case of the American Presbyterian *Psalms and Hymns* (Philadelphia, 1843) 'Hither, ye faithful, haste with songs of triumph'.

The version printed below is the one used in virtually all modern hymnbooks, although they do not always print all its seven verses. Like the Latin original, it is the work of several hands. Verses one, two, six and seven, which are the most commonly sung, are based on a translation made by Frederick Oakeley (1802–80) in 1841 for the use of his congregation at the Margaret Chapel in London. Verses three, four and five are based on a translation by William Brooke (1848–1917) for the *Altar Hymnal* of 1884. It will be noticed that even in its full form, the English translation is one verse shorter than the original Latin hymn. The fifth verse of *Adeste, fideles*, beginning '*Aeterne*

Parentis', has not found its way into general use in English. Literally translated, it reads 'We shall see the Eternal Splendour of the Eternal Father veiled in flesh, God as a child wrapped in swaddling clothes.'

Frederick Oakeley was a pioneer of liturgical reform and one of the leading figures in the choral revival in the mid-nineteenth century Church of England. When he became incumbent of the Margaret Chapel in Marylebone in 1839 he introduced the chanting of psalms to Gregorian tones and Anglican chant, the singing of Tudor settings of the communion service and the use of hymns for feast days. Among those who worshipped at the Chapel was the young William Ewart Gladstone who commented that the worship was both devout and hearty and also expressed his appreciation that the sermon never lasted for more than twenty minutes. Oakeley was hounded out of the Church of England for ritualistic practices and converted to Roman Catholicism in 1845. The Margaret Chapel, re-built as All Saints, Margaret Street, remained a centre of Anglo-Catholic worship, as it has to this day.

Oakeley's translation of *Adeste, fideles*, which began 'Ye faithful, approach ye', was never published but achieved considerable popularity through its use at the Margaret Chapel. A slightly altered version, beginning 'O come all ye faithful, joyfully triumphant', and published in Murray's *Hymnal* in 1852, was widely taken up in hymnbooks throughout the English-speaking world and forms the basis of the most popular verses of the hymn as it is now sung. The second line of the first verse was altered to 'Rejoicing, triumphant' in the *Parish Hymn Book* of 1863 and to the familiar 'Joyful and triumphant' soon afterwards in other books.

William Brooke, a Londoner who was born a Baptist but joined the Church of England in his late teens, was a keen student of hymnology and contributed hymns to many Victorian periodicals and collections. When the *Altar Hymnbook* of 1884 published the revised version of Oakeley's translation of the first and last pairs of verses of the original, Brooke supplied a translation of the middle four verses in order to provide a translation of the full text.

The tune to which 'O come, all ye faithful' is universally sung is that found in all the early manuscripts of '*Adeste, fideles*'. Whether John Wade composed it himself or copied it from another source is not clear. It appears in early manuscripts in both triple and duple time. There is a marked similarity between the tune for *Adeste, fideles* and the air '*Rage inutile*' from the comic opera, *Le Comte d'Acajou*, by Charles Simon Favart which was produced in Paris in 1744. There is some debate as to whether Wade was copying or parodying Favart's tune, or vice versa, or whether both composers might have been borrowing from an independent third source. The editors of the *New Oxford Book of Carols* dismiss theories floated early in the twentieth century that the tune was adapted by Handel but suggest that Thomas Arne might have had a hand in it.

Whatever its ultimate provenance, the tune was widely used in the later eighteenth century. It was first printed in England in 1782 in *An Essay on Church Plain Chant* and later appeared in Samuel Webbe's *Collection of Mottets or Antiphons* (1792). In Protestant circles the tune was used for a variety of psalms in what was called the 104th metre (that of Psalm 104 and 'O Worship the King'). In a *Selection of Psalm and Hymn Tunes* published in 1796 it was set to John Newton's hymn 'Begone, unbelief'. In this and in other later collections the tune was regularly named 'the Portugeuse hymn'. This may conceivably have been because of its regular use in the chapel of the Portugeuse Embassy in London where, as in other Roman Catholic circles, it accompanied '*Adeste, fideles*'. In his *Congregational and Chorister's Psalm and Hymn Book* (1843) Vincent Novello, who was himself organist at the Portugeuse Embassy Chapel, attributed the melody to John Reading, with the date 1680, and noted:

The piece obtained the name of 'The Portuguese Hymn' from the accidental circumstance of the Duke of Leeds . . . having heard the hymn first performed at the Portuguese Chapel (in 1795), and who, supposing it to be peculiar to the service in Portugal, introduced the melody at the Ancient Concerts, giving it the title of the 'Portuguese Hymn', by which appellation this very favourite and popular tune has ever since been distinguished; but it is by no means confined to the choir of the Portuguese Chapel, being the regular Christmas hymn 'Adeste Fidelis', that is sung in every Catholic chapel throughout England.

Others, however, maintain that the tune has Portuguese origins. An article which I wrote in *The Times* in December 1995 about the hymn's history elicited a letter from John Porter who feels that Novello has misled us about the tune:

> The most convincing explanation of its origins suggest that it was composed by Marcas Portugal (1762-1830), a Portuguese composer who produced over fifty operas and was for part of his career Chapel Master to the monarchs of Portugal. Any claim that it originated in Britain contradicts the fact that it is known as the Portuguese carol in both Italy and Spain, and the Portuguese themselves recognise it as their contribution to the international festival of Christmas.

THE PORTUGUESE HYMN was the fourth most common tune on church barrel organs built between 1790 and 1860, surpassed only by THE OLD HUNDREDTH, HANOVER and TALLIS'S CANON. The growing popularity of 'O come, all ye faithful' from the mid-nineteenth century, which was greatly boosted by its inclusion in the first edition of *Hymns Ancient and Modern* in 1861, meant that the tune became increasingly associated with this particular hymn in Protestant as well as Catholic worship. It took on its modern title of ADESTE FIDELES, while still continuing to be set to other texts. In his *Sacred Songs and Solos*, for example, Ida Sankey used it for 'How firm a foundation, ye saints of the Lord', an association which was perpetuated as recently as 1955 in the hymnbook of the Presbyterian Church of the USA.

Adeste, fideles

O come, all ye faithful,
Joyful and triumphant,
O come ye, O come ye to Bethlehem;
Come and behold him
Born the King of angels.
O come, let us adore him,
O come, let us adore him,
O come, let us adore him,
Christ the Lord.

2 God of God,
Light of Light,
Lo! he abhors not the Virgin's womb;
Very God,
Begotten, not created.

3 See how the shepherds
Summoned to his cradle,
Leaving their flocks, draw nigh to gaze!
We, too, will thither
Bend our hearts' oblations.

4 Lo, star-led chieftains,
Magi, Christ adoring,
Offer him incense, gold and myrrh;
We to the Christ-child
Bring our hearts oblations.

5 Child, for us sinners,
Poor and in the manger,
Fain we embrace thee with love and awe:
Who would not love thee,
Loving us so dearly?

6 Sing, choirs of angels!
Sing in exultation!
Sing, all ye citizens of heaven above:
'Glory to God
In the highest'.

7 Yea, Lord we greet thee,
Born this happy morning;
Jesu, to thee be glory given
Word of the Father
Now in flesh appearing.

54

O HOLY NIGHT

This carol came in fourth place in the 2005 BBC *Songs of Praise* poll despite the fact that it is found in few British hymnbooks. Long popular in the United States, it is more often sung as a performed item by a soloist than by a congregation. Among those who have recorded it are Joan Sutherland, Leontyne Price and Luciano Pavarotti as well as a host of popular artists including Perry Como, Mahalia Jackson and Nat King Cole. During a recent performance before a live audience, the Welsh mezzo-soprano, Kathryn Jenkins, managed to shatter a glass chandelier above her head.

In origin, this carol comes from France. It was written in 1847 by Placide Clappeau (1808–1877), a wine seller and amateur poet who was mayor of the small town of Roquemaure near Avignon, in response to a request from the parish priest for a poem for Christmas. He approached a friend of a friend, Adolphe Charles Adam, to provide a tune for it. Adam (1803–1856), who studied at the Paris conservatoire, had established himself as the leading comic opera composer of the day. His best-known works were the opera *Le Postillon de Lonjumeau* and the ballet *Giselle*. In its original French form, 'O Holy Night' received its first performance at midnight mass in Roquemaure parish church on Christmas Eve 1847.

The carol was an instant success and was published in an English version in London in 1855. In its native France, its use in church and liturgical settings was somewhat inhibited by the fact that Adam was Jewish and Clappeau became a freethinker in later life. However, in the United States, it became extremely popular, thanks especially to the translation into English by John Sullivan Dwight (1812–1893). A Harvard graduate, Dwight was a Unitarian minister for six years and then turned to music criticism and journalism. He spent most of his life in and around

Boston and edited *Dwight's Journal of Music* for thirty years. Much influenced by the poetry of Goethe and Schiller, whose work he translated, he was also a lover of Beethoven's music. It is Dwight's translation which appears on page 238 and which has become the standard version of 'O Holy Night'. According to some accounts, this carol was the first piece of music ever broadcast on radio.

O Holy Night

O holy night! The stars are brightly shining,
It is the night of the dear Saviour's birth.
Long lay the world in sin and error pining.
Till He appeared and the Spirit felt its worth.
A thrill of hope the weary world rejoices,
For yonder breaks a new and glorious morn.
Fall on your knees! Oh, hear the angel voices!
O night divine, the night when Christ was born;
O night, O holy night, O night divine!
O night, O holy night, O night divine!

Led by the light of faith serenely beaming,
With glowing hearts by His cradle we stand.
O'er the world a star is sweetly gleaming,
Now come the wise men from the Orient land.
The King of kings lay thus lowly manger;
In all our trials born to be our friend.
He knows our need, our weakness is no stranger,
Behold your King! Before him lowly bend!
Behold your King! Before him lowly bend!

Truly He taught us to love one another,
His law is love and His gospel is peace.
Chains he shall break, for the slave is our brother.
And in his name all oppression shall cease.
Sweet hymns of joy in grateful chorus raise we,
With all our hearts we praise His holy name.
Christ is the Lord! Then ever, ever praise we,
His power and glory ever more proclaim!
His power and glory ever more proclaim!

55

O LITTLE TOWN OF BETHLEHEM

The inspiration for this hymn came during a visit to the Holy Land by Phillips Brooks, an American Episcopalian priest. It was not quite written 'on location' as it was almost three years after being in Bethlehem that he put pen to paper but there is no doubt that, unlike many carols, it is based on the experience of being in the town of Jesus' birth at Christmas time. It has become a firm favourite and stands in seventh place in the 2005 BBC *Songs of Praise* poll.

Phillips Brooks was born in Boston in 1835 and educated at Harvard. After some years teaching Latin, he studied at the Episcopal Theological Seminary at Alexandria, Virginia, and was ordained in 1859. He was successively rector of the Church of the Advent, Philadelphia, Holy Trinity, Philadelphia and Trinity Church, Boston. Having turned down offers of professorships, the office of preacher at Harvard and the assistant bishopric of Pennsylvania, he was elected Bishop of Massachusetts in 1891 but died 18 months after his consecration.

Brooks was a man of towering physical and spiritual presence. He stood more than six feet, six inches tall and was a commanding preacher who spoke at the rate of 213 words a minute. A strong humanitarian and reformer, he was a warm admirer of Abraham Lincoln and supported the Northern cause in the American Civil War.

In the summer of 1865 Brooks took a year's leave of absence from his church in Philadelphia and began a world tour. On Christmas Eve he rode on horseback from Jerusalem to Bethlehem, pausing in the field where the angels' appearance to the shepherds is said to have taken place. Later in the evening he attended the service at the Church of the Nativity on the supposed site of Jesus' birth-place and was deeply moved by the experience. Back home in Philadelphia, he drew on his memories of this visit when writing a hymn in 1868 for the members of his Sunday School to sing at Christmas.

Taken up by several late nineteenth-century American hymnal editors, 'O little town of Bethlehem' found its way into the 1906 *English Hymnal* and has remained a favourite on both sides of the Atlantic ever since. In his study of *The English Hymn* Richard Watson notes:

> Brooks skillfully brings the reader from the contemplation of the scene itself to an awareness of its meaning for the individual believer. The transition is managed with consummate skill: from the silence of the night and the mystery of the Incarnation to the reception of Christ by the meek soul is a step which Brooks achieves by recalling the singer to 'this world of sin', in which there are meek souls, but there is also sin and misery. Brooks knows that 'Misery cries out to Thee', and his Christmas hymn is a hope that the situation will change, that through the coming of Christ and the spread of Christian values, society will become better. That hope must be the aim of all people of goodwill, and it becomes a part of that unmystical and high-minded morality that is a major feature of American hymn-writing at this time.

Three tunes are associated with this carol. North Americans generally sing it to ST. LOUIS, the melody which was written for it by Brooks' organist at Holy Trinity, Philadelphia, Lewis Redner. The story goes that after several weeks' fruitless effort to come up with a suitable tune, Redner awoke on Christmas Day 1868 with the melody ringing in his ears, fully formed and harmonized and that it was sung for the first time at a service two days later. In Britain 'O little town of Bethlehem' is usually sung either to CHRISTMAS CAROL, composed by Walford Davies, organist of the Temple Church, London, in 1905 in a setting for choirs but later adapted for congregational use, or, more commonly, to FOREST GREEN, an arrangement by Ralph Vaughan Williams of the tune of a traditional English folk ballad 'The Ploughman's Dream'. Vaughan Williams copied the tune down from the singing of a farm labourer in Forest Green, near Ockley in Surrey and paired it with 'O little town of Bethlehem' in the *English Hymnal*, of which he was music editor.

O little town of Bethlehem,
How still we see thee lie!
Above thy deep and dreamless sleep
The silent stars go by.
Yet in thy dark streets shineth
The everlasting light
The hopes and fears of all the years
Are met in thee to-night.

2 O morning stars, together
Proclaim the holy birth,
And praises sing to God the King,
And peace to men on earth;
For Christ is born of Mary;
And, gathered all above,
While mortals sleep, the angels keep
Their watch of wondering love.

3 How silently, how silently,
The wondrous gift is given!
So God imparts to human hearts
The blessings of his heaven.
No ear may hear his coming;
But in this world of sin,
Where meek souls will receive him, still
The dear Christ enters in.

4 Where children pure and happy
Pray to the blessed child,
Where misery cries out to thee,
Son of the mother mild;
Where charity stands watching
And faith holds wide the door,
The dark night wakes, the glory breaks,
And Christmas comes once more.

5 O holy Child of Bethlehem
Descend to us we pray;
Cast out our sin, and enter in,
Be born in us today.
We hear the Christmas angels
The great glad tidings tell:
A come to us, abide with us,
Our Lord Emmanuel.

56

O TANNENBAUM

I print this carol in its original German version rather than in English for several reasons. While it is still widely sung as a Christmas song in Germany, in Britain it is virtually unknown and the tune carries connotations that are political rather than Christmassy. North Americans do sing 'O Christmas tree' but for them the tune of *O Tannenbaum* brings to mind echoes of the Civil War as much as of the festive season. Another reason for printing this carol in German is that it is entirely devoid of explicitly Christian content and I suppose in a rather cowardly way I hope that this method of presenting it may deflect the criticisms of those who feel that its pagan propaganda should have no place in a book devoted to Christmas hymns and carols.

More than any other item in this book, *O Tannenbaum* takes us back beyond the Christian appropriation of mid-winter festivities to their pagan origins. The evergreen tree (which is what *Tannenbaum* means) belongs with mistletoe and the yule log to the ancient celebrations marking the winter solstice which were particularly marked among the Teutonic and Celtic peoples of northern Europe. Evergreens are obvious symbols of fertility and regeneration and it is not surprising that their veneration should have played a major part in these pre-Christian festivities.

O Tannenbaum also belongs to the world of nineteenth-century romanticism. It was written in 1824 by Ernst Anschütz, a Leipzig schoolmaster, for his charges to sing around the Christmas trees that were becoming a feature of every German home. The practice of bringing a fir tree into the house at Christmas time and decorating it with brightly coloured balls and candles seems to have begun in the Rhineland in the late Middle Ages. Popular German tradition had Luther as the inventor of the Christmas tree but this was one of several legends developed in the nineteenth century as nationalism and romanticism combined to invest this symbol of Germanic tradition with a particular aura and power. It was, of course, the German Prince Albert who brought the Christmas tree to Britain when he set up a decorated fir tree in the great hall at Windsor Castle in 1841. Within a decade, few British homes were without a tree in the drawing room and the practice rapidly spread across the Atlantic.

Anschütz based *O Tannenbaum* on an old German folk-song 'O Dannenbom' which serenades the fir tree for its green leaf in winter as in summer. The first verses of the two songs are very similar in their content and message. In his second verse, Anschütz introduced a distinct Christmas theme, wholly missing from the older song, although he avoided expressing any overtly Christian sentiment and there is no reference to the birth of Jesus anywhere in his text. The third verse enlists the tree as an educational aid which will teach hope and love and faithfulness to those who gaze on it in wonder. For readers whose German may be a little shaky, here is an English verse translation made by Walter Ehret of Scarsdale, New York, in 1963 for his *International Book of Christmas Carols*:

O Christmas tree, O Christmas tree,
With faithful leaves unchanging!
Not only green in summer's heat
But in the winter's snow and sleet:
O Christmas tree, O Christmas tree,
With faithful leaves unchanging!

O Christmas tree, O Christmas tree,
Of all the trees most lovely!
Each year you bring renewed delight,
A-gleaming in the Christmas night:
O Christmas tree, O Christmas tree,
Of all the trees most lovely!

O Christmas tree, O Christmas tree,
Your leaves will surely teach me
That hope and love and faithfulness

Are precious things I can possess:
O Christmas tree, O Christmas tree,
Your leaves will surely teach me.

The *Galliard Book of Carols* contains a translation by Bernard Braley, beginning 'O Christmas tree, O Christmas tree, the tree for every season', which attempts to give a more Christological focus to the carol by including the lines: 'Throughout the year, your lively green/Reminds us of the Christ unseen'. Another very free translation of *O Tannenbaum* is also worthy of mention. Henry Wadsworth Longfellow turned the poem into a complaint about the behaviour of a fickle lover, contrasted with the constancy of the tree which he identified as a hemlock, a species of fir well known in North America (botanical name *Abies Canadensis*):

O hemlock tree! O hemlock tree!
How faithful are thy branches!
Green not alone in summer time,
But in the winter's snow and rime!
O hemlock tree! O hemlock tree!
How faithful are thy branches!

O maiden fair! O maiden fair!
How faithless is thy bosom!
To love me in prosperity,
And leave me in adversity!
O maiden fair! O maiden fair!
How faithless is thy bosom!

Anschütz wrote *O Tannenbaum* to fit the melody of a popular song, '*Es lebe doch*', published in 1799. It had, in turn, borrowed the melody of a traditional students' song, '*Lauriger Horatius quam dixisti verum'*. The tune has had a vigorous life as bearer of political propaganda in Britain and the United States. It is best known on this side of the Atlantic as the melody of the Red Flag ('The people's flag is deepest red'), the anthem of the Labour movement written in 1889 by James Connell, an Irish poacher turned sheep farmer turned politician, and still sung with varying degrees of enthusiasm and embarrassment at the end of every Labour Party conference. Liberal Democrats have their own version, sung less often but with more gusto, which begins 'The people's flag is slightly pink, not deepest red as people think'. During the American Civil War, the melody of *O Tannenbaum* was enlisted to the Confederate cause through its use for James Randall's song, 'The despot's heel is on thy shore, Maryland, my Maryland', written in 1861 'to fire the Southern heart' after Unionist troops had marched through Baltimore. We have moved a long way from Christmas trees but why should the pagans have all the good tunes?

O Tannenbaum, O Tannenbaum,
Wie grün sind deine Blätter!
Du grünst nicht nur zur Sommerzeit,
Nein, auch im Winter, wenn es schneit.
O Tannenbaum, O Tannenbaum,
Wie grün sind deine Blätter!

O Tannenbaum, O Tannenbaum,
Du kannst mir sehr gefallen.
Wie oft hat doch zur Weihnachtszeit
Ein Baum von dir mich hoch erfreut.
O Tannenbaum, O Tannenbaum,
Du kannst mir sehr gefallen.

O Tannenbaum, O Tannenbaum,
Dein Kleid soll mich was lehren:
Die Hoffnung und Beständigkeit
Gibt Trost und Kraft zu jeder Zeit.
O Tannenbaum, O Tannenbaum,
Du kannst mir sehr gefallen.

57

OF THE FATHER'S LOVE BEGOTTEN

This fine processional hymn which speaks so majestically and sonorously about Christ in all his attributes, human and divine, has a complex genesis. Derived from a Latin poem written around the year 400, it was wedded to a later medieval liturgical melody in the middle of the nineteenth century. The translation presented here is a composite effort, representing the work of three Victorian hymnodists. Elements from another translation made early in the twentieth century have also been incorporated into several modern hymnbooks.

The poem on which the hymn is based was written by Aurelius Clemens Prudentius who lived from 349–410. Biographical details on him can be found in the note about 'Bethlehem of noblest cities' (No. 12). It is to be found in the collected edition of his works known as the *Cathemerinon*, which provides hymns to be sung at various times of the day and on certain days of the year, and comes from a 37-stanza *Hymnus omnis horae* (Hymn for every hour) beginning '*Da puer, plectrum*'.

A portion of the poem, dealing with the Incarnation and beginning '*Corde natus ex parentis*', seems to have been taken up for liturgical use in the church around the ninth century. In the Mozarabic (Spanish) rite and in some other European rites, verses from it were sung on the feast of the Circumcision of Christ (1 January) and on feast days associated with the Virgin Mary. At York six verses were sung at Compline from Christmas Eve to Epiphany and at Hereford verses of '*Corde natus*' were sung at the services of prime, terce, sext and none (the so-called lesser hours) throughout the same period. Part of the hymn is contained in the Hereford Breviary. The concluding doxology (verse 9) and the refrain '*Saeculorum saeculis*' (translated here as

'Evermore and evermore') were added later and first appear in eleventh-century manuscripts.

Prudentius' majestic exposition of the Christian understanding of the nature and purpose of Christ covers the pre-existent Logos begotten of God before time, his work in the creation of the world '*per verbum*', his assumption of human flesh in order to save the human race from sin and death, the Virgin Birth, the foreshadowing of his coming by the Old Testament prophets, his role as judge of the living and the dead and his adoration by all creation, animate and inanimate.

It is not surprising that when the Oxford Movement prompted a revival of the early office hymns of the church, this comprehensive and well-written treatment of the Christmas message in all its theological complexity was one of the first texts to be translated and brought into use in the mid-Victorian Church of England. The first translation seems to have been made by Beresford Hope for his 1844 *Hymns of the Church*. It began 'Son Eternal of the Father'. When J.M. Neale (on whom see notes to No.1) translated six verses of '*Corde natus*' for the enlarged edition of his *Hymnal Noted* (1854), he took over several of Hope's lines. Neale's translation was in turn incorporated and amended in the version of the hymn prepared in 1861 by Henry Baker for the first edition of *Hymns Ancient and Modern* of which he was editor. Baker extended the hymn to nine stanzas, taking three additional verses from the Hereford Breviary text.

The hymn as it is printed on page 254 is the composite version which appeared in the first two editions of *Hymns Ancient and Modern*. Verses one, four, five, six and eight are Neale's, as altered by Baker, and two, three, seven and nine are by Baker. Neale's original translation began 'Of the Father's heart begotten', a more accurate rendering of the Latin '*corde*' than either the first line given in the 1859 trial edition of *Hymns Ancient and Modern*, 'Of the Father's will begotten', or that finally resolved on by Baker, 'Of the father's love begotten'. Neale's original versions of verses five and six ran:

He is here, Whom seers in old time
Chanted of while ages ran:
Whom the writings of the Prophets
Promised since the word began:
Then foretold, now manifested
To receive the praise of men.

Praise him, O ye Heaven of heavens!
Praise Him, Angels in the height!
Every power and every virtue
Sing the praise of God aright:
Let no tongue of man be silent,
Let each heart and voice unite.

Other translations made in the mid-nineteenth century include 'Born of God the Father's bosom', 'Yea, from the Almighty mind He sprung' and 'Offspring of the Eternal Father'. None of these had the same popularity as the Baker-Neale-Hope version which is probably the nearest that there is to a *textus receptus* for this hymn. Few hymnbooks, however, have chosen to reproduce it in its entirety or in its original form. Indeed, it underwent considerable alteration in subsequent editions of *Hymns Ancient and Modern* with verse three being dropped, verses five and six being reversed and the following textual alterations being made:

Verse 5
This is He whom seers and sages
Sang of old with one accord;
Whom the writings of the Prophets
Promised in their faithful word

Verse 7
Hail, thou judge of souls departed!
Hail, thou King of them that live!
Who at last in judgement coming

Verse 8
Now let old and young men's voices
Join with boys' thy name to sing,

Matrons, virgins, little maidens
In glad chorus answering

While several modern hymnbooks base their (usually truncated) versions of this hymn on the Baker-Neale-Hope text, others rely on a translation made by Roby Furley Davis (1866-1937) for the 1906 *English Hymnal*. Its first line echoes Neale's original:

Of the Father's heart begotten,
Ere the world from chaos rose,
He is Alpha: from that Fountain
All that is and hath been flows;
He is Omega, of all things
Yet to come the mystic Close.

There is much to commend in Davis' translation. It was chosen by David Willcocks for his 1963 arrangement of six verses of the hymn which appeared in *Carols for Choirs*. Space precludes the quotation of all its nine verses here. It can be found in its entirety only in the original edition of the *English Hymnal* (at No.613) – the *New English Hymnal* prints only seven verses. Let me just give the opening couplets of each verse and also the whole of its concluding stanza, which translates a verse in Prudentius' poem powerfully expressing the whole creation's praise of Christ which did not find its way into *Hymns Ancient and Modern*:

Verse 2 By his word was all created;
He commanded and 'twas done

Verse 3 He assumed this mortal body,
Frail and feeble, doomed to die

Verse 4 O how blest that wondrous birthday,
When the Maid the curse retrieved

Verse 5 This is he, whom seer and sibyl
Sang in ages long gone by

Verse 6 Sing ye heights of heaven, his praises;
Angels and Archangels, sing!

Verse 7 Hail! thou Judge of souls departed;
Hail! of all the living King

Verse 8 Now let old and young uniting
Chant to thee harmonious lays

Verse 9 Let the storm and summer sunshine,
Gliding stream and sounding shore,
Sea and forest, frost and zephyr,
Day and night their Lord adore;
Let creation join to laud thee
Through the ages evermore.

Several hymnal editors have cherry picked what they consider the best bits of these various translations and strung them together. This is the approach adopted by the editors of the *New Oxford Book of Carols* who have also added some lines of their own for good measure.

The haunting plainsong melody DIVINUM MYSTERIUM (also known as CORDE NATUS) to which this hymn is almost always set began life as a trope sung during the *Sanctus* in praise of the Blessed Sacrament. Tropes were musical interpolations in the medieval liturgy originally consisting of vocalized ornament on a single syllable but later with words set to them. This particular tune is first found in twelfth and thirteenth-century manuscripts in Italy and Germany set to the words '*Divinum mysterium*'. There is some suggestion that it may have evolved from the chant of the Christmas sequence, '*Votis pater*'.

J.M. Neale and his colleague, Thomas Helmore, the musical editor of the *Hymnal Noted*, discovered the tune in the sixteenth-century Finnish collection *Piae Cantiones* and paired it with the translation of Prudentius' hymn. It has proved a happy marriage although there are differing views about whether it should be sung in triple time with a pronounced rhythmic stress or in a more free-flowing chant style. The editors of the *New Oxford Book of Carols* advocate singing the hymn to the chant that was used for the Latin verses when they were sung at York and Hereford, which is still extant, but I doubt that it will supplant DIVINUM MYSTERIUM.

Corde natus ex Parentis

Of the Father's love begotten
Ere the worlds began to be,
He is Alpha and Omega,
He the source, the ending he,
Of the things that are, that have been,
And that future years shall see,
Evermore and evermore.

2 At his word they were created;
He commanded; it was done:
Heaven and earth and depths of ocean
In their threefold order one;
All that grows beneath the shining
Of the light of moon and sun,
Evermore and evermore.

3 He is found in human fashion,
Death and sorrow here to know,
That the race of Adam's children,
Doomed by Law to endless woe,
May not henceforth die and perish
In the dreadful gulf below,
Evermore and evermore.

4 O that birth for ever blessed!
When the Virgin, full of grace,
By the Holy Ghost conceiving,
Bare the Saviour of our race,
And the Babe, the world's Redeemer,
First revealed his sacred face,
Evermore and evermore.

5 This is he whom seers in old time
Chanted of with one accord;
Whom the voices of the Prophets
Promised in their faithful word;
Now he shines, the long-expected:
Let creation praise its Lord,
Evermore and evermore.

6 O ye heights of heaven, adore him;
Angel-hosts, his praises sing;
Powers, dominions, bow before him,
And extol our God and King:
Let no tongue on earth be silent
Every voice in concert ring,
Evermore and evermore.

7 Righteous Judge of souls departed!
Righteous King of them that live!
On the Father's throne exalted
None in might with thee may strive;
Who at last in vengeance coming
Sinners from thy face shalt drive,
Evermore and evermore.

8 Thee let men, Thee let young men,
Thee let boys in chorus sing;
Matrons, virgins, little maidens
With glad voices answering;
Let their guileless songs re-echo
And the heart its praises bring,
Evermore and evermore.

9 Christ, to thee, with God the Father,
And, O Holy Ghost, to thee,
Hymn and chant and high thanksgiving
And unwearied praised be,
Honour, glory and dominion,
And eternal victory,
Evermore and evermore.

58

ON CHRISTMAS NIGHT ALL CHRISTIANS SING

This jolly little piece, which came thirteenth in the 2005 BBC *Songs of Praise* poll. is generally known as the Sussex Carol because that is where it was collected by two of the leading enthusiasts of the early twentieth-century folksong revival. However, it should perhaps properly be called the Irish or even the Low Countries carol, having made its first appearance as 'Another short caroll for Christmas Day' in a *Smale Garland of Pious and Godly Songs* written and published by an Irish bishop, Luke Wadding, in Ghent in 1684. It is not entirely clear whether Wadding was its author or whether it is of late medieval provenance.

Much less is known about Luke Wadding than about his sixteenth-century Franciscan namesake with whom he should not be confused. In 1683, while in exile in Ghent, he was consecrated to the Roman Catholic diocese of Ferns, covering County Wexford in Ireland, and he seems to have remained bishop there until 1691. Versions of the carol, differing considerably from Wadding's text, appeared in Harward of Tewkesbury's *Choice Collection of Christmas Songs* (1790), J. Guest's *A New Carol Book* (Birmingham, c. 1830) and in the *Good Christmas Box* of 1847.

In 1904 the folk-song enthusiasts, Cecil Sharp and Ralph Vaughan Williams, noted down the carol from the singing of Mrs Verrall of Monk's Gate, near Horsham in West Sussex. It is her version, printed in the *Journal of the Folk Song Society* in 1905, and subsequently taken up in a good number of carol books, which is printed below.

The tune CHRISTMAS NIGHT is the one to which Mrs Verrall sang the carol. It was one of eight traditional carols arranged for unaccompanied singing by Vaughan Williams in

1920. This is not the only fine tune contributed by Mrs Verrall to English hymnody. The stirring MONK'S GATE, to which John Bunyan's pilgrim hymn 'Who would true valour see' is almost invariably sung, was another melody which Vaughan Williams heard her singing at her home in December 1904 and subsequently arranged for congregational use.

The Sussex Carol

On Christmas Night all Christians sing,
To hear the news the angels bring:
News of great joy, news of great mirth,
News of our merciful King's birth.

2 Then why should men on earth be so sad,
Since our Redeemer made us glad
When from our sin he set us free,
All for to gain our liberty?

3 When sin departs before his grace,
Then life and health come in its place;
Angels and men with joy may sing,
All for to see the new-born King.

4 All out of darkness we have light,
Which made the angels sing this night:
'Glory to God and peace to men,
Now and for evermore, Amen.'

59

ON THE FIRST DAY OF CHRISTMAS

This delightful song derives from a game of forfeits traditionally played on Twelfth Night. Each person taking part had to remember all the objects mentioned by previous players and add an extra item to the list. Anyone failing to repeat correctly what had gone before would have to perform a forfeit.

This particular version of the song seems to have been popular on Tyneside in the eighteenth and nineteenth centuries and appears on several broadsides printed in Newcastle during that period. William Husk claimed that his inclusion of it in his *Songs of the Nativity* (1864) marked its first appearance in a collection of carols, although he noted that in a broadside of c. 1770 it was entitled 'An Old English Carol'.

Various theories have been advanced as to the meaning of the very diverse set of persons and objects sent as tokens of love over the twelve days of the Christmas season. They may well be Christian symbols and it has been suggested that the song, or at least this version of it, has its origins in the post-Reformation period and was devised by Roman Catholics as a coded checklist of the basic tenets of their faith during the period when they were forbidden from openly practising their religion. Specifically, it may have been designed as a vehicle for teaching young people the elements of Catholicism in a way that would not arouse Protestant hostility or suspicion.

Going in descending order, the twelve drummers drumming have been taken to represent either the twelve points of belief in the Apostles' Creed or the twelve minor prophets (neither of which I propose listing for you here). The eleven pipers suggest the eleven disciples left to announce the good news of Jesus' resurrection after Judas had hanged himself. The ten lords a-leaping seem most likely to signify the ten commandments. The nine ladies dancing could be the nine fruits of the Spirit listed by St Paul – love, joy, peace, patience, kindness, goodness, fidelity, gentleness and self-control. The eight maids a-milking suggest the Beatitudes. The seven swans a-swimming represent the seven works of mercy. The six geese a-laying stand for the six days of creation. The five gold rings are thought to represent either the first five books of the Old Testament (the Pentateuch) or the five obligatory sacraments of the Roman Catholic Church. The four calling birds match up with the four Gospels. The three French hens have been taken as symbols both of the gifts given by the three wise men to the infant Jesus and of the virtues of faith, hope and charity mentioned in St Paul's Epistle to the Corinthians. The two turtle doves may have the most literal meaning – this was the sacrifice that Mary and Joseph made when Jesus was born – or they may signify the Old and New Testaments.

The partridge in the pear tree is the most puzzling of the gifts to explain in terms of Christian symbolism. It has been suggested that some medieval artists took the partridge to symbolize Christ but I have found no evidence to support that theory – it is the pelican rather than the partridge which often symbolized Christ. Another explanation is that the partridge is a symbol of the Devil who reveals to Herod that the Virgin Mary is standing behind a sheaf of corn. Pointing out that in folk-lore the partridge is an emblem of evil and the pear a symbol of fertility, Erik Routley speculates that 'the presence of the Evil one in the genealogical tree would appear to be a reference to Man in his fallen state awaiting Redemption through the Passion of Christ'. It is also possible that this particular item in the list of lover's gifts has no religious significance and survives from an earlier version of the song, perhaps tying in with the tradition that a girl who walks backwards towards a pear tree on Christmas Eve and goes round it three times will see the image of her future husband.

There is also a less involved and theological explanation for the first five items in the list. They may all refer to birds. The pear tree may simply be a corruption of *perdix*, the French word for partridge. The calling birds, which appear as colly-birds in some versions of the song, could be blackbirds, doves (from the

French *colombe*), or even quails (*cailles*), the French hens and turtle doves what they seem and the gold rings either goldfinches (sometimes known as goldspinks) or gulderers (turkeys). Yet another, and slightly less convincing, explanation is that the song relates to the stocking and running of a country estate with the partridge in a pear tree symbolizing a plot of wooded land suitable for breeding game birds.

The Geordie version of 'The Twelve Days of Christmas', which has become standard in most books of carols and nursery rhymes, is not the only one. In other parts of the country, different gifts were listed. In versions of the song collected in Sussex, for example, the four birds are canaries, there are eight deer a-running, ten ladies skipping, eleven bears a-baiting and twelve parsons preaching! In Somerset Cecil Sharp noted down several variants of the partridge in a pear tree, including 'part of a Juniper tree', 'part of a June apple tree' and 'pass through a Junipear Tree'.

The song is not just confined to the British Isles. Numerous versions have been collected in France, many of which have a gastronomic flavour. One which comes from the town of Cambresis, for example, has the partridge in the pear tree and the two turtle dove but then goes on to mention three wood pigeons, four ducks, five rabbits, six hares, seven hounds, eight shorn sheep, nine horned oxen, ten turkeys, eleven hams and twelve small cheeses. A version found in the west of France provides even more of a gourmet's feast with stuffing, two breasts of veal, three joints of beef, four pigs' trotters, five legs of mutton, six partridges with cabbage, seven rabbits on spits, eight plates of salads, nine dishes for a chapter of canons, ten full casks of wine, rounded off with eleven beautiful full-breasted maidens but ending rather ominously with twelve musketeers.

It may well be that 'The Twelve Days of Christmas' is ultimately of Gallic origin. Routley felt that its 'refined and chivalrous tone, and the fact that it has always been such a favourite with the French, would lead one to suspect that its source lies among the songs of the troubadours of Languedoc'. He points out that the snatch of melody that accompanies the enumeration of the gifts is almost identical with that used by French minstrels in the twelfth and thirteenth centuries and suggests that the dancing ladies and leaping lords are the leotards and jacquelines of '*La grace sautée*' from French ballet.

Several other traditional carols take a similar numerical approach and go through the twelve days of Christmas. 'A New Dial', a carol first found in an almanack printed in 1625, which begins 'In those twelve days let us be glad' gives a cumulative list of God's gifts beginning with One God, one Baptism and one Faith. It continues with two Testaments, three persons in the Trinity, four Evangelists, five senses, six days to labour, seven liberal arts, eight beatitudes, nine muses, ten commandments and eleven thousand virgins suffering death for Jesus' sake (a reference to the story of St Ursula) and twelve disciples and articles of the Creed.

A similar check-list of key Christian doctrines can be found in the traditional song 'Green grow the rushes-O'. Here twelve stands for the apostles, eleven for those who went up to heaven, ten for the Commandments, nine for the bright shiners (probably the nine ranks of angels), eight for the April rainers (perhaps another reference to angels or to the eight souls saved from the flood in Noah's Ark), seven for the stars in the sky (possibly those in the Ursa Major group or the ones mentioned in Revelation 1.16), six for the proud walkers (thought by some to be a corrupt reference to the six water pots in the miracle at Cana and by others to be a corruption of 'workers' and so tie in with the six days of labour decreed by God for man), five for the symbol at your door (the pentagram was used as a charm to ward off the Evil One), four for the Gospel makers, three for the rivals (perhaps the persons of the Trinity or the wise men), two for the lily-white boys (Jesus and John the Baptist, but please don't write to ask me why they should be clothed in green). The line 'One is one and all alone and ever more shall be so' provides a nice encapsulation of the doctrine of monotheism.

This song is in much demand as the basis for advertising jingles. In December 1996 *The Times* launched a promotional campaign with a full page advert headed 'The 12 Prizes of

Christmas' in which the following words appeared under the traditional tune: 'Twelve cases of Lanson, eleven shopping trips at Warner Bros, ten Philips cordless phones, nine hampers of Cockburn's, eight Wedgwood gift sets, seven whirlpool microwaves, six Fortnum and Mason hampers, five sets of Butler and Wilson jewellery, four Psion personal organizers, three nights at Claridges for two, two tickets to Spain, and a shopping trip to New York'. The Royal Bank of Scotland has also hi-jacked the song to promote its direct banking service. A glossy brochure replete with coloured pictures of milkmaids, drummers, leaping lords and other features of the traditional list, offers twelve goodies for the discerning customer, including amendment of direct debits, the ability to switch funds between accounts and the ordering of replacement cards and PIN numbers – hardly as romantic as French hens and turtle doves but a testimony to the hold that this particular Christmas song has on the popular imagination.

Mercifully, after all that I have found to comment on with regard to this song, there is very little to be said about the tune to which it is generally sung. Nobody knows how old it is or where it comes from although the scholarly editors of the *New Oxford Book of Carols* observe that bars 18-19 date only from Frederick Austin's 1909 arrangement, that E is sometimes found for F in the seventh note (they print the tune in the key of F), and that the pause on 'rings' tends to lengthen from verse to verse. They also provide an alternative tune which is still sung by the men of the Copper family in Sussex.

The Twelve Days of Christmas

On the first day of Christmas
My true love sent to me,
A Partridge in a pear tree.

2 On the second day of Christmas
My true love sent to me,
Two turtle doves,
And a Partridge in a pear tree.

3 On the third day of Christmas
My true love sent to me,
Three French hens, Two turtle doves
And a Partridge in a pear tree.

4 On the fourth day of Christmas
My true love sent to me,
Four calling birds, Three French hens,
Two turtle doves, and a Partridge in a pear tree.

5 On the fifth day of Christmas
My true love sent to me,
Five gold rings, four calling birds, three French hens,
Two turtle doves, and a Partridge in a pear tree.

6 On the sixth day of Christmas
My true love sent to me,
Six geese a-laying, Five gold rings,
Four calling birds, Three French hens,
Two turtle doves, and a Partridge in a pear tree.

7 On the seventh day of Christmas
My true love sent to me,
Seven swans a-swimming,
Six geese a-laying, etc.

8 On the eighth day of Christmas
My true love sent to me,
Eight maids a-milking,
Seven swans a-swimming, etc.

9 On the ninth day of Christmas
My true love sent to me,
Nine drummers drumming,
Eight maids a-milking, etc.

10 On the tenth day of Christmas
My true love sent to me,
Ten pipers piping,
Nine drummers drumming, etc.

11 On the eleventh day of Christmas
My true love sent to me,
Eleven ladies dancing,
Ten pipers piping. etc.

12 On the twelfth day of Christmas
My true love sent to me,
Twelve lords a-leaping,
Eleven ladies dancing,
Ten pipers piping,
Nine drummers drumming,
Eight maids a-milking,
Seven swans a-swimming,
Six geese a-laying,
Five gold rings,
Four calling birds,
Three French hens,
Two turtle doves,
And a partridge in a pear tree.

60

ONCE IN ROYAL DAVID'S CITY

This Victorian gem retains its place as one of the most popular of all Christmas hymns, standing in eighth place in the 2005 BBC *Songs of Praise* poll, even if its didactic moralizing tone is hardly in keeping with the spirit of our age. Since 1919 it has been the opening item in the Christmas Eve service of nine lessons and carols at King's College, Cambridge, and for many listeners and viewers around the world the sound of the lone treble voice singing its first verse marks the moment when Christmas really begins.

It is one of the many hymns still in circulation which were written more than 150 years ago by the redoubtable Mrs C.F. Alexander. Born in Dublin in 1818, the daughter of an English army officer, she spent much of her childhood mixing with the Anglo-Irish aristocracy. When she was seven her father became agent to the Earl of Wicklow and it may well have been the grand houses and the almost feudal society of southern Ireland that inspired the much-criticized and much-misunderstood verse of her well-known children's hymn, 'All things bright and beautiful' about the 'rich man in his castle' and 'the poor man at his gate'. Although she appears in all hymnbooks with her married name, Cecil Frances Humphreys wrote most of her hymns before her marriage at the age of 32 to a moderate Tractarian clergyman, William Alexander, who was to end his dazzling ecclesiastical career as Archbishop of Armagh and Primate of all Ireland. She died in 1895.

'Once in Royal David's city' first appeared in her *Hymns for Little Children* which was published in 1848 and went through more than 100 impressions in the next fifty years. The profits from the book went to an institute for the deaf at Strabane which she was instrumental in founding. Like many of her hymns, it was written with a primarily didactic purpose in order to implant in the minds of the young through simple verse the essential doctrines of the Christian faith. This aim underlay her 1848 volume which was based on the Church Catechism and provided fourteen hymns to explain the different sections of the Apostles' Creed. 'Once in Royal David's city' was designed to amplify and explain the statement 'I believe in Jesus Christ...who was born of the Virgin Mary'. The opening statement of the Creed, 'I believe in God the Father Almighty, Maker of heaven and earth' was dealt with in 'All things bright and beautiful' and 'There is a green hill far away' sought to unpack the full significance of 'He was crucified, dead and buried'.

In marked contrast to the almost docetic tone of 'Away in a manger' with its statement that 'the Little Lord Jesus, no crying he makes', Mrs Alexander's hymn fully acknowledges Jesus' humanity, noting that 'tears and smiles like us he knew'. Its call on Christian children to be 'mild, obedient, good as he' perhaps grates somewhat on modern congregations, likewise its emphasis on the quality of obedience exemplified by Jesus and it is noticeable that verse three has been dropped from several recent British hymnals, including *Rejoice and Sing*, *Baptist Praise and Worship* and from many American books.

This hymn also displays another characteristic of Victorian hymnody in general, and Mrs Alexander's work in particular, in its idolization of childhood. This is particularly evident in the closing couplet which seems almost literally to make children into little angels. This is a common theme in hymns written by women authors for children in the mid-nineteenth century, especially those which portray Jesus, as this one does, leading his children on 'to the place where he has gone'. Another striking example is Jemima Thompson's 'I think when I read that sweet story of old' which incites the young to look forward to arriving in 'that beautiful place He is gone to prepare for all who are washed and forgiven' and assures them that 'many dear children are gathering there, for of such is the kingdom of heaven'. In my study of Victorian hymnody, *Abide With Me*, I have suggested that what may seem to our eyes a rather mawkish association of children with heaven may have in large part been a pastoral response to the high infant mortality rates in Victorian Britain.

The tune IRBY to which 'Once in Royal David's city' is universally sung was composed for it by Henry Gauntlett and first appeared set to Mrs Alexander's verses and arranged as a unison melody with simple piano accompaniment in 1849 in a pamphlet entitled *Christmas Carols, Four Numbers*. It was included in the 1858 musical edition of *Hymns for Little Children* and three years later in the first edition of *Hymns Ancient and Modern* where it was given the name IRBY for reasons unknown. There are at least three localities in England called IRBY but none has any apparent connection with Gauntlett, who is one of the most prolific-ever composers of hymn tunes. Born in Wellington, Shropshire, in 1805, he became organist of Olney Church in Buckinghamshire at the age of nine and choirmaster five years later. After practising as a solicitor in London, he took early retirement in 1846 to devote all his time and energies to music. He served as organist to several London churches, notably Union Chapel in Islington, and helped to edit many hymnals. His output of hymn tunes is said to have exceeded 10,000 but few of them are still sung today.

Once in Royal David's city
Stood a lowly cattle shed,
Where a mother laid her Baby
In a manger for his bed.
Mary was that mother mild,
Jesus Christ her little child.

2 He came down from earth to heaven
Who is God and Lord of All
And his shelter was a stable
And his cradle was a stall,
With the poor and mean and lowly
Lived on earth our Saviour holy.

3 And through all his wondrous childhood
He would honour and obey
Love, and watch the lowly maiden
In whose gentle arms he lay.
Christian children all must be
Mild, obedient, good as he.

4 For he is our childhood's pattern
Day by day like us he grew;
He was little, weak and helpless;
Tears and smiles like us he knew;
And he feeleth for our sadness,
And he shareth in our gladness.

5 And our eyes at last shall see him,
Through his own redeeming love;
For that Child so dear and gentle
Is our Lord in heaven above;
And he leads his children on
To the place where he is gone.

6 Not in that poor lowly stable,
With the oxen standing by,
We shall see him, but in heaven,
Set at God's right hand on high,
When, like stars, his children crowned
All in white shall wait around.

61

OUTLANDERS, WHENCE COME YE LAST?

This item has only ever appeared in two carol books and then not in its original form which is how it is printed here. Yet it deserves inclusion as one of two interesting excursions into Christmas carol writing by an eminent Victorian agnostic (the other being 'Masters in this hall', No. 51).

These verses first appeared in 1868 in William Morris' book, *The Earthly Paradise*, a collection of 24 lengthy epic poems, two for each month of the year, taken from classical, medieval, Norse and Eastern legends and supposedly told by a group of wanderers who have fled from a city struck with plague to an Atlantic island where Greek and North European cultures meet. The overall atmosphere of the work, which was enormously popular with late Victorian readers, is dream-like and escapist.

'Outlanders, whence come ye last?' occurs as a self-contained song within one of the two poems for September, 'The Land East of the Sun and West of the Moon', which is set in Norway during the time of King Magnus. It is recalled by one of the central characters, John, as an ancient Christmas song.

As laid out with its repeated refrain in the second and fourth line of every verse, the piece has a definite carol-like quality and it caught the eye of H.R. Bramley and John Stainer as they were casting around for material to include in their 1871 collection, *Christmas Carols New and Old*. Their version of the carol began with Morris' third verse and was set to a tune by the great Victorian hymn-tune composer, John Bacchus Dykes. Morris' Merry England-style socialism was also calculated to appeal to Percy Dearmer and a truncated version of 'Outlanders, whence come ye last?' found its way into the *Oxford Book of Carols* (1928).

Like Bramley and Stainer, Dearmer cut out Morris' first two verses and began his version 'From far away we come to you'. He also for some reason omitted the verse beginning 'News, news of the Trinity'. While keeping the running refrain through the verses, he also added a chorus at the end of each verse:

From far away we come to you,
To tell of great tidings strange and true.

In the *Oxford Book of Carols* 'From far away we come to you' took pride of place in the section devoted to 'carols by modern writers and composers'. Ralph Vaughan Williams, the book's musical editor, composed a unison tune for it. I doubt that it has been very much sung and it is not in the *New Oxford Book of Carols*. It is, nonetheless, worth preserving as a literary oddity. For all its slightly self-consciously archaic language and medieval romanticism, Morris' carol has a certain poetic quality and an appealing simplicity.

Outlanders, whence come ye last?
Through what green seas and great have ye passed?

2 From far away, O masters mine,
We come to bear you goodly wine.

3 From far away we come to you,
The snow in the street and the wind on the door,
To tell of great tidings strange and true.
Minstrels and maids stand forth on the floor:
From far away we come to you,
To tell of great tidings strange and true.

4 News, news of the Trinity,
And Mary and Joseph from over the sea!

5 For as we wandered far and wide,
What hap to you deem there should us betide?

6 Under a bent when the night was deep,
There lay three shepherds tending their sheep:

7 'O ye shepherds, what have ye seen,
To slay your sorrow and heal your teen?'

8 'In an ox-stall this night we saw
A babe and a maid without a flaw:

9 'There was an old man there beside;
His hair was white and his hood was wide:

10 'And as we gazed this thing upon,
Those twain knelt down to the little one.

11 'And a marvellous song we straight did hear,
That slew our sorrow and healed our care.'

12 News of a fair and a marvellous thing,
Nowell, nowell, nowell, we sing.

62

PAST THREE O'CLOCK

This is a marvellously atmospheric piece which makes one almost able to feel the cold night and hear the waits singing in the streets. I am sorry to say that it is in large part a twentieth-century concoction but at least the refrain is traditional.

'Past three o'clock' is largely the work of George Ratcliffe Woodward, whom we have already encountered as the author of 'Ding, dong merrily on high' (No. 18). He wrote the verses for *The Cambridge Carol Book* (1924) which he edited together with the musician, Charles Wood. The refrain is a traditional waits' cry, dating at least from the seventeenth century, and deriving from their function of calling out the hours through the night. It is found, attributed to the London waits, in a book of tunes for dancing published in 1665 and occurs at the end of a late seventeenth-century ballad, 'Song of the York Waits', quoted in William Chappell's *Popular Music of the Olden Time* (1853), and in the *New Oxford Book of Carols*, which is worth reproducing in full as it gives a good picture of the waits in their heyday:

In a winter's night,
By moon or lanthorn light,
Through hail, rain, frost or snow,
Their rounds the music go;
And each in frieze or blanket
(For either Heaven be thanked),
Lined with wine a quart,
Or ale a double tankard
... Candles, four in a pound,
Lead up the jolly Round,
Whilst cornet shrill i'th'middle
Marches, and merry fiddle,
Curtal with deep hum,hum,

Cries, 'We come, we come, come!'
And theorbo loudly answers,
'Thrum, thrum, thrum, thrum, thrum.'
But, their fingers frost-nipt,
So many notes are o'er-slipt
... Then, Sirs, to hear their music
Would make both me and you sick.
And much more to hear a roopy fiddler call
(With voice, as Moll would cry,
'Come, shrimps or cockles buy!'),
'Past three, fair frosty morn,
Good morrow, my masters all.'

Woodward was not the first to take the waits' traditional refrain and add verses to turn it into a song. A volume of *Old English Ditties* published by William Chappell in 1881 included a version of 'Past three o'clock' with non-Christmas verses by John Oxenford.

The tune of 'Past three o'clock' is at least traditional even if most of the words are not. It is found in the seventeenth-century sources.

Past three o'clock,
And a cold frosty morning:
Past three o'clock:
Good morrow, masters all!

Born is a Baby,
Gentle as maybe,
Son of th'eternal
Father supernal.

2 Seraph quire singeth,
Angel bell ringeth,
Hark how they rime it,
Time it and chime it!

3 Mid earth rejoices
Hearing such voices
Ne'ertofore so well
Carolling 'Nowell'.

4 Hinds o'er the pearly,
Dewy lawn early
Seek the high stranger
Laid in the manger.

5 Cheese from the dairy
Bring they for Mary,
And, not for money,
Butter and honey.

6 Light out of star-land
Leadeth from far land
Princes to meet him,
Worship and greet him.

7 Myrrh from full coffer,
Incense they offer;
Nor is the golden
Nugget withholden.

8 Thus they: I pray you,
Up, sirs, nor stay you
Till ye confess him
Likewise, and bless him.

63

PEOPLE, LOOK EAST

This Advent carol has an unusual feature seldom found in hymns. Its first line contains a complete sentence and the substantial part of another one. More seriously, it also contains some exciting theology. Its theme of commanding different parts of creation to herald and praise Jesus' birth is not unique (a similar approach underlies 'All Creatures of Our God and King') but there are several original touches about the way that it is done. Several hymns have birds, stars and angels praising their maker but I cannot think of any others that tell the furrows to be glad! Indeed, the image presented in verse two of the earth giving up its strength to nourish the seed provides an interesting and unusual expression of the sacrificial cycle of self-giving that underlies all creation and growth. Also striking and original are the portrayals of Christ at the end of each verse as 'love the guest', 'love the rose', 'love the bird', 'love the star' and 'love the Lord'.

'People look East' was one of several carols written for the 1928 *Oxford Book of Carols* by Eleanor Farjeon, who was a friend of the editor, Percy Dearmer, for whom she also wrote a number of hymns for *Songs of Praise*, notably 'Morning has broken' (*Daily Telegraph Book of Hymns*, No. 5–6).

Eleanor Farjeon was born in London in 1881. Her father was a novelist, playwright and journalist of Jewish descent and her mother came from an American theatrical family. After flirting with both spiritualism and theories of reincarnation, she was received into the Roman Catholic Church on her seventieth birthday.

The tune to which this carol is sung, and for which it was written, comes from France and goes back at least as far as the beginning of the seventeenth century. It first appears in a collection entitled *La Clef des Chansonniers* (1717) set to a song beginning 'L'Echelle du temple' and included among a group of tunes described as being more than a century old. It later became associated with a Besançon carol, possibly dating from the eighteenth century, which began '*Berger, secoue ton sommeil profond*!' and was translated into English, probably in the early nineteenth century, to form the carol 'Shepherds! Shake off your drowsy sleep'.

Carol of the Advent

People, look East. The time is near
Of the crowning of the year.
Make your house fair as you are able,
Trim the hearth and set the table.
People, look East, and sing today:
Love the Guest is on the way.

2 Furrows, be glad. Though earth is bare,
One more seed is planted there:
Give up your strength the seed to nourish,
That in course the flower may flourish.
People, look East, and sing today:
Love the Rose is on the way.

3 Birds, though ye long have ceased to build,
Guard the nest that must be filled.
Even the hour when wings are frozen
He for fledging-time has chosen.
People, look East, and sing today:
Love the Bird is on the way.

4 Stars, keep watch. When night is dim
One more light the bowl shall brim,
Shining beyond the frosty weather,
Bright as sun and moon together.
People, look East, and sing today:
Love the Star is on the way.

5 Angels, announce to man and beast
Him who cometh from the East.
Set every peak and valley humming
With the Word, the Lord is coming.
People, look East, and sing today:
Love the Lord is on the way.

64

PERSONENT HODIE

This jaunty Latin carol, which probably dates from the fifteenth or sixteenth century, is a parody of an earlier medieval song.

It is first found in *Piae Cantones*, the rare Finnish collection of 1582 whose rediscovery by J.M. Neale and others in the mid-nineteenth century did so much to fire the revival of traditional carols in Victorian times. It appears in only one other known source – a Swedish *psalmer* of 1619 where it is translated into the vernacular.

'*Personent hodie*' parodies an earlier medieval song in honour of St Nicholas which began '*Intonent hodie voces ecclesie*'. St Nicholas, who is said to have been bishop of Myra and to have been present at the first Council of Nicaea (325) is the patron saint of Russia, sailors and children, to whom he traditionally brings gifts on his feast day, 6 December.

The editors of the *New Oxford Book of Carols* point out that the striking repetition of syllables in the sixth line of each verse (which is not clear from the text as given below but will be well known to anyone who has sung this carol) may well be related to the fact that in the original song they referred to trios. For example in the third verse, which referred to three boys drowned in a barrel whom the saint restored to life, the words '*subersum puerum*' (the drowned boy) were sung as '*subersum, sum, sum puerum*' – a jokey representation of the drowned trio. The fourth verse of the original song, which told of three girls whom he saved from prostitution by giving each a bag of gold as a dowry, included the phrase '*Reddens vir, vir, virginibus*'.

In '*Personent hodie*' these repeated phrases ('*Et de vir,vir,vir*' in the first verse, '*Perdidit, dit, dit*' in the second, and so on,) seem slightly comical and are reminiscent of the repeated phrases in the fuguing anthems of the eighteenth century which so irritated John Wesley, like 'Stir up this stu, stu, stupid heart of mine' and

'O for a man, O for a man, O for a mansion in the sky' (which became known, for obvious reasons, as the spinster's prayer).

For those whose Latin may be a little rusty, let me offer a literal translation of this hymn:

1. May the voices of boys sound out today, joyfully praising him who is born to us, given by Almighty God and brought forth from a virgin's womb.
2. He is born in the world; he is wrapped round with bands; he is placed in a manger in an animals' stable, the ruler of the heavens; the Prince who destroyed the spoils of Hell.
3. Three wise men came, they offer gifts and seek the little one, following a star, adoring him and offering to him gold, frankincense and myrrh.
4. Let all the clerics, and likewise the boys, sing like the angels: 'You have come into the world. For that reason I pour out praise. Glory to God in the highest.'

The references to boys have led the editors of the *New Oxford Book of Carols* to speculate that '*Personent hodie*' may have been written to be sung on Holy Innocents Day (28 December) when choristers with their boy bishop traditionally took over the service.

There have been several English translations of this carol. The *Faber Book of Carols*, which calls it 'The Boys' Carol' has one by John Parkinson beginning 'Sing aloud on this day', the *New Oxford Book of Carols* uses Jane Joseph's 'On this day earth shall ring', *Carols for Today* features Michael Perry's 'Shout aloud, girls and boys' and the 1965 *Penguin Book of Christmas Carols* includes one which begins 'Let the boys' cheerful noise'.

The tune which always accompanies the carol, whether sung in Latin or in English, is that found in *Piae Cantiones*. It is presumably also the tune to which the earlier '*Intonent hodie*' was sung. A very similar melody is found in the Moosburg Gradual of 1360. In 1916 Gustav Holst provided a fine setting of the tune for his Whitsun music festival at Thaxted parish church in Essex. It has been taken up in several modern carol collections.

The Boys' Carol

Personent hodie
Voces puerulae
Laudenates iucunde
Qui nobis est natus,
Summo Deo datus,
Et de virgineo
Ventre procreatus.

2 In mundo nascitur;
Pannis involvitur;
Praesepi ponitur
Stabulo brutorum
Rector supernorum;
Perdidit spola
Princeps Infernorum.

3 Magi tres venerunt;
Munera offerunt;
Parvulum inquirunt,
Stellulam sequendo,
Ipsum adorando,
Aurum, thus et myrrham
Ei offerendo.

4 Omnes clericuli,
Pariter pueri,
Cantent ut angeli:
'Advenisti mundo:
Laudes tibi fundo
Ideo: Gloria
In excelsis Deo'.

65

QUELLE EST CETTE ODEUR AGRÉABLE

This is very much the foreign language section of my collection. After '*Personent hodie*', here is a carol in French and there is another Latin one to follow!

I have printed this one in its original language because the French is not difficult (I will not insult your intelligence by offering a translation) and has a vivid poetic quality which I do not find in any of the English verse translations.

'*Quelle est cette odeur*' almost certainly dates from the seventeenth century and is thought to come from Lorraine. It dramatizes the appearance of the angels to the shepherds as recorded in St Luke's Gospel. The editors of the *New Oxford Book of Carols* suggest that it was originally written to be sung by four solo voices and choir, with verse one being sung by the first shepherd, verse two by the second shepherd, verse three by the third shepherd, verse four by the choir of angels, verse five by Gabriel and verse six either by the angels' choir or by all.

Several English translations can be found in modern carol books. *Carols Old and New*, *Carols for Choirs* and the *University Carol Book* favour A.B. Ramsay's 'Whence is that goodly fragrance flowing, Stealing our senses all away?'. The latter book also includes K.W. Simpson's 'What is this fragrance softly stealing? Shepherds! It sets my heart astir', which is also found in the *Faber Book of Carols*. The editors of the *New Oxford Book of Carols* have provided their own translation, 'Shepherds, what fragrance all perfuming, Sweetly our senses now doth seize'.

The tune, usually now identified as QUELLE EST CETTE ODEUR, first appears in both English and French sources in the early eighteenth century. It is found in a printed work in the British Library dating from around 1710 and in a French collection, *La Clef des Chansonniers*, published in 1717. The tune was much used for secular songs in this period. Thomas d'Urfey, a dramatist and poet, incorporated it in 1719 in his *Wit and Mirth: Or Pills to Purge Melancholy* and John Gay famously used it for his drinking song 'Fill every glass' in the Beggar's Opera of 1728. In France, C.S. Favart incorporated it in his 1741 comic opera, *La Chercheuse d'esprit*.

Another French carol on the same subject is worthy of mention here. '*Quittez, pasteurs, Vos brebis, vos houlettes*' dates from the early eighteenth century and is set to a traditional Besançon melody. It has found its way into many modern English carol collections, variously translated as 'O Shepherds, leave your peaceful flock a-grazing', 'O leave your sheep, Your lambs that follow after', 'O leave your sheep, where ewes with lambs are feeding' and 'Ye shepherds, leave your flocks upon the mountains'.

Quelle est cette odeur agréable,
Bergers, qui ravit tous nos sens?
S'exhale t'il rien de semblable
Au milieu des fleurs du printemps?
Auelle est cette odeur agréable,
Bergers, qui ravit tous nos sens?

2 Mais quelle éclatante lumière
Dans la nuit vient frapper les yeux?
L'astre du jour, dans sa carrière,
Fût-il jamais si radieux?
mais quelle éclatante lumière
Dans la nuit vient frapper les yeux?

3 Voici beaucoup d'autres merveilles!
Grand Dieu! qu'entends-je dans les airs?
Quelles voix! Jamais nos oreilles
N'ont entendu pareil concerts.
Voici beaucoup d'autres merveilles!
Grand Dieu! qu'entends-je dans les airs?

4 Ne craignez rien, peuple fidèle,
Écoutez l'Ange du Seigneur;
Il vous annonce une merveille
Qui va vous combler de bonheur.
Ne craignez rien, peuple fidèle,
Écoutez l'Ange du Seigneur;

5 A Bethléem, dans une crêche,
Il vient de vous naître un Saveur;
Allons, que rien ne vous empêche
D'adorer votre Rédempteur!
A Bethléem, dans une crêche,
Il vient de vous naître un Saveur.

6 Dieu tout-puissant, gloire eterenelle
Vous soit rendue jusqu'aux cieux!
Que la paix soit universelle,
Que la grâce abonde en tous lieux!
Dieu tout-puissant, gloire éternelle
Vous soit rendue jusqu'aux cieux!

66

QUEM PASTORES LAUDAVERE

Like '*Quelle est cette odeur*', this carol is probably better known for its tune than for its words. QUEM PASTORES LAUDAVERE has achieved considerable popularity set to J.M. Neale's 'Jesus, kind above all other' (itself a translation of a Latin original, *Jesus noster, Jesus bonus*), Percy Dearmer's 'Jesus, good above all other' and, to a lesser extent, Fred Kaan's 'Father, who in Jesus found us', all of which were written with this tune in mind.

The original Latin carol which has been associated with the tune for nearly 600 years, is still sung, however, and certainly deserves a place in a book such as this.

Both words and tune of '*Quem pastores laudavere*' are first found in a manuscript dated 1410 in the possession of Hohenfurth Abbey in Germany. The carol was printed, in the form reproduced below, in Valentin Triller's *Ein schlesich Singbuchlein aus gottlicher Schrifft* (Breslau, 1555) and in other mid-sixteenth century German songbooks.

The grammatical construction is difficult because the whole carol is a single sentence with the main verb (*resonet*) not occurring until the third line of the last verse. Roughly translated, it reads:

1. To him whom the shepherds praised, being told by the angels: 'Now let fear be banished from you: the King of Glory is born'.
2. To him to whom the wise men journeyed, carrying gold, frankincense and myrrh and offered these things sincerely to the victorious Lion (of Judah).
3. To Christ the King, born of God, given to us through Mary, let resound right worthily 'Praise, honour and glory'.

Later versions of the carol add an extra stanza, interpolated between verses two and three, which adds a new sentence enjoining those singing it to rejoice with Mary and the heavenly hierarchy of angels as they praise the infant in reverent tones and with sweet melody:

Exsultemus cum Maria
In coelesti hierarchia:
Natum promant voce pia
Dulci cum melodia;

The editors of the *New Oxford Book of Carols* point out that in Catholic and Lutheran liturgies, *Quem pastores laudavere* was performed both as a conventional Christmas hymn and, until the eighteenth century, as one of the distinctive *Wechelgesänge* of Germanic Christmas hymnody. These songs were performed by four boys (or groups of boys in unison, or even small consorts or choirs) who stood holding candles, ideally in high galleries on four sides of the church. Each sang one line of each four-line stanza, so that the tune seemed to revolve in the air, as if sung by circling angels, and each 'angelic' voice evoked the 'pastoral' response of the equivalent verse of the hymn '*Nunc angelorum gloria*' from the main choir below. In Lutheran churches *Wechelgesänge* were a feature of Christmas Eve vespers and the torchlit *Christnacht* (Christmas Night) ante-communion service, when the annunciation to the shepherds was a central theme.

In a songbook produced by a Leipzig church cantor in the 1630s '*Quem pastores*' was divided among three choirs, presumably sited in high galleries, each of which sang one of the first three lines of each verse, with all three combining for the final line.

Numerous English translations have been made of '*Quem pastores laudavere*'. The most widely used is probably that by the Congregational minister and Biblical scholar, George Bradford Caird (1917-84), 'Shepherds came, their praises bringing' which is found, *inter alia*, in *Baptist Praise and Worship*, *Carols for Today*, *Hymns for Today's Church*, *Rejoice and Sing*, *Sunday School Praise* and *Church Family Worship*. *Hymns Ancient and Modern* favours C.S. Phillips' 'Thou whom shepherds worshipped, hearing/ Angels tell their tidings cheering', the *Church Hymnary* uses James Quinn's 'Angel voices, richly blending,/Shepherds to the manger sending' and the *University Carol Book* gives J. O'Connor's 'Shepherds tell your beauteous story/How the dazzling angel glory'. *Carols for Choirs 2* has an arrangement of the carol by John Rutter with English words by Imogen Holst beginning 'Shepherds left their flocks astraying'. Other translations to be found in current hymn and carol books include 'He whom shepherds apprehended' in the *Penguin Book of Christmas Carols*, 'Shepherds came to sing and praise him' in *Hymns and Congregational Songs* and 'Shepherds sang their praises o'er him' in the *New Oxford Book of Carols*. Perhaps with such a plethora of different English versions in use, there is something to be said for simply giving the Latin original here.

Quem pastores laudavere,
Quibus angeli dixere,
Absit vobis jam timere,
Natus est rex gloriae.

2 Ad quem magi ambulabant,
Aurum thus myrrham portabant,
Immolabant haec sincere
Nato regi gloriae.

3 Christo regi, Deo nato,
Per Mariam nobis dato,
Merito resonet vere
Laus, honor et gloria.

67

REJOICE AND BE MERRY

This carol, which is often known as 'the gallery carol', belongs to the great tradition of west-gallery music, so called because it was associated with the choirs and bands sited in the west galleries of churches before the advent of organs in the mid-nineteenth century. Further information on the gallery tradition, which flourished from the 1750s to 1850s, can be found in the notes to 'Arise and hail' (No.8).

'Rejoice and be merry' comes from Dorset and probably dates from the early or mid-eighteenth century. It is one of two carols – the other being the Yeoman's Carol, 'Let Christians all with joyful mirth' – discovered in an old west-gallery song book in the early years of the twentieth century by Rev. L.J.T. Darwall, a Dorset vicar. Both carols were taken up in the *English Carol Book* of 1919. The present whereabouts of the tune book that Darwall discovered are not known.

Dorset seems to have been a particularly rich source for west gallery carols. A recently published collection, *Carols of the West Country* (1996) contains several from the county, including two in similar spirit to this one, 'Rejoice! the promised Saviour's come!' and 'Rejoice with us, mankind, and sing'. It may simply be that the Dorset carols have been better preserved than those from other counties thanks to the efforts of Thomas Hardy and other members of his family who collected texts and tunes.

The tune of 'Rejoice and be merry', which comes from the same source as the words, has an identical first line to that of 'Tomorrow shall be my dancing day' (No. 90).

The Gallery Carol

Rejoice and be merry in song and in mirth;
O praise our Redeemer, all mortals on earth!
For this is the birthday of Jesus our King,
Who brought us salvation: his praises we'll sing.

2 A heavenly vision appeared in the sky;
Vast numbers of angels the shepherds did spy,
Proclaiming the birthday of Jesus our King,
Who brought us salvation: his praises we'll sing.

3 Likewise a bright star in the sky did appear,
Which led the wise men from the East to draw near;
They found the Messiah, sweet Jesus our King,
Who brought us salvation: his praises we'll sing.

4 And when they were come, they their treasures unfold,
And unto him offered myrrh, incense and gold.
So blessed for ever be Jesus our King,
Who brought us salvation: his praises we'll sing.

68

REMEMBER, O THOU MAN

This is another carol which was popular with west-gallery choirs in Dorset. Thomas Hardy, who learned it from his mother, quotes a four-verse version in his novel *Under the Greenwood Tree,* after first describing how the members of the Mellstock band rehearsed it in preparation for their annual Christmas Eve carol-singing round the village:

'Better try over number seventy-eight before we start, I suppose,' said William, pointing to a heap of old Christmas-carol books on a side table.

'Number seventy-eight was always a teaser – always. I can mind him since I was growing up a hard boy-chap'.

'But he's a good tune and worth a mint o' practice,' said Michael.

'He is; though I've been mad enough wi' that tune at times to seize him and tear an all to linnet. Ay, he's a splendid carrel – there's no denying that.'

'The first line is well enough,' said Mr.Spinks; 'but when you come to "O, thou man" you make a mess o't.'

'We'll have another go into en, and see what we can make of the martel. Half an hour's hammering at en will conquer the toughness of en, I'll warn it'.

Later in the novel, Hardy describes the carol being sung outside the village school.

'Number seventy-eight,' he softly gave out as they formed round in a semicircle, the boys opening the lanterns to get a clearer light, and directing their rays on the books.

Then passed forth into the quiet night an ancient and time-worn hymn, embodying a quaint Christianity in words orally transmitted from father to son through several generations down to the present characters, who sang them out right earnestly.

'Remember, O thou man' probably dates from the sixteenth century. It first appears in the 'Country Pastimes' section of Thomas Ravenscroft's *Melismata: musical phansies fitting to court, citie and countrey humours to 3,4 and 5 voyces* (1611) where it is entitled 'A Christmass Carroll'.

It is the version found in Ravenscroft's collection, which is as near as we have to an original text for this carol, that I have chosen to reproduce below. There are numerous other versions. One published in an appendix of 'Hymns for Divine Musick' in a sermon preached in 1733 by Arthur Bedford, a leading liturgical reformer and advocate of church music, omits Ravenscroft's first verse and begins 'O remember Adam's fall, O thou man, O thou man'. It follows Ravenscroft's verses three, four and five fairly closely but adds a new second verse:

O remember, O thou man,
O thou man, O thou man!
O remember O thou man,
Thy time misspent!
O remember O thou man,
How thou from thy God didst run,
And his presence thou didst shun
Therefore repent!

Sandys prints yet another version in his 1833 collection of Christmas carols. There, the sixth line of the first verse is changed from 'How thou art dead and gone' to 'How thou camest to me then' and there is an extra penultimate verse:

In a manger laid he was,
O thou man, O thou man!
In a manger laid he was,
At this time present.
In a manger laid he was,
Between an ox and an ass,
And for all our trespass,
Therefore repent.

The version quoted by Hardy in *Under the Greenwood Tree* broadly follows verses two, three, eight and nine of Ravenscroft's text. All the known versions of this carol share the same sombre admonitory theme. It stands in marked contrast to most carols in having relatively little sense of joy and concentrating heavily on the reality of sin and death. Despite its somewhat gloomy tone, it is not just a period piece and has found its way, in a version which begins: 'Remember, mortal man' into the *New Catholic Hymnal*.

The tune which Hardy's musicians found so difficult, FANCY DAY, was probably a derivative of one which accompanied the carol in Ravenscroft's *Melismata*. The tune found in the appendix to Bedford's sermon is different and the carol appears in early nineteenth-century Cornish manuscripts set to two melodies which are different again.

Remember, O thou man,
O thou man, O thou man!
Remember O thou man,
Thy time is spent!
Remember O thou man,
How thou art dead and gone,
And I did what I can:
Therefore repent!

2 Remember Adam's fall,
O thou man, O thou man!
Remember Adam's fall
From heaven to hell!
Remember Adam's fall,
How we were condemned all
To hell perpetual
There for to dwell.

3 Remember God's goodness,
O thou man, O thou man!
Remember God's goodness
And promise made!
Remember God's goodness,
How he sent his Son, doubtless,
Our sins for to redress:
Be not afraid!

4 The angels all did sing,
O thou man, O thou man!
The angels all did sing,
Upon the shepherds' hill!
The angels all did sing:
Praises to our heavenly King,
And peace to men living
With a good will!

5 The shepherds amazed were,
O thou man, O thou man!
The shepherds amazed were
To hear the angels sing!
The shepherds amazed were
How it should come to pass
That Christ Jesus our Messiah
Should be our king!

6 To Bethlehem did they go,
O thou man, O thou man!
To Bethlehem did they go,
The shepherds three;
To Bethlehem did they go,
To see whether it were so or no,
Whether Christ were born or no,
To set man free.

7 As the angels before did say,
O thou man, O thou man!
As the angels before did say,
So it came to pass;
As the angels before did say,
They found a babe, whereas it lay
In a manger, wrapt in hay,
So poor he was.

8 In Bethlem was he born,
O thou man, O thou man!
In Bethlem was he born,
For mankind's sake;
In Bethlem was he born:
For us that were forlorn,
And therefore took no scorn
Our flesh to take.

9 Give thanks to God alway,
O thou man, O thou man!
Give thanks to God alway,
With hearts most joyfully!
Give thanks to God alway
For this, our happy day;
Let all men sing and say:
'Holy, holy!'

69

SEE AMID THE WINTER'S SNOW

Here is a very Victorian hymn which firmly sets the Nativity story in wintertime and almost has the Lamb of God appearing through the snow. It displays other hallmarks of Victorian sentimentality and didacticism , idealizing childhood, presenting Jesus as 'meek and mild' and asking him to teach us to emulate his 'sweet humility'. It is not a carol for the politically correct (or the ultra-Protestant) and both verses six and seven have disappeared from most modern hymnals. So, more puzzlingly, have verses three and four. However, it remains a firm popular favourite, coming twelfth in the 2005 BBC *Songs of Praise* poll.

'See amid the winter's snow' was the work of Edward Caswall whose biographical details are covered in the notes to 'Bethlehem, of noblest cities' (No. 12). He wrote it shortly after his entry into the Birmingham Oratory and it first appeared in a book of *Easy Hymn Tunes* in 1851. It was re-printed in his *The Masque of Mary, and Other Poems* (1858) under the title 'Christmas' and in his collected *Hymns and Poems* in 1873.

The last verse with its strong Mariology has, not surprisingly, failed to make it into Protestant hymnbooks. Curiously, given its Catholic provenance, this hymn has proved much more appealing to Nonconformist than to Anglican hymnal editors. It has never appeared in *Hymns Ancient and Modern* nor the *English Hymnal* and failed to impress Percy Dearmer enough to warrant inclusion in *Songs of Praise.* Methodist, Baptist, Congregational, Presbyterian and United Reformed Church hymnals have all included it, however, although often in a truncated form, omitting verses three, four, six and seven.

Where these verses have been retained, they have often been toned down. *Baptist Hymns and Worship*, for example, renders verses five and six as follows:

Sacred infant, all divine,
Grace and tender love combine,
Bringing you from highest bliss
Down to such a world as this!

Holy child with gentle face,
Saviour of our fallen race,
Ever teach us so that we
Learn your deep humility.

The editors of *Hymns and Psalms*, who retain the first five verses of the original, wisely change the phrase 'tender lamb', with its suggestion of the Sunday roast, to 'Lamb of God' in the third line of verse one. For some strange reason, they also make the angels' message less definite by changing 'the Saviour's birth' to 'a Saviour's birth' in the fourth line of verse four.

In his study of *The English Hymn* Dick Watson points out how Caswall uses the same device in this hymn as he does in verse three of 'Bethlehem of noblest cities', namely the use of the word 'See' to take attention away from the beholder and on to the subject. He further observes:

His dislike of the evangelical attention to the soul and its salvation means that a hymn such as 'See, amid the winter's snow' is remarkably chaste in its presentation of the Christmas scene. Its plain character comes from its verse-form, with seven-syllable couplets neatly arranged to give precision and order. It develops into a dialogue between the singers and the shepherds ('Say, ye holy shepherds, say' . . . 'As we watched at dead of night'), and then into a reflection on the divine love. It eschews any reference to the individual: the singers are too busy taking part in the drama, asking the shepherds questions and exclaiming at the wonder of the Incarnation.

. . . .The skill of Caswall's hymn, its clever balancing of one mode against another, of one couplet against another, and of one name against another, allows both the portrayal of the Christmas story and the reflection upon it to be clearly articulated. The theology, as might be expected, deals with the coming of light out of darkness, with the sunrise and the happy dawn.

Some hymnals erroneously give the first line of this hymn as 'See amid the winter snow'. Presbyterians in particular seem to have something against the first verse – presumably it is either the snow or the tender lamb that they dislike Both the revised and third edition of the Church of Scotland's *Church Hymnary* and the United Reformed Church's *Rejoice and Sing* begin the hymn with the second verse. The fourth edition of the *Church Hymnary* (2005) begins with Caswall's first verse but changes the opening line to 'See! in yonder manger low'.

The tune HUMILITY which fits this hymn so well was written for it by John Goss and appeared in Bramley and Stainer's *Christmas Carols, New and Old* (1871). Goss was born in 1800 in Fareham, Hampshire where his father was organist. He was a chorister at the Chapel Royal and later became organist of St Luke's Church, Chelsea. From 1838 to 1872 he was organist of St Paul's Cathedral. He died in Brixton in 1880. His best-known hymn tune is almost certainly the affirmative PRAISE MY SOUL for Henry Lyte's 'Praise my soul, the king of heaven'. HUMILITY must rank close behind it. Percy Dearmer, who like many twentieth-century churchmen was very sniffy about Victorian tunes, singled it out as being unusually good for its period. Commenting on the 24 tunes composed by contemporary church musicians for Bramley and Stainer's *Christmas Carols, New and Old*, he observed that 'of these, little perhaps, except the tune by Sir John Goss, deserves to survive'. With my well-known affection for Victorian hymn tunes, I would put it rather differently but I certainly agree that HUMILITY provides an absolutely superb setting for Caswall's verses, greatly enhancing their spiritual power and effectiveness – just as so many Victorian tunes do!

See amid the winter's snow,
Born for us on earth below,
See, the tender lamb appears,
Promised from eternal years!
Hail, the ever-blessed morn!
Hail, redemption's happy dawn!
Sing through all Jerusalem,
Christ is born in Bethlehem!

2 Low within a manger lies
He who built the starry skies,
He who, throned in height sublime,
Sits amid the cherubim!

3 Say, ye holy shepherds, say:
What your joyful news today?
Wherefore have ye left your sheep
On the lonely mountain steep?

4 'As we watched at dead of night,
Lo! we saw a wondrous light;
Angels, singing "Peace on earth",
Told us of the Saviour's birth.'

5 Sacred infant, all divine,
What a tender love was thine
Thus to come from highest bliss
Down to such a world as this!

6 Teach, oh teach us, holy Child,
By thy face so meek and mild,
Teach us to resemble thee
In thy sweet humility!

7 Virgin Mother, Mary blest,
By the joys that fill thy breast,
Pray for us that we may prove
Worthy of the Saviour's love.

70

SEE HIM LYING ON A BED OF STRAW

According to its author, this infectiously jaunty carol in calypso rhythm became popular through a technical blunder. A BBC engineer managed to wipe the tape of the King's College Carol service in the days before it went out live. The BBC had hastily to organize an alternative programme and brought in the singer Cliff Richard. One of the items which he chose to sing was 'See him lying on a bed of straw'. It made an instant 'hit' and has since established itself as a firm favourite, coming tenth in the 2005 BBC *Songs of Praise* poll of Britain's most popular carols.

'See him lying on a bed of straw' was written by Michael Perry, an Anglican clergyman with a particular interest in hymnody. Born in 1942 in Beckenham, Kent, he was educated at Dulwich College, Southampton University and Ridley Hall, Cambridge. He was ordained into the Church of England ministry in 1965 and served curacies at St Helens in Lancashire and Bitterne, Southampton. He was vicar of Bitterne from 1972 to 1981, rector of Eversley, Hampshire from 1981 to 1989 and vicar of Tonbridge, Kent from 1989 until his untimely death from an inoperable brain tumour in December 1996.

Michael Perry was much involved with the Jubilate group, set up in the early 1960s to promote a more up-to-date style of Anglican church music. The group, which later became a non-profit making company called Jubilate Hymns, published two volumes of *Youth Praise* in the 1960s and a collection called *Psalm Praise* in 1973. In 1982 it produced a pioneering modern language hymnal, *Hymns for Today's Church*, in which several traditional hymns were shorn of their archaisms. This was followed in 1986 by *Carols for Today* which gave carols the same treatment as well as adding new ones to the repertoire.

Perry wrote his Calypso Carol in 1964 for an end-of-term

concert at Oak Hill College in London where he was a theological student. Among those who took part in its first performance was a future Archbishop of Canterbury, George Carey, who was then a tutor in doctrine at the college. The inspiration for the carol came from a question that Peter Hancock, then curate at Christ Church, Beckenham, had asked a group of young people at Christmas: 'How would you like to be born in a stable?' That gave Michael Perry the idea for the first line 'See him lying on a bed of straw'. He got the idea of setting the carol to a calypso rhythm from another member of the Jubilate Group, Richard Bewes, who wrote calypsos about cricket and for church social events.

The Calypso Carol, as it has become known, first appeared in print in the Jubilate Group's *Youth Praise 2* in 1969. In this early version it began 'See him a-lying on a bed of straw' and in verse four 'Thy' and 'Thine' were used instead of 'your'. The version which appears below is that found in *Hymns for Today's Church* and in most current hymnals. The editors of *Baptist Praise and Worship,* anxious to avoid exclusive language, have felt it necessary to alter the second line of the refrain to 'To see the Lord of love again' and to alter the third verse to:

Angels, sing again the song you sang,
Sing the glory of God's gracious plan;
Sing that Bethl'em's little baby can
Be the Saviour of us all.

This carol has been translated into Welsh, Swedish and German. It is particularly popular in the Caribbean and appeared on a set of four Christmas stamps produced by the English designer Jennifer Toombs for the Windward Islands. The five cent stamp was based on the line 'See him lying on a bed of straw', the thirty cent one on 'Star of silver, sweep across the skies', the 55 cent one on 'Angels, sing again the song you sang' and the $3 one on 'Mine are riches, from your poverty'. Michael Perry was amused to tune into the radio one day and hear a BBC announcer describe his work as 'that traditional folk carol from the West Indies'.

Although Perry later described this carol as 'fairly artless', it manages to pack some serious theology into its catchy rhythms and contains several Biblical references. The line 'mine are riches from your poverty' is a nice encapsulation of the message in 2 Corinthians 8.9: 'For ye know the grace of our Lord Jesus Christ, that, though he was rich, yet for your sakes he became poor, that ye through his poverty might be rich.' Perry dates the beginning of his serious hymn-writing career from this carol. He went on to write several more popular Christmas hymns, including 'Come and sing the Christmas story this holy night!' but none has achieved quite the popularity of this one.

The tune CALYPSO CAROL was written by Michael Perry at the same time as the words. It has been given various harmonizations and arrangements, including some specifically for children and a cathedral anthem setting by John Bertalot.

Calypso Carol

See him lying on a bed of straw:
A draughty stable with an open door;
Mary cradling the babe she bore –
The Prince of glory is his name.
O now carry me to Bethlehem
To see the Lord of love again:
Just as poor as was the stable then,
The Prince of glory when he came.

2 Star of silver, sweep across the skies,
Show where Jesus in the manger lies;
Shepherds swiftly from your stupor rise
To see the Saviour of the world!

3 Angels, sing again the song you sang,
Bring God's glory to the heart of man:
Sing that Bethlehem's little baby can
Be salvation to the soul.

4 Mine are riches, from your poverty;
From your innocence, eternity;
Mine, forgiveness by your death for me,
Child of sorrow for my joy.

71

SING LULLABY!

This is one of the very few carols in this collection which I did not know before researching and making my selection. In fact, it appears in a large number of modern carol and hymnbooks and, having discovered its gentle beauty and subtle linking of Jesus' Nativity and Passion, I am delighted to include it.

'Sing lullaby!' was written by Sabine Baring-Gould to fit the melody of a Basque carol, '*Oi Betleem*'. As a boy of fifteen, he had spent the winter of 1850–1 in Bayonne with his family. His father hired a local schoolmaster to make a collection of Basque dance tunes. The tunes came back to Baring-Gould 45 years later when he heard Bizet's opera *Carmen* for the first time and it may have been this that inspired him to translate a number of Basque carols. Some, like 'The angel Gabriel from heaven came'(No. 74) kept fairly close to the original. In this case, however, his words represent a complete departure from the original which is a hymn in praise of the town of Jesus' birth, slightly in the style of 'O little town of Bethlehem'. Baring-Gould chose instead to write a lullaby, which fits the tune well. What distinguishes it from other lullaby carols is the way he foreshadows the passion, crucifixion and resurrection of Jesus. The way that he suggests the infant should be allowed to sleep in peace, dreaming of Easter, is particularly effective in illustrating the continuum of incarnation and atonement, crucifixion and resurrection.

Sabine Baring-Gould was born in Exeter in 1834, educated at Clare College, Cambridge, and ordained into the Church of England in 1861. After serving two curacies in Yorkshire, he became rector of East Mersea in Essex in 1871. He succeeded his father as squire of Lew Trenchard in Devon and in 1881 presented himself to the living there as rector. He remained there until his death at the age of 90. An enthusiastic collector of folk songs, Baring-Gould wrote several novels and a number of hymns, including 'Onward, Christian soldiers'.

This carol has been regularly used in the Festival of Nine Lessons and Carols at King's College, Cambridge, although it did not appear in a hymnbook until *Christian Praise* in 1957. It is to be found in the *New Oxford Book of Carols*, the *University Carol Book*, the *Galliard Book of Carols and in Carols for Today* and *Hymns for Today's Church*. The only change that the editors of the last two books have made is to alter 'gladsome' to 'joyful' in the fifth line of the last verse.

The tune, often known as THE INFANT KING, is the traditional Basque melody which accompanied '*Oi Betleem*!'. It was collected by Charles Bordes, a leading figure in the French folk-song revival, and appeared in his volume *Douze Noels populaires* in the series *Archives de la tradition basque* (1895). The tune is usually sung to Baring-Gould's words in an arrangement made by Edgar Pettman (1865–1943), organist of St James', Piccadilly, and a prolific composer of Christmas carols.

Sing lullaby!
Lullaby baby, now reclining:
Sing lullaby!
Hush, do not wake the infant king;
Angels are watching, stars are shining
Over the place where he is lying:
Sing lullaby!

2 Sing lullaby!
Lullaby baby, sweetly sleeping:
Sing lullaby!
Hush, do not wake the infant king;
Soon will come sorrow with the morning,
Soon will come bitter grief and weeping:
Sing lullaby!

3 Sing lullaby!
Lullaby, baby, gently dozing:
Sing lullaby!
Hush, do not wake the infant king;
Soon comes the cross, the nails, the piercing,
Then in the grave at last reposing:
Sing lullaby!

4 Sing lullaby!
Lullaby! Is the baby waking?
Sing lullaby!
Hush, do not stir the infant king,
Dreaming of Easter, gladsome morning,
Conquering death, its bondage breaking:
Sing lullaby!

72

SING THIS NIGHT

This is the second carol by John Rutter to feature in this collection. I first came across it when singing in the choir of my local church in the early 1990s and immediately fell in love with its sense of immediacy and that great line 'Hurry to Bethlehem and see the son of Mary!'.

Rutter wrote what he called the 'Star Carol' in 1972 in circumstances that he has described in a letter to me:

> The Star carol was written with the Bach Choir's famous Christmas Family Carol concerts in mind; these have been a very popular event in London's Royal Albert Hall for many years now. Sir David Willcocks made it his custom to invite the young children in the audience up on the stage for part of the concert to join with the choir in singing some familiar carols, but one year he asked me whether I could write a new carol for them to learn on the spot and sing, with the help of the adult choir. Hence, the verses of the Star carol are for adult mixed choir and the refrain is simple and suitable for young children to pick up after one or two hearings.

Both the words and music of this carol are by John Rutter.

The Star Carol

Sing this night, for a boy is born in Bethlehem,
Christ our Lord in a lowly manger lies;
Bring your gifts, come and worship at his cradle,
Hurry to Bethlehem and see the son of Mary!
See his star shining bright
In the sky this Christmas Night!
Follow me joyfully;
Hurry to Bethlehem and see the son of Mary!

2 Angels bright, come from heaven's highest glory,
Bear the news with its message of good cheer:
'Sing, rejoice, for a King is come to save us,
Hurry to Bethlehem and see the son of Mary!'

3 See, he lies in his mother's tender keeping;
Jesus Christ in her loving arms asleep.
Shepherds poor, came to worship and adore him,
Offer their humble gifts before the son of Mary.

4 Let us all pay our homage at the manger,
Sing his praise on this joyful Christmas Night;
Christ is come, bringing promise of salvation;
Hurry to Bethlehem and see the son of Mary!

73

STILLE NACHT!

This almost certainly deserves the accolade of the world's favourite carol. It has been translated into 230 languages. It is often voted No.1 in surveys of the most popular carols in Britain although it was pipped into second place by 'In the bleak mid-winter' in the 2005 BBC *Songs of Praise* poll. A Gallup poll in December 1996 found that 21 per cent of respondents named 'Silent Night' as their favourite carol – more than twice as many as voted for the joint runners-up, 'Away in a manger' and 'O come, all ye faithful', which each received nine per cent.

The hymn is shrouded in romance and legend. The story often goes that it was written in some haste on Christmas Eve 1818 by the parish priest and organist of the tiny Austrian village of Oberndorf after a mouse had eaten through the organ wires. 'Stille nacht' was rustled up for the two men to sing to a guitar accompaniment at Midnight Mass.

It is certainly true that the carol was the work of the priest and organist at Oberndorf, that it was originally written for two male voices and guitar and that it was first sung at the Midnight Mass in St Nicholas' Church on 31 December 1818. However, thanks to the recent discovery of a manuscript by the author, we now know that its genesis was rather less rushed and romantic than tradition would have us believe.

The words are the work of Joseph Mohr. Born in 1792 in a poor quarter of Salzburg to a young girl whose soldier lover had deserted her before his birth, Mohr was taken in by local clergy and sang as a boy in St Peter's Church where Michael Haydn directed the music. After reading theology at Salzburg, he was ordained into the Roman Catholic Church and in 1815 became curate in the Alpine village of Mariapfarr, 100 kilometres south of Salzburg. It was there that he wrote his six-verse carol which is striking in its frequent references to fatherhood and complete absence of references to Mary or motherhood. It has been suggested that the reference in the first verse to Jesus as '*Holder Knab im lockigten Haar*' ('the sweet boy with curly hair') was probably inspired by a seventeenth-century fresco in the church at Mariapfarr.

Mohr's studies at Salzburg had been disrupted by the Franco-Bavarian invasion of Austria under Napoleon. In 1816 the Bavarian forces who had been occupying Mariapfarr retreated, signalling the end of the Napoleonic occupation. This may explain the optimistic tone of Mohr's verses with their message that God keeps his promise to protect man from harm and their unusual and striking description of Jesus as '*die Völker der Welt*' (the peoples of the world).

Mohr's upbringing had left him with bad lungs and in 1817 he was forced to quit Mariapfarr with its severe mountain climate for the milder air of the riverside village of Oberndorf, 25 kilometres north of Salzburg. Here he seems to have developed a great affinity with the boatmen who made up a high proportion of his parishioners. A letter from a superior in the church complained that 'he gambles and drinks at night and sings amongst other things unwholesome songs. He jokes with members of the opposite sex, doesn't behave in a spiritual manner and goes out with women'. From Oberndorf he went on to serve as priest in several other parishes in the Salzburg diocese, ending at Wagrein, near St Johann, where he died in 1848.

The tune for Mohr's carol, which he apparently brought with him unperformed from Mariapfarr, was supplied by his organist at Oberndorf, Franz Gruber (1787–1863), who was schoolmaster at the neighbouring village of Arnsdorf. Musicologists suggest that it was based on the Siciliano form, a 6/8 beat with much use of parallel thirds and sixths used for carols in Sicily and South Italy and popularized by Corelli in his Christmas *concerto grosso*.

Priest and organist gave the first performance of their carol after midnight mass on Christmas Eve 1818 beside the crib in a side chapel of the church of St Nicholas, Oberndorf. The church was demolished in 1905 when the whole village was moved to higher ground after two disastrous floods but the 'Silent Night Chapel' now stands on its site. Every year thousands flock there to hear the hymn being sung.

'*Stille nacht*' might well have sunk without trace, alongside hundreds of other Austrian folk carols, had a manuscript copy of it not come into the hands of Josef Strasser, a glove-maker and folk-music enthusiast who had a family singing group in the best 'Sound of Music' tradition. The Strasser family performed the piece as a newly discovered Tyrolean folk carol. As a result of a concert they gave in Leipzig in 1832 the carol was published as one of a set of four Tyrolean songs. There was no mention of either author or composer in this first printed copy and it was only after recourse to the law that Mohr and Gruber were able to prove their authorship. Gruber went on to arrange the music for organ, orchestra and choir. Relatively early on, verses three, four and five were dropped in Austria and they have not generally been translated.

The first English translation, 'Stilly night, holy night' was made in 1858 for the choir of St Mark's Church, Brighton by Emily Elliott, author of 'Thou didst leave thy throne and thy kingly crown' (No.87). Of the numerous later English translations, the most widely sung is probably that by John Freeman Young (1820–85), bishop in the Episcopal Church of the USA. Like most others, it provides only three verses. It is a very free translation, introducing the virgin, for example, but captures much of the spirit of the original:

Silent night! Holy night!
All is calm, all is bright.
Round yon virgin, mother and child,
Holy infant so tender and mild,
Sleep in heavenly peace.

Silent night! Holy night!
Shepherds quake at the sight.
Glories stream from heaven afar,
Heavenly hosts sing Hallelujah,
Christ the Saviour is born.

Silent night! Holy night!
Son of God, love's pure light.
Radiant beams from thy holy face,
With the dawn of redeeming grace,
Jesus, Lord, at thy birth.

Another translation found in several hymnbooks is 'Still the night, holy the night' by Stopford A. Brooks, an Anglican priest who later became a Unitarian, which first appeared in 1881. Other translations begin 'Holy night! Peaceful night!' (Miss J.M. Campbell, 1863), 'Silent night! Hallowed night!' (*Christian Hymn Book*, 1865), 'Peaceful night, all things sleep' (Leeds carol book, 1872).

'*Stille nacht*' played a celebrated role in briefly easing the tense atmosphere in the trenches of Flanders during the First World War. The film *O What a Lovely War* movingly depicts an episode in the first Christmas of the war when its singing by German troops was taken up by the Tommies and led to a brief Christmas truce. Its later popularity in English owed much to Bing Crosby's rendition of it in the 1945 film, *The Bells of St Mary's*. It has since become an international favourite. The Silent Night Homepage on the world-wide web (http://members.tripod.com/-iago/index.html) gives the hymn in 59 different languages (a fraction of those into which it has been translated), from Afrikaans to Zulu via Bataknese, Greenlandic, Latvian, Taiwanese Ho-lo-oe and Tahitian.

More, perhaps, than any other item in this book, 'Silent night' comes close to crossing the boundary line between carol and secular Christmas song. It almost falls into the 'I'm dreaming of a white Christmas' category. This is largely because of the artistes who have recorded it and the schmaltzy treatments which it has been given. For a long time it was not regarded as a suitable carol for inclusion in hymnbooks. It was not in Bramley and Stainer's collection, the *Oxford Book of Carols* excluded it and it has never been allowed to sully the pages of *Hymns Ancient and Modern*. It is undeniably sentimental, especially when the music is added to the words but its text is wholly Christ-centred and spiritual. Erik

Routley notes that 'the real force in "*Stille nacht*" is, without doubt, the manner in which historically and stylistically it epitomizes the German Christmas, cosy and child-centred, which was first becoming part of the English scene just when it was being composed.'

'Silent night' has inevitably been parodied. Chris Fabry in his *Away with the Manger* offers the following:

Silent night, Solstice night,
All is calm, all half price.
Round yon department store,
All of us strangers,
Wondering who will get
The last Power Rangers,
Shop in heavenly peace.

Stille Nacht!

Stille Nacht! heilige Nacht!
Alles schläft; einsam wacht
Nur das traute heilige Paar.
Holder Knab im lockigten Haar,
Schlafe in himmlischer Ruh!
Schlafe in himmlischer Ruh!

2 Stille Nacht! heilige Nacht!
Gottes Sohn, o wie lacht
Lieb' aus deinem göttlichen Mund
Da uns schlägt die rettende Stund,
Jesus, in deiner Geburt!
Jesus, in deiner Geburt!

3 Stille Nacht! heilige Nacht!
Die der Welt Heil gebracht
Aus des Himmels goldenen Höhn.
Uns der Gnaden Fülle lässt sehn
Jesum in Menschengestalt,
Jesum in Menschengestalt.

4 Stille Nacht! heilige Nacht!
Wo sich heut alle Macht
Väterlicher Liebe ergoss,
Und als Bruder huldvoll unschloss
Jesus die Völker der Welt,
Jesus die Völker der Welt.

5 Stille Nacht! heilige Nacht!
Lange schon uns bedacht,
Als der Herr vom Grimme befreit
In der Vater urgrauer Zeit
Aller Welt Schonung verheiss!
Aller Welt Schonung verheiss!

6 Stille Nacht! heilige Nacht!
Hirten erst kundgemacht
Durch der Engel Alleluja,
Tont es laut bei Ferne und Nah:
Jesus der Retter is da!
Jesus der Retter is da!

74

THE ANGEL GABRIEL FROM HEAVEN CAME

Of the many carols written about the Annunciation as recorded in Luke's Gospel, this is surely one of the most beautiful. Like 'Sing lullaby!' it is based on a Basque carol and is the work of Sabine Baring-Gould (on whom see notes to No. 71). Generations of choirboys have known and loved the concluding line of the last verse as 'Most highly flavoured lady'.

'*Birjina gaztettobat zegoen*' was, like '*Oi Betleem!*', collected from the Basque region by Charles Bordes and appeared at the beginning of his volume *Douze Noels populaires* in the series *Archives de la tradition basque* (1895). It ran to six stanzas and told the story of the Angel's appearance to Mary very much as it is related in Luke 1.26–38.

Baring-Gould was clearly taken with this carol, which probably like '*Oi Betleem*' brought back memories of his holiday 45 years earlier in Bayonne. He gave it a fairly straight translation, reducing the six original stanzas to four, and adding a very Victorian and unbiblical touch by giving Gabriel 'wings as drifted snow'.

'The angel Gabriel from heaven came' was first published in 1922 in one of a series of pamphlets, each containing six carols, entitled *The University Carol Book*. It was republished in a book with the same title published in 1961. The first English hymn-book to include it seems to have been the *New Catholic Hymnal* of 1971. It has since made its way into many hymnbooks and carol collections.

The tune, which is sometimes known as GABRIEL'S MESSAGE, is the one which accompanied '*Birjina gaztettobat zegoen*' in Bordes' collection. Like the tune for 'Sing lullaby!', it is often sung in an arrangement made by Edgar Pettman (1865–1943), organist of St James', Piccadilly, and a prolific composer of Christmas carols.

The Annunciation inspired several earlier carols which have now fallen out of use. A manuscript in Balliol College, Oxford, dating from the sixteenth century, contains one which begins 'A virgyn pure, This is full sure, Gabriell did her grete'. A medieval Irish carol, beginning '*Angelus ad Virginem*' has been translated by W.A.C. Pickard as 'Gabriel to the Virgin came,/ And entered at her dwelling'. Another Latin carol, found in *Piae Cantiones*, was translated by J.M. Neale as 'Gabriel's message does away/Satan's curse and Satan's sway'.

One of the best of the early carols on this theme appears in Husk's *Songs of the Nativity* where it is described as being 'much used in the Western countries'. Although Husk notes that it is included in his collection for its popularity, rather than its literary merit, the first two of its five stanzas are worth quoting, not least because of the suggestion in the second that Joseph was an old man (on this see notes to the Cherry Tree Carol, No. 42):

The Angel Gabriel from God
Was sent from Galilee,
Unto a Virgin fair and free,
Whose name was called Mary.
And when the Angel thither came,
He fell down on his knee,
And looking up in the Virgin's face,
He said, 'All hail, Mary!'

Then sing we all, both great and small,
Noel, Noel, Noel;
We may rejoice to hear the voice
Of the Angel Gabriel.

Mary anon looked him upon,
And said, 'Sir, what are ye?'
I marvel much at these tidings
Which thou hast brought to me.
Married I am unto an old man,
As the lot fell unto me;
Therefore, I pray, depart away,
For I stand in doubt of thee.

Birjina gaztettobat zegoen

The angel Gabriel from heaven came,
His wings as drifted snow, his eyes as flame:
'All hail' said he, thou lowly maiden Mary
Most highly favoured lady! Gloria!

2 For known a blessed Mother thou shalt be;
All generations laud and honour thee:
Thy son shall be Emmanuel, by seers foretold
Most highly favoured lady! Gloria!

3 Then gentle Mary meekly bowed her head;
'To me be as it pleaseth God!' she said.
'My soul shall laud and magnify his holy Name.'
Most highly favoured lady! Gloria!

4 Of her Emmanuel, the Christ, was born,
In Bethlehem, all on a Christmas morn;
And Christian folk throughout the world will ever say:
Most highly favoured lady! Gloria!

75

THE BOAR'S HEAD IN HAND BEAR I

This has the distinction of being the earliest English carol to appear in print. There is nothing to link it with Christmas in the words but it has come to be associated with the festive season, largely, as Ko-Ko in the *Mikado* might say, because of the following remarkable set of circumstances.

The story goes that one Christmas morning in the fifteenth century a scholar from Queen's College, Oxford, named Copcot was walking out to the village of Horspath where he intended to attend Mass. As he was striding over Shotover Common a wild boar made for him. He overcame the beast by taking it by the scruff of the neck and stuffing down its throat the volume of Aristotle which he had been reading. He then calmly cut off the boar's head and carried it on his staff to the church where he left it in the porch. After Mass he took it back to his college for dinner.

This episode is commemorated in a window at Horspath Parish Church and by an annual Christmas dinner at Queen's College at which the choir sings this carol as a boar's head decorated with a garland of bay leaves and rosemary and lying on a silver platter is ceremoniously carried in to the hall by three chefs. The procession is led by a solo singer, who sings the first verse, and accompanied by torch bearers. It halts for each verse and moves forward during the refrains. After the platter has been set down on the high table, the Provost distributes the herbs among the choir and presents the solo singer with the orange that has been stuck in the boar's mouth.

The version of the carol which appears overleaf is that now sung at Queen's College. It has evolved from a text first published in 1521 as 'A caroll bringyng in the bores heed' in *Christmase Carolles Newly Emprynted at London in the flete strete* by

Jan van Wynken of Worth, an apprentice of William Caxton who had introduced printing into England just 47 years earlier. Its original third verse gave a more direct link with Christmas:

Be gladde, Lordes, bothe more and lasse,
For this hath ordeyned our stewarde
To cheer you all this Christmasse,
The Bores heed with mustarde.

Christmas feasts involving boars' heads seems to have been popular throughout Britain in the Middle Ages and Queen's College almost certainly adopted rather than invented both the feast and the carol. The open season for hunting boars ran from Christmas to Candlemas (2 February) and their use in mid-winter feasts may well have derived from the Norse custom of sacrificing a boar to Freyja, the goddess of fertility. Holinshed's Chronicle describes King Henry II himself bringing in a boar's head for the feast after his son's coronation in 1170 as heir apparent to the throne. During the reign of Elizabeth I on Christmas Day in the Inner Temple 'a fair and large boar's head' was served 'upon a silver platter with minstrelsy'.

Several other boar's head carols, possibly pre-dating the Queen's College one, survive from fifteenth-century manuscripts. Husk cites the oldest as being one that begins 'Hey! Hey! Hey! Hey! The Boar his head is armèd gay' and contains the splendid verse:

Lords, knights, and squires,
Parsons, priests, and vicars,
The boar his head is the first mess.

Another fifteenth-century manuscript contains one beginning:

At the beginning of the meat
Of a boar's head ye shall eat,
And in the mustard ye shall wet

And ye shall singen ere ye go.

An interesting version which links the boar's head much more directly with Christmas and even attempts to take it as a symbol of Christ is found in a manuscript preserved by Ritson, the antiquarian, in the sixteenth century and now in the British Library. It is headed '*In die nativitatis*' and may conceivably have been written to be sung by the singing-men of Exeter Cathedral during feasting in their common hall:

The boar's head, that we bring here,
Betokeneth a prince without peer
Is born this day to buy us dear,
Noel.
A boar is a sovereign beast,
And acceptable in every feast;
So might this Lord to be most and least,
Noel.
The boar's head we bring with song,
In worship of Him that thus sprung
Of a Virgin to redress all wrong;
Noel.

There are other boar's head carols associated with Twelfth Night revels in Oxford colleges and in the Inns of Court.

The tune of the Queen's College Boar's Head carol, which has been recorded by Maddy Prior on a disc of traditional carols, is unlikely to go back beyond the later seventeenth or early eighteenth century. It is printed in William Wallace Fyfe's *Christmas, its Customs and Carols* (1863).

The boar's head in hand bear I,
Bedecked with bays and rosemary;
And I pray you my masters be merry,
Quot estis inconvivio.
  Caput apri defero
  Reddens laudes Domino,
  Laudes Domino, Laudes Domino, Laudes Domino.

2 The boar's head, as I understand,
Is the bravest dish in all the land
When thus bedecked with a gay garland
Let us *servire cantico.*

3 Our steward hath provided this
In honour of the King of Bliss,
Which on this day to be served is
In Reginensi atrio.

76

THE FIRST GOOD JOY THAT MARY HAD

This carol was probably developed as a kind of nursery rhyme to teach children the key episodes in Jesus' life. Like the more general practice of carol-singing, its origins may well lie in the efforts of Franciscan missionaries in the fourteenth century to instruct country folk in the most basic tenets of the Christian religion using simple language. The earliest-known version is in a fourteenth-century manuscript entitled 'Joyes Fyve' where the events recounted were the Annunciation, Nativity, Resurrection, Ascension and Assumption. It began:

The first joy, as I you tell,
With Mary met Saint Gabriel,
'Hail Mary, I greet you well',
With Father and Son and Holy Ghost.

Later medieval versions extended the joys to include the Annunciation, the Visitation, the visit of the Magi, the Presentation, the coming of the Holy Spirit, the Assumption of the Blessed Virgin and the coronation of Mary in heaven. These events tied in with the principal commemorations in the liturgy of the Roman Catholic Church and may also have been added to assist people to say the Rosary and offer petitionary prayer to the Virgin.

By the late Middle Ages most versions of this song seem to have given Mary seven joys, most of which involved key events in her son's life rather than her own. This emphasis, and the popularity of the song, remained after the Reformation when the seven joys were often enumerated as the Nativity, Resurrection and Ascension, the miracles of making the lame walk, making the blind see and bringing the dead to life and the good Protestant virtue of reading the Bible.

The version given below appeared with numerous variations on carol sheets and broadsides all over Britain from the seventeenth to the nineteenth century. In the one collected by Sandys, Mary's first good joy is recorded as being 'to see her own Son Jesus to suck at her breast bone'. Sandys also gives different concluding lines for the last three verses, 'To raise the dead alive', 'To wear the Crucifix' and 'To wear the crown of Heaven'.

While the seven joys version was by far the most popular, there were also longer ones. Cecil Sharp noted down a ten-stanza version in Somerset which named the eighth joy as being 'to bring the crooked straight', the ninth as to 'turn water into wine' and the tenth, rather mystifyingly, as being 'to bring up ten gentlemen'. The longest versions run to twelve verses. In one of these, noted down by Alice Gillingham from the singing of a gypsy woman as she nursed her sleeping baby, the first joy is the Nativity, the second is seeing Jesus going to school, the third when he begins to read, the fourth seeing him reading the Bible, the fifth seeing him turn water into wine, the sixth seeing him cure lepers, the seventh when he makes the blind to see, the eighth when he carries the Crucifix, the ninth when he rises from the dead, the tenth when he opens the gates of hell, the eleventh when he ascends into heaven and the twelfth when the Holy Ghost is sent. In his *Songs of the Nativity*, William Husk notes that 'the extension of the seven joys to twelve is confined to the northern parts of the country' and quotes a ten-stanza version from Newcastle where the joys include wearing the Crown of heaven, turning darkness into light and writing without a pen. Another twelve-verse version, collected in Gloucestershire, makes the tenth joy 'to write with a golden pen', the eleventh 'to have the keys of heaven' and the twelfth 'to have the keys of hell'.

In Ireland, where the carol remained linked to Marian devotion, it was often entitled 'The Seven Rejoices of Mary' and Mary was referred to throughout as 'Our Lady'. A ten-verse American version, collected from North Carolina, is printed in the *New Oxford Book of Carols*.

Several different tunes were used to accompany this carol on broadside sheets. Bramley and Stainer printed the one which they regarded as most common. Other tunes were collected by folk-song enthusiasts in the early years of the twentieth century. Anne Gilchrist noted one down in Blackham, Sussex, which had been learned from tinker children in Ashdown Forest and came across another adapted from the nursery rhyme 'Three little kittens'. Cecil Sharp noted down different ones in Gloucestershire and Cornwall. Lucy Broadwood collected two Berkshire versions of 'The Nine Joys of Mary', one sung to the tune of 'The Banks of Sweet Dundee' and the other to a version of 'God rest ye merry, Gentlemen'.

The Seven Joys of Mary has lent itself to numerous parodies and secular imitations. Anne Gilchrist came across a scurrilous ballad about John Wesley which began 'The first good joy of Mary Anne'. W.J. Philips remembered from his youth in London in the 1880s hearing a version sung by unemployed men 'We've got no work to do-o-o, we've got no work to do'.

Joys Seven

The first good joy that Mary had,
It was the joy of one;
To see the blessed Jesus Christ
When He was first her Son.
When He was first her Son, good Man:
And blessed may He be,
Both Father, Son, and Holy Ghost,
To all eternity.

2 The next good joy that Mary had,
It was the joy of two;
To see her own son, Jesus Christ
To make the lame to go.

3 The next good joy that Mary had,
It was the joy of three;
To see her own son, Jesus Christ
To make the blind to see.

4 The next good joy that Mary had,
It was the joy of four;
To see her own son, Jesus Christ
To read the Bible o'er.

5 The next good joy that Mary had,
It was the joy of five;
To see her own son, Jesus Christ
To bring the dead to life.

6 The next good joy that Mary had,
It was the joy of six;
To see her own son, Jesus Christ
Rise from the crucifix.

7 The next good joy that Mary had,
It was the joy of seven;
To see her own son, Jesus Christ
Ascending into heaven.

77

THE FIRST NOWELL

This much-loved carol probably has its origins in late medieval times. It is said to have appeared on broadsides printed at Helston, Cornwall, in the eighteenth century, but the earliest surviving texts date only from the early nineteenth century

'The first Nowell' was first published in the 1823 revised edition of Davies Gilbert's *Some Ancient Christmas Carols*. Gilbert, who came from Helston, took it from a manuscript collection of Cornish carols made around 1817 and now in the County Record Office at Truro. William Sandys included the carol in his *Christmas Carols, Ancient and Modern* in 1833 where it is described as a West country carol 'for Christmas Day in the morning'. It is Sandys' version, which follows Gilbert's almost verbatim, which I give below. The only substantial alteration is in the opening line of verse 3 where Gilbert had 'And by the lightning of that star'.

All subsequent versions of the carol have been based on that found in Sandys' collection. It is generally shortened, with verses five, seven and nine hardly ever being sung. One small but significant change has been made to Sandys' text. The number of shepherds has been made less definite by 'certain' being substituted for 'three' in the second line of the first verse. There is, of course, no indication in the Gospel accounts as to how many shepherds there were. The figure of three seems to have derived from medieval mystery plays. Sandys noted that in the Chester Mysteries the shepherds were named as Harvey, Trowle and Tudd – clearly they were good Anglo-Saxons rather than Palestinians.

When the service of Nine Lessons and Carols was started at King's College, Cambridge, in 1918, 'The first Nowell' was chosen as the final hymn, being sung alone by the congregation as the choir moved to the altar to sing the concluding metrical Magnificat. It is a sign of its subsequent hold on the collective

British psyche that it has been frequently been parodied. Desmond Morris, the anthropologist, recalls Oxford United fans singing the praises of a player:

Graydon, Graydon, Graydon, Graydon,
Born is the king of Oxford Town.

The familiar tune of 'The first Nowell' first appeared in Sandys' book and was given its modern form by John Stainer for his *Christmas Carols, Old and New* in 1871. It has generated considerably more interest and discussion among hymnologists than the words. Erik Routley describes it as 'rather terrible' and points out that when it is sung in full, one two-line phrase is repeated 27 times. 'It is repetitive to the point of hideous boredom'.

The three virtually identical statements of one phrase are unusual in folk melody and have led to suspicions that there must have been errors in the transmission of the tune. Cecil Sharp's discovery in Camborne of another version of the carol, beginning ' "Nowell and nowell" the angels did say', provoked much debate as to whether the modern tune for 'The first Nowell' was originally a descant to a completely different melody.

The editors of the *New Oxford Book of Carols,* who have gone into the whole question in considerable detail, conclude that the tune recorded by Sandys and sung today represents a conflation of parts of the Camborne tune and the upper part of another long lost west-gallery setting of the carol. Conflation of the parts of gallery carols was common and is partly explained by the fact that the melody was often in the tenor line. What may well have happened with 'The first Nowell' is exactly what William Dewy warned the counter boys in the Mellstock Choir about when they were tackling 'Arise and hail': 'Don't ye go straying into the treble part, as ye did last year' (see notes No. 8).

The tune that we now have may well represent snatches of the treble part taken erroneously to be the melody line and transmitted as such when the carol was sung in unison. It has been suggested that 'The first Nowell' was originally sung to the tune we associate with 'On Christmas night all Christians sing' (No. 58). The words certainly go rather well to that tune but I somehow doubt that for all its repetitiveness, we will see the familiar THE FIRST NOWELL being ousted as the usual accompaniment to the carol after which it is named.

The first Nowell the angel did say
Was to three poor shepherds in fields as they lay
In fields where they lay a-keeping their sheep
On a cold winter's night that was so deep.
Nowell, Nowell, Nowell, Nowell
Born is the King of Israel.

2 They looked up and saw a star,
Shining in the east, beyond them far;
And to the earth it gave great light,
And so it continued both day and nigh.

3 And by the light of that same star,
Three wise men came from country far;
To seek for a King was their intent
And to follow the star wherever it went.

4 This star drew nigh to the north-west
O'er Bethlehem it took its rest,
And there it did both stop and stay
Right over the place where Jesus lay.

5 Then did they know assuredly
Within that house the King did lie;
One entered in for them to see
And found the babe in poverty.

6 Then entered in those wise men three,
Full reverently upon their knee,
And offered there in his presence
Their gold and myrrh and frankincense.

7 Between an ox stall and an ass,
This Child truly there born he was;
For want of clothing they did him lay
All in the manger, among the hay.

8 Then let us all with one accord
Sing praises to our Heavenly Lord,
That hath made heaven and earth of naught,
And with his blood mankind hath bought.

9 If we in our time shall do well,
We shall be free from death and Hell,
For God hath prepared for us all
A resting place in general.

78

THE HOLLY AND THE IVY

This carol, which came fourteenth in the 2005 BBC *Songs of Praise* poll, ingeniously takes the holly with its white blossom, red berries, prickle and bark as symbolic of key episodes in the life of Christ. It is first found in a broadside published in Birmingham around 1710. 'Joshua Sylevester' (thought to be a pseudonym used by William Sandys and William Husk) included it in a collection of *Christmas Carols* published in 1861. Husk also put it in his *Songs of the Nativity* (1864) and Bramley and Stainer in their *Christmas Carols, New and Old* (1871). The version which is printed on page 344 and which has become standard, was taken down in 1909 by Cecil Sharp from the singing of Mrs Mary Clayton at Chipping Camden, Gloucestershire, and published in his *English Folk Carols* in 1911. The main difference with earlier texts is the alteration of 'now are both well grown' to 'when they are both full grown' in the second line of the first verse.

Although the title suggests a parity between the two plants mentioned, ivy hardly gets a mention in the body of this carol. This is in marked contrast to its treatment in medieval carols where the interplay between the two plants is a common theme. An old folk song found in a manuscript in the Bodleian Library portrays a battle between them for mastery:

Holly and ivy made a great party
Who should have the mastery
In lands where they go.

Then spoke Holly: 'I am free and jolly,
I will have the mastery
In lands where we go'.

Then spoke Ivy, 'I am loud and proud,
I will have the mastery
In lands where we go'.

Then spoke Holly, and set him down on his knee,
'I pray thee, gentle Ivy, say me no villeny,
In lands where we go'.

In folk tradition holly is sometimes associated with good and ivy with evil. It is difficult to know how this distinction originated and it is by no means universal. Ivy was used in England as a substitute for palm branches in Palm Sunday processions and both holly and ivy were among the plants most disliked and shunned by Scottish witches, presumably because they were both seen as holy. The really evil plant, at least in the eyes of the church, was mistletoe because of its associations with pagan and Druidic rites and it is noticeable that it never appears in any medieval carol. Several medieval carols in fact gave ivy a very positive image. One used it to symbolize the Divine spouse and another, dating from the fifteenth century, was possibly written to counteract prejudice against it:

I shall tell you a reason why
Ye shall love Ivy and think no shame;
The first letter beginneth with I,
And right even so – Jesus' name.

The tussle between holly and ivy portrayed in many medieval carols may have represented the battle between the sexes rather than that between good and evil. Holly stood for maleness while ivy was seen as having female characteristics. A seventeenth-century collection of aphorisms, *The Twelve Months*, includes the observation 'Great is the contention of holly and ivy, whether master or dame wears the breeches'. There was an old Oxfordshire tradition that a man must supply a maid with ivy or she would steal his breaches. A letter in the *Gentleman's Magazine* in 1779 described the burning at Shrovetide in a village in East Kent of two effigies known as the 'Holly Boy' and the 'Ivy Girl'.

A carol which describes the decoration of a hall at Christmas with holly and the deliberate exclusion of ivy seems to have accompanied a dramatic game in which women were excluded from the company in the hall and grouped outside the door:

Holly stands in the hall, fair to behold;
Ivy stands without the door; she is full sore a-cold.
Nay, ivy, nay, it hall not be, iwys;
Let Holly habe the mastery, as the manner is.

Holly and his merry men, they dance and they sing,
Ivy and her maidens, they weep and they wring.

Ivy hath a kybe; she caught it with the cold;
So may they all have aye that with Ivy hold.

Holly hath berries as red as any rose;
The foster, the hunters keep him from the doors.

Ivy hath berries as black as any sloe;
There came the owl, and ate her as she go.

Holly hath birds, a full fair flock,
The nightingale, the woodpecker, the gentle laverock.

Good Ivy, what birds hast thou?
None but the owlet, that cries 'How! How!'

The carol that we know as 'The holly and the ivy' does not seem to draw on these medieval precedents. It displays no particular antipathy towards ivy, nor any association of it with either evil or femininity. Rather holly and ivy are bracketed together because they are evergreen and associated with Christmas decoration. The main reason for the carol's favouring of holly and virtual ignoring of ivy seems to be simply because the former plant offers so many more possibilities for illustrating and symbolizing the life and death of Christ.

The refrain of this carol is particularly intriguing. 'The rising of the sun' seems to hark back to the mid-winter solstice and to pre-Christian sun worship. As for the running of the deer, there may be some significance in the fact that both holly and ivy were among the plants at the borders of woodlands which were spared from the forester's axe because they were among the favourite food of deer. 'The playing of the merry organ' has echoes of Chaucer's *Canterbury Tales* where, in the Priest's Tale, the crowing of the poor widow's cock is described as being 'merrier than the merry organ'.

Early versions of the carol are accompanied by different tunes – Bramley and Stainer's, for example, is set to an old French carol tune. The tune that has now become standard was collected in Gloucestershire by Sharp in 1909. A choral arrangement of it by Walford Davies, published in 1913, was popularized through the broadcasts of the King's College carol services. Other arrangements have been made by Martin Shaw and Allen Percival.

Another carol, which was taken down in the early twentieth century by the Rev. G.H. Doble in St Day, near Redruth, Cornwall, has considerable similarities to 'The holly and the ivy' although it uses different images and dispenses with the ivy altogether. It is known as the Sans Day carol:

Now the holly bears a berry as white as the milk,
And Mary bore Jesus, who was wrapped up in silk:

And Mary bore Jesus Christ, our Saviour for to be,
And the first tree in the greenwood, it was holly, holly, holly!
And the first tree in the greenwood, it was the holly.

Now the holly bears a berry as green as the grass,
And Mary bore Jesus, who died on the cross.

Now the holly bears a berry as black as the coal,
And Mary bore Jesus, who died for us all.

Now the holly bears a berry, as blood is it red,
Then trust we our Saviour, who rose from the dead.

Yet another carol about holly and ivy, which makes much of their evergreen qualities, is found in a sixteenth-century collection where it is set to a tune attributed to Henry VIII:

'Green grow'th the holly',
So doth the ivy;
Though winter blasts blow ne'er so high,
Green grow'th the holly.

A modern version of 'The holly and the ivy' appears in several current hymnbooks, including *Hymns and Psalms*. Written by Emily Chisholm (1910-) 'in a mood of nostalgia' while on a holiday in the Black Forest as an Advent carol and first published in *New Orbit* in 1972, it begins:

The holly and the ivy
Are dancing in a ring,
Round the berry-bright red candles
And the white and shining King.

Now, here at last after so many excursions, is the familiar standard version of the carol for which you have been waiting so patiently.

The holly and the ivy,
When they are both full grown,
Of all the trees that are in the wood,
The holly bears the crown.
The rising of the sun
And the running of the deer,
The playing of the merry organ,
Sweet singing in the choir.

2 The holly bears a blossom
As white as the lily flower,
And Mary bore sweet Jesus Christ
To be our sweet Saviour.

3 The holly bears a berry
As red as any blood,
And Mary bore sweet Jesus Christ
To do poor sinners good.

4 The holly bears a prickle
As sharp as any thorn,
And Mary bore sweet Jesus Christ
On Christmas Day in the morn.

5 The holly bears a bark
As bitter as any gall,
And Mary bore sweet Jesus Christ
For to redeem us all.

6 The holly and the ivy,
When they are both full grown,
Of all the trees that are in the wood,
The holly bears the crown.

79

THE LORD AT FIRST DID ADAM MAKE

This carol took pride of place in Davies Gilbert's 1822 collection, *Some Ancient Christmas Carols*, one of the most important pioneering volumes in the nineteenth-century revival of traditional English carols. Like 'Adam lay ybounden' (No.4) and 'Remember, O thou man' (No.68), it starts the Christmas story not in Bethlehem but in the Garden of Eden and so shows the full background to and need for God's descent to earth in human form and Jesus' salvific mission.

Its provenance is unknown. The fact that it specifically mentions Christmas Eve suggests that it was originally sung at home rather than in church. Christmas Eve services were unknown in Protestant England until late in the nineteenth century. It probably comes from the West of England.

The hymn is printed here as it appears in Gilbert. A version published by Sandys eleven years later varies in several respects. Its opening line is 'The Lord at first had Adam made', and its third verse runs:

'For in the day thou dost it touch,
Or dost it then come nigh,
And if that thou dost eat thereof
Then surely thou shalt die.'
But Adam, he did take no heed
To that same only thing,
But did transgress God's holy law,
And sore was wrapped in sin.

In the fourth verse, Sandys has 'to' rather than 'for' in the second line and 'From death, and hell, and thrall' in line six. In the fifth verse he has 'redeemed from hell' in the fourth line, which certainly rhymes better than 'thrall' with 'well', and 'do the thing that's right' in line six. The sixth verse begins 'Now for the benefits that we/Enjoy from Heaven above' and ends 'And when we die in heaven we shall/Enjoy our living Lord'. In the seventh verse, Sandys substitutes 'hungry sort' for 'hungry souls'.

Sandys gives two tunes for this carol, both of which are included in the *Oxford Book of Carols* and the *New Oxford Book of Carols*. Both are in the minor key and sound starkly atonal to modern ears. About the first, the editors of the more recent Oxford collection comment: 'There is a rough, peasant musicality about the setting as a whole to which a middle-class Georgian editor could hardly aspire.'

For Christmas Eve

The Lord at first did Adam make
Out of the dust and clay,
And in his nostrils breathed life,
E'en as the Scriptures say.
And then in Eden's paradise
He placed him to dwell,
That he within it should remain,
To dress and keep it well.
Now let good Christians all begin,
An holy life to live,
And to rejoice and merry be,
For this is Christmas Eve.

2 And then within the garden he
Commanded was to stay,
And unto him in commandment
These words the Lord did say:
'The fruit which in the garden grows
To thee shall be for meat,
Except the tree in the midst thereof,
Of which thou shalt not eat.'

3 'For in the day that thou shalt eat,
Or to it then come nigh,
And if that thou dost eat thereof
Then surely thou shalt die.'
But Adam, he did take no heed
Unto that only thing,
But did transgress God's holy law,
And so was wrapped in sin.

4 Now mark the goodness of the Lord,
Which he for mankind bore:
His mercy soon he did extend,
Lost man for to restore.
And then, for to redeem our souls
From death and hellish thrall,
He said his own dear Son should be
The Saviour of us all.

5 Which promise now is brought to pass
Christians, believe it well;
And by the coming of God's dear Son
We are redeemed from thrall.
Then if we truly do believe
And do the thing aright,
Then, by his merits, we at last
Shall live in heaven bright.

6 Now for the blessings we enjoy
Which are from heaven above,
Let us renounce all wickedness
And live in perfect love.
Then shall we do Christ's own command,
Ev'n his own written word,
And when we die in heaven shall
Enjoy our living Lord.

7 And now the tide is nigh at hand
In which our Saviour came;
Let us rejoice and merry be
In keeping of the same.
Let's feed the poor and hungry souls,
And such as do it crave;
Then, when we die, in heaven sure
Our reward we shall have.

80

THE MOON SHINES BRIGHT

This is not, as might appear from its first line, a song about Charlie Chaplin but rather a carol found in many eighteenth- and nineteenth-century broadsides, especially in the West Country. Variously entitled 'the Waits' Carol' and 'the Bellman's Song', it seems to have derived from verses sung by the bellmen or watchmen who went round at night crying out the hours. One version has the last two lines of the first verse as 'And hark! the bellman of the night/ Bids us awake and pray'.

The emphasis throughout the carol is on the death of Jesus, suggesting that the carol belongs to Lent rather than Christmas. There is, indeed, no mention of the Nativity and it is only the last line that anchors it to the Christmas season, or more precisely, the New Year. In fact, it probably did start as a Lenten carol although it also seems to have been sung in early summer. A May-time carol from Hertfordshire quoted in an *Every-day Book* published in 1821 incorporates several verses from 'The moon shines bright' and ends with the stanza:

And now our song is almost done
And we can no longer stay,
So bless you all both great and small
As we wish you a joyful May.

The third verse of this carol seems to be a variation of the first verse of the hymn, 'Jerusalem, my happy home', based on a passage in the *Meditationes* of St Augustine and found in a manuscript in the British Library dating from the late sixteenth century:

Jerusalem, my happy home,
Name ever dear to me,

When shall my labours have an end?
Thy joys when shall I see?

In his *Songs of the Nativity* William Husk printed a ten-verse version of 'The moon shines bright' with the following extra stanzas inserted between verses six and seven:

Instruct and teach your children well,
The while that you are here;
It will be better for your soul
When your corpse lies on the bier.

Today you may be alive and well,
Worth many a thousand pound,
Tomorrow dead and cold as clay,
Your corpse laid under ground.

With one turf at your head, O man,
And another at your feet,
Thy good deeds and thy bad, O man,
Will altogether meet.

'The moon shines bright' may go back to the sixteenth century and it has been suggested that it could be the carol to which Shakespeare refers in the song 'It was a lover and his lass' in *As You Like It*:

This caroll they began that hour,
With a hey, and a ho, and a hey nonino,
How that a life was but a flower,
In the spring time, the only pretty ring time..

Little is known about the origins of the tune to which this carol is now always set. It was published in Bramley and Stainer's *Christmas Carols, New and Old* in 1871 but probably dates from the eighteenth century or even earlier.

The Waits' Carol

The moon shines bright, and the stars give a light,
A little before the day
Our Lord, our God, He called on us,
And bade us awake and pray.

2 Awake, awake, good people all,
Awake and you shall hear,
Our Lord, our God, died on the cross
For us whom He loved so dear.

3 O fair, O fair Jerusalem,
When shall I come to thee?
When shall my sorrows have an end,
Thy joy that I may see.

4 The fields were green as green could be,
When from His glorious seat
Our Lord, our God, He watered us,
With His heavenly dew so sweet.

5 And for the saving of our souls
Christ died upon the cross:
We ne'er shall do for Jesus Christ
As he hath done for us.

6 The life of man is but a span
And cut down in its flower;
We are here today, and tomorrow are gone,
The creatures of an hour.

7 My song is done, I must be gone,
I can stay no longer here.
God bless you all, both great and small,
And send you a happy New Year.

81

THE RACE THAT LONG IN DARKNESS PINED

This great Scottish paraphrase of Isaiah's prophecy of the coming of the Prince of Peace who will bring darkness out of light has rightly found its way into the Advent or Christmas sections of many hymnals.

It is the work of John Morison, a minister who was much involved in writing and campaigning for the paraphrases of Scripture passages which were somewhat reluctantly taken up in the eighteenth century by a Church of Scotland still thirled to an exclusive diet of metrical psalmody. Born in Cairnie, Aberdeenshire, in 1750, Morison was educated at King's College, Aberdeen, and taught in several schools in Caithness. He submitted 24 pieces to the committee of the Church of Scotland set up in 1742 to prepare and collect paraphrases to be sung in worship. Seven of his paraphrases were accepted, including this one and two others which are still popular in Scotland, 'Come, let us to the Lord our God with contrite hearts return' and ''Twas on that night when doomed to know'. In 1780 Morison was ordained as the minister of Canisbay, on the north coast of Caithness. At the General Assembly of 1781 he was appointed a member of the committee to revise the paraphrases. It was in the volume of *Scottish Paraphrases* produced by that committee in 1781, which remains the standard text for paraphrases, that 'The race that long in darkness pined' first appeared in the form in which I print it on page 354.

Morison was not the only person to paraphrase the text of Isaiah 9:2–8 which begins 'The people that walked in darkness have seen a great light; they that dwell in the land of the shadow of death, upon them hath the light shined.' It memorably inspired one of the great choruses in Handel's *Messiah* and was paraphrased earlier in the eighteenth century by Isaac Watts. It was Morison who did it best, however, although not well enough for Anglicans who have their own much amended version, first produced for the first edition of *Hymns Ancient and Modern* which begins:

The people that in darkness sat
A glorious light have seen;
The light that shined on them who long
In shades of death have been.

Even Presbyterians are not as keen on Morison's paraphrase as they once were. The current edition of the *Church Hymnary* omits verses two and three, while *Rejoice and Sing* rather perversely sticks to Morison for verses one, four, five and six but takes the Anglican version of verse two:

To hail Thee, Sun of Rightenousness,
The gathering nations come,
Rejoicing as when reapers bear
Their harvest treasures home.

Because this paraphrase is in common metre, there are a vast number of tunes to which it can be sung. Anglicans, Methodists and members of the United Reformed Church, or at least their hymnal editors, seem to favour the traditional metrical psalm tune DUNDEE which I feel is too wistful and which most Scots associate with 'I to the hills will lift mine eyes'. Something more affirmative is needed. The revised edition of the *Church Hymnary* favoured TIVERTON by Jacob Grigg, first found in a selection of psalm tunes published in 1795. The third edition has substituted CREDITON, a tune by Thomas Clark found in a book of psalm tunes for country choirs published around 1810. It would certainly be my choice. The fourth edition of the *Church Hymnary* offers both TIVERTON and ST MAGNUS (NOTTINGHAM) by Jeremiah Clarke.

Paraphrase xix

The race that long in darkness pined
Have seen a glorious light;
The people dwell in day, who dwelt
In death's surrounding night.

2 To hail Thy rise, Thou better Sun!
The gathering nations come,
Joyous, as when the reapers bear
The harvest treasures home.

3 For Thou our burden hast removed,
And quelled the oppressor's sway,
Quick as the slaughtered squadrons fell
In Midian's evil day.

4 To us a Child of hope is born;
To us a Son is given;
Him shall the tribes of earth obey,
Him all the hosts of heaven.

5 His name shall be the Prince of Peace,
For evermore adored,
The Wonderful, the Counsellor,
The great and mighty Lord.

6 His power increasing still shall spread,
His reign no end shall know;
Justice shall guard his throne above,
And peace abound below.

82

THE VIRGIN MARY HAD A BABY BOY

This simple but affecting carol comes from the West Indies. It was collected by Edric Connor on the island of Trinidad in 1942 from the singing of James Bryce, who at the age of 94 was still working on a grapefruit plantation for the paltry sum of one shilling and eight pence a day. Bryce, whose parents and grandparents had been slaves, died the year after the song was collected.

Edric Connor noted that 'The Virgin Mary had a baby boy' was the only West Indian negro carol which he encountered during several years of research on the folk songs of his native Caribbean. It was first published in his *Collection of West Indian Spirituals and Folk Tunes* in 1945.

While the verses have an unmistakable calypso rhythm, the chorus has a more African sound and may have been brought over to the West Indies by negro slaves.

The virgin Mary had a baby boy,
The virgin Mary had a baby boy,
The virgin Mary had a baby boy
And they say that his name is Jesus
He come from the glory,
He come from the glorious kingdom,
He come from the glory,
He come from the glorious kingdom,
O yes, believer! O yes, believer!
He come from the glory,
He come from the glorious kingdom.

2 The angels sang when the baby was born,
The angels sang when the baby was born,
The angels sang when the baby was born,
And they say that his name is Jesus.

3 The shepherds came when the baby was born,
The shepherds came when the baby was born,
The shepherds came when the baby was born,
And they say that his name is Jesus.

4 The wise men came when the baby was born,
The wise men came when the baby was born,
The wise men came when the baby was born,
And they say that his name is Jesus.

83

THE WISE MAY BRING THEIR LEARNING

Several of the hymnbooks which include this delightful children's hymn do not place it in the Christmas section. However, I have no hesitation in including it in a book of Christmas hymns and carols since it seems to me to belong firmly to the Epiphany season with its recurrent theme of the treasures offered to Jesus the King. I am glad to say that my feelings are echoed by the editors of *Church Family Worship* where it is placed alongside 'As with gladness men of old' in the section devoted to The Wise Men.

Not that this song is suitable only for singing at Christmas. Its essential message that the greatest treasures that we bring to Jesus are the duties we have to do each day, hearts that love him and thankful praise, makes it a song for all times and seasons. Its Christmas feel is, however, enhanced by its tune, TYROLESE, an Austrian carol melody originally associated with the carol '*Ihr Hirten, stehet alle auf*'. The *Oxford Book of Carols* used the tune for another carol, known as Falan-Tiding which begins 'Out of the orient crystal skies/A blazing star did shine'. TYROLESE and 'The wise may bring their learning' were first brought together in 1951 by the editors of the *BBC Hymn Book* and have remained paired ever since.

The authorship of this carol is unknown although I would be prepared to take a small bet that it was written by a woman in the latter part of the nineteenth century. It first appeared in a collection of children's hymns entitled *Praise for Children* published in 1881 and was taken up in the *Congregational Church Hymnal* of 1887. The version I give below is the original with all its Victorianisms ('young souls meekly striving to walk in holy ways' and 'the little duties we have to do each day'). Most modern hymnbooks which still include this hymn, and not a few do, prefer the modernized and less child-centred version produced by the compilers of the *BBC Hymn Book*. It reverses the order of the second and third verses and renders them as follows:

We'll bring the many duties
We have to do each day;
We'll try our best to please him,
At home, at school, at play:
And better are these treasures
To offer to our King
Than richest gifts without them;
Yet these we all may bring.

We'll bring him hearts that love him,
We'll bring him thankful praise,
And souls for ever striving
To follow in his ways:
And these shall be the treasures
We offer to the King,
And these are gifts that ever
Our grateful hearts may bring.

There are certain similarities between 'The wise may bring their learning' and the the opening verse of a hymn by Christina Rossetti, although for her the question raised in the mind of a child contemplating the wise men is not so much what gifts he or she may offer Jesus, but rather what can act as a guiding star or angel. Here are the first two verses of the Rossetti hymn.

The shepherds had an angel,
The wise men had a star;
But what have I, a little child,
To guide me home from far,
Where glad stars sing together
And singing angels are?

Lord Jesus is my guiding star,
My beacon-light in heaven;
He leads me step by step along
The path of life uneven;
He, true light, leads me to that land
Whose day shall be as seven.

The wise may bring their learning,
The rich may bring their wealth,
And some may bring their greatness,
And some their strength and health:
We too would bring our treasures
To offer to the King;
We have no wealth or learning,
What gifts then shall we bring?

2 We'll bring him hearts that love him,
We'll bring him thankful praise,
And young souls meekly striving
To walk in holy ways:
And these shall be the treasures
We offer to the King,
And these are gifts that even
The poorest child may bring.

3 We'll bring the little duties
We have to do each day;
We'll try our best to please him,
At home, at school, at play:
And better are these treasures
To offer to our King
Than richest gifts without them;
Yet these a child may bring.

84

THERE'LL BE A NEW WORLD BEGINNIN' FROM TONIGHT

Most of the carol texts in this book do not suffer too much from being shorn of their tunes. I have to admit that this one does. It really needs its racy melody, preferably complete with the 'Pink a ping, pang pong' which follows the first, second and fifth line of the refrain in the second part of Malcom Sargent's arrangement, to do it justice. Those who do not know it, and cannot sing along subliminally as they read the text, will, I fear, be unable to appreciate just how effective it can be. You need to get into your Country and Western gear and into the 'ay-ay-yipee' idiom of the old cowboy trail songs. The editors of one of the many books in which this appears suggest that 'coconut shells might provide an appropriate accompaniment'.

Both words and music were written by Cyril Broadhurst (1908–1981) , an American composer and playwright who wrote more than a hundred country and western songs. 'There'll be a new world beginnin' from tonight' was the concluding song in his one-act play, *The Cowboy Christmas*, which was first performed in thc Bellevue Stratford Hotel in Philadelphia in 1942. The play transferred the Nativity story from Bethlehem to the American Wild West and told the story of three cowboys, camping with their cattle, who followed a strange, luminous bright star which led them to a barn where they saw a baby in a manger and sensed the beginning of something new for the world.

The Cowboy Christmas was written and performed under the auspices of the Oxford Group, the spiritual and moral reform movement instituted in the 1920s by Frank Buchman, a Lutheran minister originally from Pennsylvania. The group got its name when he took a team of Oxford Rhodes Scholars to

South Africa in 1928. Ten years later Buchman launched a worldwide movement under the title Moral Re-Armament. The Oxford Group has always made much use of drama and music in spreading its message of the need for individual and corporate moral reformation. The first performance of *The Cowboy Christmas* is said to have helped to end a labour strike in a Philadelphia factory supplying vital materials for the allied effort in the Second World War. Representatives of both management and labour attended the play and were deeply moved by its message of reconciliation and love.

The Cowboy Carol, as it has become known, was first published with a musical arrangement by Frances Roots Hadden in *A Treasury of Christmas Music* published by Blandford's in 1949. It came to the attention of the great arranger and conductor, Sir Malcolm Sargent, who wrote to the Oxford Group in January 1951 asking for permission to arrange the carol for the Royal Choral Society. Sargent's arrangement for mixed voices without accompaniment was first performed by the Royal Choral Society at their Christmas concert in the Royal Albert Hall in December 1951 and was published by Oxford University Press the following year. A later arrangement by Sargent with accompaniment was published in 1958 – an old invoice in the OUP archives in Oxford reveals that the total bill for printing, folding, trimming and supplying paper for 3000 copies came to the princely sum of nineteen pounds, seven shillings and sixpence – those were the days! The Cowboy Carol was recorded in 1957 by HMV who erroneously described it as 'traditional' and in 1963 the Royal National Institute for the Blind produced a braille version.

The Cowboy Carol

There'll be a new world beginnin' from tonight!
There'll be a new world beginnin' from tonight!
When I climb up to my saddle
Gonna take him to my heart!
There'll be a new world beginnin' from tonight!

2 Right across the prairie,
Clear across the valley,
Straight across the heart of every man,
There'll be a right new brand of livin'
That'll sweep like lightning fire
And take away the hate from every land.

3 Yoi, yippee! We'e gonna ride the trail!
Yoi, yippee! We'e gonna ride today!
When I climb up to my saddle,
Gonna take him to my heart,
There'll be a new world beginnin' from tonight.

85

THERE'S A STAR IN THE EAST

Like 'Go, tell it on the mountain' (No. 25), this carol fits into the category of a negro spiritual. Based on St Luke's account of the angels' appearance to the shepherds to announce the good news of Jesus' birth, it was collected from the singing of slaves in the American south during the period of the US Civil War.

'Rise up, shepherd and follow', as it is generally known, first appeared in *Slave Songs of the United States*, a collection edited by W.F. Allen, C.P. Ware and L.McK. Garrison, and first published in 1867. It was described there as 'a Christmas Plantation Song', having been collected in the slave plantations of Georgia and South Carolina.

As in many other spirituals, it is possible to discern in the verses of this carol a yearning for deliverance from slavery and oppression. This perhaps lies at the root of its urgent repeated call to 'Rise up . . . and follow'.

The editors of the *New Oxford Book of Carols* point to the similarity of its tune to those of several British folk songs, including a Welsh carol. An arrangement of 'Rise up, shepherd and follow' by John Rutter, which appears in both *A Little Carol Book* and *100 Carols for Choirs* has become very popular.

There's a star in the East on Christmas morn,
Rise up, shepherd and follow!
It'll lead to the place where the Saviour's born:
Rise up, shepherd and follow!

Leave your sheep and leave your lambs,
Rise up, shepherd and follow!
Leave your ewes and leave your rams,
Rise up, shepherd and follow!
Follow, follow,
Rise up, shepherd and follow!
Follow the Star of Bethlehem,
Rise up, shepherd and follow!

2 If you take good heed to the angels words,
Rise up, shepherd and follow!
You'll forget your flocks, you'll forget your herds,
Rise up, shepherd and follow!

86

THIS IS THE TRUTH SENT FROM ABOVE

This carol, much favoured in choirs and places where they sing, is probably of late seventeenth- or early eighteenth-century origin and, like so many others, seems to have particular associations in the West of England. As with 'The Lord at first did Adam make' (No.79), it has the virtue of recounting the whole Christian drama of salvation from its beginning with the story of creation and the fall.

It appears in a longer sixteen-verse version in *A Good Christmas Box* (1847), one of the many Victorian collections which did so much to preserve traditional English carols. In the early years of the twentieth century, Cecil Sharp collected a version at Donnington Wood, Shropshire, and Vaughan Williams noted one down from the singing of a Mr W. Jenkins of King's Pyon, Herefordshire.

For *Carols for Today* (1987) the Jubilate Group changed the opening line to 'Christ is the Truth sent from above' and provided a substantially altered version of verses two, six and seven.

The gentle and lyrical tune to which this carol is usually set is the one which Ralph Vaughan Williams heard it being sung to in Herefordshire. He published it in 1919 in his *Eight Traditional English Carols*. Cecil Sharp collected an entirely different tune in Shropshire and published it in his *English Folk-carols* in 1911. This latter tune was often used for William Cowper's powerful hymn 'There is a fountain filled with blood'. Both tunes are given in the *New Oxford Book of Carols*.

This is the truth sent from above,
The truth of God, the God of love;
Therefore don't turn me from the door,
But hearken all, both rich and poor.

2 The first thing that I will relate,
That God at first did man create;
The next thing which to you I tell
Woman was made with him to dwell.

3 Then after that 'twas God's own choice
To place them both in paradise,
There to remain from evil free
Except they ate of such a tree.

4 But they did eat, which was a sin,
And thus their ruin did begin -
Ruined themselves, both you and me,
And all of our posterity.

5 Thus we were heirs to endless woes
Till God the Lord did interpose;
And so a promise soon did run:
That he's redeem us by his Son.

6 And at this season of the year
Our blest Redeemer did appear,
And here did live, and here did preach,
And many thousands he did teach.

7 Thus he in love to us behaved,
To show us how we must be saved;
And if you want to know the way,
Be pleased to hear what he did say:

8 'Go preach the Gospel,' now he said,
'To all the nations that are made!
And he that does believe on me,
From all his sins I'll set him free.'

9 O seek!, O seek of God above
That saving faith that works by love!
And, if he's pleased to grant thee this,
Thou'rt sure to have eternal bliss.

10 God grant to all within this place
True saving faith, that special grace
Which to his people doth belong:
And thus I close my Christmas song.

87

THOU DIDST LEAVE THY THRONE

This piece could have appeared as appropriately in *The Daily Telegraph Book of Hymns* as in the present collection. Few hymn-books identify it as a Christmas hymn although I am glad to say that *Church Family Worship* places its (much altered) version, beginning 'Lord, you left your throne and your kingly crown' in the section on The Wise Men and it appears, alongside 'Rudolph the red nosed reindeer', on 'Tim's Christmas Page', a major US website of carols.

In fact, this hymn seems to me as much about Christ's birth as about his life and work, which is the section into which it is usually slotted in most hymnbooks. This is not just because of the explicit references to Bethlehem and the Nativity in verse one and to the angels in verse two. Its whole theme, and there is no carol that does it better, is the doctrine of kenosis, the self-emptying by which Jesus divested himself of his power and majesty and came to earth in weakness and humility. It is the doctrine expressed in Philippians 2.6–8:

> Christ Jesus, who, though he was in the form of God, did not count equality with God a thing to be grasped, but emptied himself, taking the form of a servant, being born in the likeness of men.

Jesus' birth in a stable is central to a kenotic Christology and Christmas is the time more than any other when Christians should be celebrating this divine paradox at the heart of their faith and pondering the message of self-emptying love. This hymn also has a strong Advent theme. The sixth line of verse two echoes the Collect for the first Sunday in Advent in the Book of Common Prayer: 'in the time of this mortal life, in which thy Son Jesus Christ came to visit us in great humility'.

'Thou didst leave thy throne' is the work of Emily Elliott. Born in Brighton in 1836, she wrote many of her hymns for the choir of St Mark's Church in that town where her father was rector. She edited the children's magazine of the Church Missionary Society and was much involved in supporting missionary work. She died in London in 1897.

This hymn was first printed privately in 1864 for use in St Mark's, Brighton, and was first published in 1870 in the *Church Missionary Juvenile Instructor*, of which Emily Elliott was editor. For her *Chimes for Daily Service* (1880), the author altered the words of the refrain in the last two verses. For verse four she substituted:

O come to my heart, Lord Jesus!
Thy cross is my only plea

and for verse five:

And my heart shall rejoice, Lord Jesus,
When thou comest and callest on me.

Hymns and Psalms, *Rejoice and Sing* and *Baptist Praise and Worship* are among the modern hymnbooks which include these variations. Anglican hymnals tend to keep the refrain in its original state.

The tune MARGARET was composed for this hymn by Timothy Matthews and first appeared in *Children's Hymns and Tunes*, a collection published by SPCK in 1876. Matthews was another clergy child, being born in Colmworth Rectory in 1826 and educated at Bedford Grammar School and Gonville and Caius College, Cambridge. He studied music under Sir George Elvey and after a curacy at Nottingham was rector of North Coates from 1869 to 1907. He died in 1910.

Thou didst leave thy throne and thy kingly crown
When thou camest to earth for me;
But in Bethlehem's home was there found no room
For thy holy Nativity:
O come to my heart, Lord Jesus;
There is room in my heart for thee.

2 Heaven's arches rang when the angels sang,
Proclaiming thy royal degree;
But in lowly birth didst thou come to earth,
And in great humility:
O come to my heart, Lord Jesus;
There is room in my heart for thee.

3 The foxes found rest, and the bird had its nest
In the shade of the cedar tree;
But thy couch was the sod, O thou Son of God,
In the desert of Galilee:
O come to my heart, Lord Jesus;
There is room in my heart for thee.

4 Thou camest, O Lord, with the living word
That should set thy people free;
But with mocking scorn and with crown of thorn
They bore thee to Calvary:
O come to my heart, Lord Jesus;
There is room in my heart for thee.

5 When the heavens shall ring, and the angels sing,
At thy coming to victory,
Let thy voice call me home, saying, 'Yet there is room,
There is room at my side for thee:'
O come to my heart, Lord Jesus;
There is room in my heart for thee.

88

THOU WHOSE BIRTH ON EARTH

We have already encountered the Christmas musings of one great Victorian free-thinker in William Morris' 'Masters in this hall' (No.51) and 'Outlanders, whence come ye last?' (No.61). Here is a carol by another of the same hue, Algernon Charles Swinburne.

Born in the year of Queen Victoria's accession, 1837, Swinburne was educated at Eton and Balliol College, Oxford. He established a close friendship with Dante Gabriel Rossetti and other members of the Pre-Raphaelite brotherhood. He learned his poetic craft from William Morris with whom he shared a passion for heroic liberal causes. If Swinburne had a religion it was perhaps that of sexual love about which he wrote passionately and lyrically in his poems and ballads. He died, exhausted by a life of excess, in 1909.

This poem is an unusually orthodox statement of Christian belief on the part of one who was more usually at home attacking Christianity, as in the brutally pagan 'Hymn to Proserpine' and 'Before a Crucifix', or ruminating on the melancholy consequences of spiritual feeling set adrift from an objective in God, as in 'A Forsaken Garden'.

'Thou whose birth on earth' was taken up along with the poems of other non-believers like Thomas Hardy and William Morris by Percy Dearmer and appeared as a Christmas hymn in *Songs of Praise* where it took its place between a seventeenth-century poem 'The holy Son of God most high' and Nahum Tate's 'While shepherds watched their flocks by night'. The compilers of the 1949 *Public School Hymn Book* included Swinburne's carol, as did Erik Routley in his *University Carol Book*. It has not, as far as I am aware, appeared in any subsequent book. I have resurrected it here partly because of its novelty value but also because it does have some powerful mystical phrases and presents the Christmas drama in an unusual and intriguing way.

The tune to which it has generally been set is French and comes from a Tournai manuscript.

Thou whose birth on earth
Angels sang to men,
While thy stars made mirth,
Saviour, at thy birth,
This day born again;

2 As this night was bright
With thy cradle-ray,
Very light of light,
Turn the wild world's night
To thy perfect day.

3 Thou, the Word and Lord,
In all time and space
Heard, beheld, adored,
With all ages poured
Forth before thy face.

4 Lord, what worth in earth
Drew thee down to die?
What therein was worth,
Lord, thy death and birth?
What beneath thy sky?

5 Yet thy poor endure,
And are with us yet.
Be thy name a sure
Refuge for thy poor,
Whom men's eyes forget.

6 Bid our peace increase,
Thou that madest morn;
Bid oppressions cease;
Bid the night be peace;
Bid the day be born!

89

THREE KINGS FROM PERSIAN LANDS AFAR

This Epiphany carol has become deservedly popular in recent years. The text is a translation by William Mercer (1811–73; in a rare lapse, the *New Oxford Book of Carols* erroneously gives his date of birth as 1836) of a German hymn, '*Drei Kön'ge wandern aus Morgenland*' by Peter Cornelius (1824–74) who wrote both the words and music of numerous songs and of three operas, the best known of which was *Der Barbier von Bagdad* (1858).

Cornelius first wrote his carol about the three kings as a simple ballad. He sketched it in 1859 and published it in 1871 in a set of six *Weihnachtslieder*. When Cornelius showed the carol to his friend Franz Liszt, he suggested using the melody of Philip Nicolai's chorale, *Wie schön leuchtet der Morgenstern* ('How brightly beams the Morning Star', No. 34 in this book) as a piano accompaniment.

In several English books, notably the *Oxford Book of Carols*, Cornelius' hymn appears in Mercer's translation, as on page 377, with the accompaniment based on Nicolai's chorale. In others words are set to the chorale, based on Nicolai's text, so providing a chorus which runs under the soloist singing Cornelius' hymn. The best-known arrangement in this form is probably that by Ivor Atkins which appears in *Carols for Choirs 1* (1961). Hugh Keyte, Andrew Parrott and Clifford Bartlett provide another one in the *New Oxford Book of Carols*.

In these arrangements, the choir sings this translation of '*Wie schön leuchtet der Morgenstern*' by H.N. Bate (1871–1941):

How brightly shines the morning star
With mercy beaming from afar;
The host of heaven rejoices:

O Righteous Branch, O Jesse's Rod!
Thou Son of Man and Son of God!
We, too, will lift our voices:

Jesus, Jesus! Holy, holy,
Yet most lowly, draw thou near us:
Great Emmanuel, come and hear us!

The tune for the solo verses of 'Three kings from Persian lands afar' remains the one originally written by Cornelius. There is another translation of the verses by Erik Routley which begins 'Three kings have wandered from Eastern land'.

There is, of course, no Biblical warrant for the notion of three kings coming from Persian lands. Matthew, the only canonical Gospel writer to mention the coming of travellers from the East to worship the infant Jesus, writes only of an unspecified number of *Magi*, or wise men, and does not identify their nationality. The deduction that there were three of them derived from Matthew's mention of three gifts – gold, frankincense and myrrh – although there is nothing in his account to suggest that there was one gift per man. Their elevation to the status of kings and their identification with 'Persian lands' probably rested on an interpretation of Old Testament prophecy, notably verses from Psalm 72 which still ring out in Scottish churches during Advent in the form of the metrical psalm 'His large and great dominion shall from shore to shore extend' which would undoubtedly have found a place in this volume had it been larger:

The kings of Tarshish and of the isles shall bring presents:
The kings of Sheba and Seba shall offer gifts.
Yea, all kings shall fall down before him:
All nations shall serve him.

Those wishing to know more about how the legend of the three kings developed, and specifically how they came to be given their names, are invited to skip to the introduction to 'We three kings of Orient are' (No. 94) where they will find the story continues.

Three kings from Persian lands afar
To Jordan follow the pointing star,
And this the quest of the travellers three:
Where the new-born King of the Jews may be?
Full royal gifts they bear for the King;
Gold, incense, myrrh are their offering.

2 The star shines out with a steadfast ray;
The kings to Bethlehem make their way,
And there in worship they bend the knee,
As Mary's child in her lap they see;
Their royal gifts they show to the King;
Gold, incense, myrrh are their offering.

3 Thou child of man, lo! to Bethlehem
The kings are trav'lling, travel with them!
The star of mercy, the star of grace,
Shall lead thy heart to its resting place.
Gold, incense, myrrh thou canst not bring
Offer thy heart to the infant King!
Offer thy heart!

90

TOMORROW SHALL BE MY DANCING DAY

These verses seem to belong to the genre of dance songs from which the modern carol as we know it developed. Although the earliest extant source for 'Tomorrow shall be my dancing day' is William Sandys' *Christmas Carols, Ancient and Modern* (1833), it almost certainly goes back to medieval times.

The clue to its origins probably lies in the third line of the opening verse: 'To see the legend of my play'. This suggests that it was originally written for one of the medieval mystery plays and belongs in the same tradition as the Coventry carol (No.49). It has close parallels with a number of fifteenth-century 'cradle prophecy' carols in which the infant Christ foretells his future to his mother while sitting on her lap.

The editors of the *New Oxford Book of Carols* find particularly striking similarities between the language and style of this carol and surviving examples of the three-day religious plays which were performed in the Cornish language in the fourteenth and fifteenth centuries. They conclude:

> It seems possible that 'Tomorrow shall be' was devised to be sung and danced at the conclusion of the first day of a three-day drama, translated from the Cornish, which may itself have made use of the 'lover' and 'beloved' theme. The actor portraying Christ would have sung the verses and the whole company and audience the repeats of the refrains. The song would naturally have become familiar through repeated local use, and may even have been sung at Christmas: carols of the Passion were not unknown in the Christmas season. The increased popularity of 'Redemption' carols, following the eighteenth-century rise of the Methodist and Evangelical movements, would in any case have made it a natural choice for domestic carollers and village waits, by which time it would have lost the initial refrain and its origins within the drama would probably have been forgotten.

Aside from the strong emphasis on dance, reinforced by the fact that every verse ends with that word, perhaps the most striking aspect of this carol, which involves Jesus telling the story of his own life in a graphic way, is the use of the imagery of love, understood not in a spiritualized sense but very much as *eros*, the love of humans. There is, of course, good Biblical precedent for this in the erotic language of the *Song of Songs*. In his comments on the carol, Erik Routley seizes on this quality:

> For sheer passionate humanity, nothing comes near 'Tomorrow shall be my dancing day'... Nowhere are the staggering incongruities of the religion of the middle ages so shamelessly revealed as they are in this product of their genius. Nowhere is human love so boldly used as a type of the divine love ... The words of 'My dancing-day' expose the last positive quality, perhaps the single fundamental quality of the old ballad-carols, which is that they are world-affirming, not world-denying.

The *Oxford Book of Carols* divided this carol into three parts, suggesting that verses one and two were suitable for general use, verses three to seven for singing during Lent and verses eight to 11 for use at Easter and Ascensiontide. Many books print severely abbreviated forms of the carol for Christmas use only. The closing couplet in which the ascended Christ invites us all to join in the general dance is reminiscent of the portrayal of God in a late sixteenth-century poem by Sir John Davies entitled 'Orchestra, or a Poem of Dancing':

> Dancing, bright lady, then began to be
> When the first seeds whereof the world did spring,
> The fire air earth and water did agree
> By Love's persuasion, nature's might king,
> To leave their first discorded combating
> And in a dance such measure to observe
> And all the world their motion should preserve.

Since when they still are carried in a round,
And changing come one in another's place;
Yet do they neither mingle nor confound,
But every one doth keep the bounded space
Wherein the dance doth bid it turn or trace.
The wondrous miracle doth Love devise,
For dancing is love's proper exercise.

Or if this all, which round about we see,
As idle Morpheus some sick brains hath taught,
Of individual notes compacted be,
How was this goodly architecture wrought?
Or by what means were they together brought?
They err that say they did concur by chance;
Love made them meet in a well-ordered dance.

This dance theme fits well with the findings of quantum physics that sub-atomic particles are in a state of constant motion, neither entirely random nor wholly determined but involving a delicate and beautifully balanced interplay of chance and necessity. It also fits with the process theologians view of God luring all his creatures by a persuasive love rather than coercing and cajoling them. The idea of the dance of creation is one that Christians would do well to recover from its Biblical and medieval roots. It is, of course, a strong motif in Eastern religions, particularly in Hinduism where Shiva is regarded as Lord of the Dance of Creation, the one who maintains the cosmos in life and who is also the presence contained in nature. The idea of Jesus as the 'Lord of the Dance' has, of course, been taken up and expressed by Sydney Carter, whose 'I danced in the morning when the world was begun', which the author himself calls a carol, would undoubtedly have found a place in this collection, were it not already in the *Daily Telegraph Book of Hymns* (No. 55).

Tomorrow shall be my dancing day;
I would my true love did so chance
To see the legend of my play,
To call my true love to the dance.
Sing, O my love, O my love, my love,
This have I done for my true love.

2 Then was I born of a virgin pure;
Of her I took fleshly substance.
Thus was I knit to man's nature,
To call my true love to the dance.

3 In a manger laid and wrapped I was,
So very poor; this was my chance,
Betwixt an ox and a silly poor ass,
To call my true love to my dance.

4 Then afterwards baptized I was;
The Holy Ghost on me did glance,
My Father's voice heard from above
To call my true love to my dance.

5 Into the desert I was led,
Where I fasted without substance;
The devil bade me make stones with bread,
To have me break my true love's dance.

6 The Jews on me they made great suit,
And with me made great variance,
Because they loved darkness rather than light,
To call my true love to my dance.

7 For thirty pence Judas me sold,
His covetousness for to advance:
'Mark, whom I kiss, the same do hold!'
The same is he shall lead the dance.

8 Before Pilate the Jews me brought,
Where Barabbas had deliverance;
They scourged me and set me at nought,
Judged me to die to lead the dance.

9 Then on the cross hanged I was,
Where a spear my heart did glance;
There issued forth both water and blood,
To call my true love to my dance.

10 Then down to hell I took my way
For my true love's deliverance,
And rose again on the third day,
Up to my true love and the dance.

11 Then up to heaven I did ascend,
Where now I dwell in sure substance
On the right hand of God, that man
May come unto the general dance

91

UNTO US A BOY IS BORN

The Latin carol, '*Puer nobis nascitur*', of which this carol is a translation, was used in the medieval liturgy. Each ecclesiastical office ended with a ritual exchange, to plainchant, between a single voice and the whole choral body to the text '*Benedicamus Domino – Deo gracias*'. The *Benedicamus* versicle became the occasion for extended verse tropes suitable to particular seasons. '*Puer nobis nascitur*' originated as such an embellishment to be sung during the Christmas season.

The earliest text of '*Puer nobis nascitur*' is found in the Moosburg Gradual (1355-60), a large manuscript volume copied for the Augustinian College of St Castulus in Moosburg, Germany and containing songs and tropes for liturgical use. The song is also found in a fifteenth-century Trier manuscript and in the Finnish collection *Piae Cantiones* (1582). The third verse was inserted to be used on the feast of Holy Innocents' Day (28 December).

The translation given here, which is the one most widely used today, was made by Percy Dearmer for the *Oxford Book of Carols* (1928). For *Songs of Praise* Dearmer amended the last verse to:

He the Source and he the End!
Let the organ thunder
While our happy voices rend
The jocund air asunder!

Several hymnbooks suggest giving verses one and five to all, verses two and four to treble voices and verse three to men.

An earlier translation by George Ratcliffe Woodward (1848-1934), which is still found in some modern books (including the *Oxford Christmas Carol Book*) has the virtue of preserving some of the original Latin in the last verse and showing how it fitted in with the original purpose of carrying the *Benedicamus*, although its third verse is slightly clumsy and archaic:

Unto us is born a Son,
King of choirs supernal;
See on earth His life begun,
Of lords the Lord eternal.

Christ from heaven descending low
Comes, on earth a stranger;
Ox and ass their Owner know,
Becradled in a manger.

This did Herod sore affray
And grievously bewilder,
So he gave the world to slay,
And slew the little childer.

Of His love and mercy mild,
This the Christmas story,
And O that Mary's gentle child
Might lead us up to glory!

O and A and A and O
Cum cantibus in choro;
Let the merry organ go,
Benedicamus Domino.

The tune, known as PUER NOBIS NASCITUR or OMEGA AND ALPHA, is that which accompanies '*Puer nobis nascitur*' in both the Moosburg Gradual and *Piae Cantiones*. It has been widely taken up and sung across the Continent. In France it was sung as a Latin *noel* from the sixteenth century and there are organ settings by Lebègue and Dandrieu. In Germany it is sung to the text '*Uns ist geborn ein Kindelein*'.

Puer nobis nascitur

Unto us a boy is born!
King of all creation
Came he to a world forlorn,
The Lord of every nation.

2 Cradled in a stall was he
With sleepy cows and asses;
But the very beast could see
That he all men surpasses.

3 Herod then with fear was filled:
'A prince', he said, 'in Jewry!'
All the little boys he killed
At Bethlem in his fury.

4 Now may Mary's son, who came
So long ago to love us,
Lead us all with hearts aflame
Unto the joys above us.

5 Omega and Alpha he!
Let the organ thunder,
While the choir with peals of glee
Doth rend the air asunder.

From the *Oxford Book of Carols.*

92

WASSAIL, WASSAIL ALL OVER THE TOWN

Like 'Here we come a wassailing' (No. 33), this jolly song belongs to the tradition of making 'luck visits' around the neighbourhood at Christmas time. As we have seen, the word 'wassail' means 'good health to you'. It is tempting to suggest that as well as providing the root for such words as 'health', 'hale' and 'hallo', its second syllable also gives us the origin of 'ale' since there always seem to be copious quantities of liquor around whenever wassailers gather and their songs make much of the pleasures of drink.

This song exists in numerous different variations. The one printed here is known as the Gloucestershire Wassail and is found in the original and new Oxford books of carols. It is something of a composite construction. The first four verses were taken down by Ralph Vaughan Williams from the singing of an old man in Gloucestershire and the last three by Cecil Sharp from Mr Isaac Bennett at Little Sodbury in the same county. It goes back well before then, however. William Husk printed a six-verse version (basically similar to verses one, three, five, six seven and eight) in his *Songs of the Nativity* and noted that on New Year's Eve, 1864, it was sung in the little village of Over, near Gloucester, by a party of wassailers from the neighbouring village of Minsterworth. At the end of the eighteenth century the Rev John Brand wrote of the carol being sung by Gloucestershire wassailers carrying a large bowl decorated with ribbons and garlands.

A little exegesis is called for to explain some of the references in the carol. Cherry and Dobbin are both horses, Broad May, Fillpail and Colly cows. In Brand's copy these names were left blank so that they could be supplied by singers as local circumstances required. In Husk's version, it is Dobbin's right ear rather than his eye which is toasted, and the animal with the right eye is identified as Smiler. Cherry, Broad May and Colly are missing but Fillpail does make an appearance for her long tail. 'The small' in verse seven is a reference to small beer, the watery second brew considered fit only for women, servants and children.

Different versions of this song, sometimes with variant tunes, are found in other parts of the country. One collected by A.L. Lloyd from a Welsh singer in 1947 begins very similarly to the Gloucestershire version:

A wassail, a wassail throughout all this town!
Our cup it is white and our ale it is brown;
Our wassail is made of a good ale and true,
Some nutmeg and ginger, the best we could brew.

The third verse of this Welsh version strongly suggests that it comes from the tradition of wassailers going round orchards to bless them and encourage good crops:

We hope that your apple trees prosper and bear,
So we may have cider when we call next year;
And where you've one barrel I hope you'll have ten,
So we can have cider when we call again.

This practice is still kept up in the village of Stoke Gabriel in Devon where each year around Twelfth Night local wassailers go through the orchards singing loudly and banging pots and pans to wake the trees from their winter slumbers and drive out the evil spirits that would stop the boughs from fruiting. Copious quantities of cider are poured over the trees' roots and slices of cider-soaked toast are thrust high into their branches with long-handled forks.

Another version of the song is still popular in the village of Drayton in Somerset where wassailers make luck visits to the larger houses in the neighbourhood on Twelfth Night. The following version of the Somerset song was transcribed in September 1903 by Cecil Sharp from the singing of a Miss Quick in the Drayton vicarage:

Wassail, O wassail all over the town!
The cup it is white and the ale it is brown;
The cup it is made of the good ashen tree,
And so is the ale of the best barley.
For it's your wassail, and it's our wassail,
And I'm jolly, come to our jolly wassail!

2 There was an old man, and he had an old cow,
And how for to keep him he could not tell how.
He built up a barn to keep his cow warm
For no harm, boys, harm, no harm, boys, harm
And a cup of good liquor will do us no harm.

3 The missus and master were sitting by the fire,
Not thinking we poor travellers were travelling in the mire;
Come fill up our bowl and we'll be gone from here.
For it's your wassail, and it's our wassail,
And I'm jolly, come to our jolly wassail!

4 O maid, maid, maid, with your silver headed pin,
Pray open the door and let us all in,
And then you will see how merry we shall be.
For it's your wassail, and it's our wassail,
And I'm jolly, come to our jolly wassail!

5 We're not come here for to eat or to drink,
But to keep up the custom until another year.
Come fill up our bowl and we'll be gone from here.
For it's your wassail, and it's our wassail,
And I'm jolly, come to our jolly wassail!

When Sharp published this wassail in his 1909 collection of *Folk Songs from Somerset* he considerably altered it, expanding the three line verses to four lines (so that verse two, for example, ended with the line 'And a drop or two of cider will do us no harm') and substituting for the fifth verse one from the neighbouring village of Langport:

The girt dog of Langport he burnt his long tail,
And this is the night we go singing wassail:
O master and missus, now we must be gone;
God bless all in this house till we do come again.

The 'girt dog' of Langport appears to be a reference to the Danish invasion of that town in the ninth century. Langport was supposedly the furthest west that the Danes penetrated in their invasion of England before being repulsed by King Alfred in 878 at the Battle of Ethandun (Edington in Wiltshire).

But enough of Somerset. It is high time to return to the Gloucestershire version of the Wassail Song you were, patient readers, promised long ago. Its tune, incidentally, is that 'sung by an old person in the county' to Vaughan Williams.

The Gloucestershire Wassail

Wassail, wassail all over the town!
Our toast it is white, and our ale it is brown,
Our bowl it is made of the white maple tree;
With the wassailing bowl we'll drink to thee.

2 So here is to Cherry and to his right cheek,
Pray God send our master a good piece of beef,
And a good piece of beef that may we all see;
With the wassailing bowl we'll drink to thee.

3 And here is to Dobbin and to his right eye,
Pray God send our master a good Christmas pie,
And a good Christmas pie that may we all see;
With the wassailing bowl we'll drink to thee.

4 So here is to Broad May and to her broad horn,
May God send our master a good crop of corn,
And a good crop of corn that may we all see;
With the wassailing bowl we'll drink to thee.

5 And here is to Fillpail and to her left ear,
Pray God send our master a Happy New Year,
And a happy New Year as e'er he did see,
With the wassailing bowl we'll drink to thee.

6 And here is to Colly and to her long tail,
Pray God send our master he never may fail
A bowl of strong beer; I pray you draw near,
And our jolly wassail it's then you shall hear.

7 Come, butler, come fill us a bowl of the best,
Then we hope that your soul in heaven may rest;
But if you do draw us a bowl of the small,
Then down shall go butler, bowl and all.

8 Then here's to the maid in the lily white smock,
Who tripped to the door and slipped back the lock!
Who tripped to the door and pulled back the pin,
For to let these jolly wassailers in.

93

WATCHMAN, TELL US OF THE NIGHT

This fine Advent hymn, despite being the work of a leading nineteenth-century British hymn writer, is not much sung in the United Kingdom today. In the United States, by contrast, it is very popular. I first made its acquaintance through a recording made by the Mormon Tabernacle Choir, although strangely it is not in the hymnbook of the Church of Jesus Christ of Latter Day Saints.

The author, John Bowring, was born in Exeter in 1792. A Unitarian in religious belief and a strong radical in politics, he was appointed editor of the *Westminster Review* in 1825 and subsequently represented the Clyde Burghs, Kilmarnock and Bolton in the House of Commons where he was actively involved in the campaign for free trade and the abolition of the corn laws and spoke on fiscal, educational and commercial issues. Thereafter he served in the foreign and colonial service as commercial attaché in Paris, consul in Canton and Hong Kong and governor of Hong Kong. He died in 1872. His collected works run to 36 volumes. He is remembered today chiefly for his hymns 'God is love, His mercy brightens' and 'In the cross of Christ I glory'.

This hymn nicely combines the tradition of the watchmen, precursors of the waits, and that of the star pointing to the place of Jesus' birth. Although the word 'Christ' does not feature, there is a pretty unequivocal reference to 'the Son of God' which shows the catholicity and Trinitarianism of this particular Unitarian's faith.

The tune to which 'Watchman, tell us of the night' is most usually sung in the United States is ABERYSTWYTH. Composed by Joseph Parry (1841–1903), professor of music at University College, Aberystwyth, for the Welsh hymn '*Beth sydd imi yn y byd'*, and first published in the 1879 hymnbook of the Welsh Congregational Union, it is most commonly associated in the British Isles with Charles Wesley's 'Jesus, lover of my soul'. The *Hymnbook* of the Presbyterian Church of the USA additionally sets 'Watchman, tell us of the night' to ST. GEORGE'S, WINDSOR, written in 1858 by Sir George Elvey (1816–93), organist at St George's Chapel, Windsor, for the hymn 'Hark! the song of Jubilee' and now generally associated in Britain with the harvest hymn 'Come, ye thankful people, come'.

Watchman, tell us of the night,
What its signs of promise are:
Traveller, o'er yon mountain's height,
See that glory-beaming star!
Watchman, doth its beauteous ray
Aught of joy or hope foretell?
Traveller, yes; it brings the day,
Promised day of Israel.

2 Watchman, tell us of the night;
Higher yet that star ascends:
Traveller, blessedness and light,
Peace and truth, its course portends.
Watchman, will its beams alone
Gild the spot that gave them birth?
Traveller, ages are its own,
And it bursts o'er all the earth!

3 Watchman, tell us of the night,
For the morning seems to dawn:
Traveller, darkness takes its flight;
Doubt and terror are withdrawn.
Watchman, let thy wanderings cease;
Haste thee to thy quiet home.
Traveller, lo, the Prince of Peace,
Lo, the Son of God is come!

94

WE THREE KINGS OF ORIENT ARE

Following a British carol which is now almost exclusively sung in North America, here is an American one from the same date that is probably more popular on this side of the Atlantic. It is almost certainly based more on fiction than fact but that hasn't stopped it from being a favourite for Nativity plays and school carol concerts. It also lends itself very well to parody and various versions of a more or less irreverent nature have been known to circulate round classrooms and playgrounds.

Both the words and tune of 'We three kings' were written by John Henry Hopkins. Born in 1820, the son of an iron-master turned lawyer turned parson who was elected the first bishop of Vermont, he followed his father into Episcopalian orders and became rector of Christ's Church, Williamsport, Pennsylvania. It was there, around 1857, that he wrote his Christmas hymn about the three wise men. It was first published in his *Carols, Hymns and Songs* in 1865 and gained popularity in Britain after being selected by Bramley and Stainer as the sole North American contribution to their *Christmas Carols New and Old* in 1871. Hopkins died in 1891.

Hopkins wrote this hymn to be sung by a trio of male voices with the refrain set for a full SATB chorus. The first and last verses are set in parts, with Gaspard singing the tenor line and carrying the tune, Melchior singing the middle baritone line and Balthazar the bass. Verse two is a solo for Gaspard, verse three for Melchior and verse four for Balthazar.

The three kings first received names in the Armenian Infancy Gospel which dates from the sixth century. It identified them as Melkon (which became Melchior as it came to Europe), the king of the Persians, Gaspar, the king of the Hindus and Balthazar, king of the Arabs. In the Armenian account, the three kings are described as arriving from Persia with 12,000 soldiers on horseback and the gifts which they bring are very much more complex than those enumerated by Matthew. Melkon offers not only myrrh but aloes, rare fabrics, and books written and sealed by the finger of God which foretold the birth of Christ and which had descended from Adam to the Persian Magi at the time of Cyrus. Gaspar offers nard and cinnamon as well as incense and Balthazar gold, silver, sapphires and pearls.

As the legend of the three kings travelled from the Near East to Europe in the early middle ages, the gifts were simplified and also associated with different kings. By the eighth century, when the story was well established in Europe, Gaspard was associated with gold, taken to symbolize the royal status of the infant Jesus, Melchior with frankincense, its use in temple worship reinforcing the sense of Jesus' divinity, and Balthazar with myrrh, the main spice used for embalming and so having clear associations with death.

Further embellishments were made to the story of the three kings during the Middle Ages. In the twelfth century three embalmed bodies in a perfect state of preservation found buried under a church near Milan were declared to be those of the kings. They were transferred to Cologne Cathedral where they became the object of veneration and pilgrimage. Further stories grew up around the kings – that they had chosen Prester John, the great figure of medieval romance, as their temporal successor and had brought with them jewels which had belonged to Alexander the Great and which the Queen of Sheba had found in King Solomon's palace. A late fifteenth-century chronicle identified Gaspard (now often called Caspar) as an Ethiopian with the result that he was portrayed as a black man in many of the great Renaissance paintings of the Adoration of the Magi.

When so much of the Nativity story proves to be rather flimsy when it is chipped away by academics, it is reassuring to find that modern science has attempted to come to the aid of 'the star of wonder' that features so prominently in this carol and in Christmas myth. In a lecture to the Cambridge Philosophical Society in 1991, subsequently published as an article in the

Quarterly Journal of the Royal Astronomical Society and in revised form in the *Tyndale Bulletin* in 1992, Colin Humphreys, Professor of Materials Science at Cambridge University, has argued that the star which the wise men saw over Bethlehem may well have been a 'broom star', a comet with a tail looking as though it was sweeping the sky clean, which Chinese astronomers recorded in 5BC. The comet appears to have been continuously visible for 70 days which would have given the kings long enough to travel from their Oriental homes to Bethlehem.

Another explanation for the star has been offered by David Hughes of Sheffield University who points out that a rare conjunction of the planets Jupiter and Saturn took place in 7 BC. An American astronomer, Roger Sinnott, has discovered an even rarer conjunction between Jupiter and Venus on 17 June in the year 2 BC when he thinks people living in Babylon would have seen the two planets approaching so closely that they would seem to merge into one, 'gleaming like a great beacon over Judea into the west'.

In several modern versions of this carol, the last lines of verse five are altered to:

Alleluya, alleluya,
Earth to the heaven replies.

We three kings of orient are;
Bearing gifts we traverse afar,
Field and fountain, moor and mountain,
Following yonder star:

O star of wonder, star of night,
Star with royal beauty bright,
Westward leading, still proceeding,
Guide us to thy perfect light.

2 Born a king on Bethlehem plain,
Gold I bring, to crown him again,
King for ever, ceasing never,
Over us all to reign:

3 Frankincense to offer have I,
Incense owns a deity nigh;
Prayer and praising, all men raising,
Worship, him God most high:

4 Myrrh is mine; its bitter perfume
Breathes a life of gathering gloom;
Sorrowing, sighing, bleeding, dying,
Sealed in the stone-cold tomb.

5 Glorious now behold him arise,
King and God and sacrifice,
Heaven sings 'Alleluya',
'Alleluya' the earth replies.

95

WHAT CHILD IS THIS WHO LAID TO REST

Like 'Watchman, tell us of the night', this carol is more popular in the United States than in the land where it was written. Maybe the tune to which it is set, GREENSLEEVES, is just too hackneyed on this side of the Atlantic. If so, that is a pity for it is a carol with a strong message and some fine imagery.

The hymn was written around 1865 by William Chatterton Dix, whom we have already encountered as the author of 'As with gladness men of old' (No.9 – see the notes on this carol for his biography). It appeared in Bramley and Stainer's *Christmas Carols, New and Old* in 1871. It is found in most of the major American denominational hymnals. British hymn-books have been less enthusiastic, although it does appear in several recent collections, including the United Reformed Church's *Rejoice and Sing* where the language is updated. In the penultimate line of the first verse, for example, 'laud' becomes 'praise' and the opening line of verse two is changed to 'Why lies he in so poor a place'. For some reason the URC editors do not like the phrase 'the Word Made Flesh' in the penultimate line of verse two and they change it to 'the Saviour comes', so losing the echo of the prologue to John's Gospel. Their egalitarian and Protestant sensibilities are also offended by the references to peasant, king and Virgin in the third verse, line two of which is altered to 'All tongues and people own him' and line six to 'While Mary sings a lullaby'. The new BBC *Songs of Praise* collection (1997), which also includes 'What child is this', follows most of the changes made in *Rejoice and Sing* although it is content to leave the opening line of verse two in its original form.

The tune GREENSLEEVES, to which this carol has always been sung since its first publication, almost certainly dates from the sixteenth century. It is popularly attributed to Henry VIII but is more likely to be one of several melodies that developed over the standard Italian dance basses which came to England around 1550. The earliest extant appearance of the tune is in a fantasia by William Byrd dating from the early 1580s. By the end of the seventeenth century GREENSLEEVES had lost its bass and developed melodic variations which departed from the original harmony.

GREENSLEEVES has carried many texts over its 450 years or so of existence. They include at least one other Christmas (or more properly New Year) carol, which appeared in a collection of *New Christmas Carols* published in 1642 as 'A Caroll for New-yeares day. To the tune of Greene Sleeves':

The old yeare now away is fled,
The new year it is entered:
Then let us now our sins downe tread,
And joyfully all appeare!
Let's merry be this holy day,
And let us now both sport and play;
Hang sorrow! Let's cast away!
God send you a happy new yeare!

A much more recent Christmas carol set to the tune is Michael Perry's 'When shepherds watched and angels sang' which appears in *Hymns for Today's Church* and *Church Family Worship* (1986):

When shepherds watched and angels sang
And Judah's hills with glory rang,
Then Christ was born the Son of Man
On Christmas Day in the morning:
Christ was born the Son of Man
On Christmas Day, on Christmas Day;
Christ was born the Son of Man
On Christmas Day in the morning.

A less spiritual version of Greensleeves, which I think may come from an early *Private Eye* record, goes as follows:

I woke up this morning and got out of bed
With a very strong urge to paint the shed,
I fell off the ladder and broke my head,
And now my new jacket's got green sleeves.

What child is this who laid to rest,
On Mary's lap is sleeping?
Whom angels greet with anthems sweet
While shepherds watch are keeping?
This, this is Christ the King,
Whom shepherds guard and angels sing:
Haste, haste to bring him laud,
The Babe, the Son of Mary!

2 Why lies he in such mean estate
Where ox and ass are feeding?
Good Christians fear: for sinners here
The silent Word is pleading.
Nail, spear shall pierce him through,
The Cross be borne for me, for you;
Hail! hail the Word made Flesh,
The Babe, the Son of Mary!

3 So bring him incense, gold and myrrh;
Come, peasant, king, to own him!
The King of Kings salvation brings:
Let loving hearts enthrone him!
Raise, raise the song on high!
The Virgin sings her lullaby.
Joy! joy! for Christ is born,
The Babe, the Son of Mary!

96

WHAT SWEETER MUSIC CAN WE BRING

This carol was written by the seventeenth-century English poet, Robert Herrick, and, according to its title, sung to the King (probably Charles I) in the Banqueting Hall in Whitehall. It belongs to a group of seventeenth-century English poems which have been re-discovered and set as hymns in the twentieth century. Others include George Herbert's 'Teach me my God and king', Henry Vaughan's 'My soul, there is a country' and Samuel Crossman's 'My song is love unknown'.

Robert Herrick was born in 1591 in London and was apprenticed for ten years to his uncle who was a goldsmith. He went up to Cambridge in 1613 and was ordained into the Church of England in 1623. In 1627 he accompanied a military expedition to the Isle of Rhé as chaplain to the Duke of Buckingham and in 1629 became vicar of Dean Prior in Devonshire. He was ejected from his living in 1647 but returned in 1662. He died in 1674.

Herrick wrote well over a thousand poems, which he grouped together in two collections, 'Noble Numbers', covering sacred subjects, and 'Hesperides', made up of largely secular material, which were published together in a single volume in 1648. 'What sweeter music' rather surprisingly comes from the latter collection.

'What sweeter music' is printed at the end of these notes as Herrick wrote it and as it is printed in his *Poetical Works,* with the spelling modernized. It was shortened to make a four-verse carol with refrain by the editors of the *Oxford Book of Carols*, Percy Dearmer, Ralph Vaughan Williams and Martin Shaw. They called it 'Herrick's Carol' and set it to a tune from a seventeenth century German nativity play. More recently, John Rutter has made a fine arrangement, for SATB and organ or strings, which is very popular with choirs. This shortened version of the carol runs as follows:

What sweeter music can we bring
Than a carol, for to sing
The birth of this our heavenly King?
Awake the voice! Awake the string:

We see him come, and know him ours,
Who with his sunshine and his showers
Turns all the patient ground to flowers.

Dark and dull night, fly hence away,
And give the honour to this day,
That sees December turned to May,
If we may ask the reason, say.

The darling of the world is come,
And fit it is we find a room
To welcome him. The nobler part
Of all the house here is the heart.

Which we will give him, and bequeath
This holly and this ivy wreath,
To do him honour who's our King,
And Lord of all this revelling.

The *Oxford Book of Carols* made carols out of two other poems by Herrick. The first, offered as a carol for Candlemas Eve, traditionally the end of the Christmas season, deals with the dreary business of taking down the Christmas decorations:

Down with the rosemary and bays,
Down with the mistletoe;
Instead of holly, now upraise
The greener box, for show.

The other Herrick poem included in the *Oxford Book of Carols*, which comes from his 'Noble Numbers', makes an original if distinctly cumbersome Christmas ditty:

In numbers, and but these few,
I sing thy birth, O Jesu,
Thou pretty baby, born here,
With superabundant scorn here,
Who for thy princely port here,
Hadst for thy place
Of birth, a base
Out-stable for thy court here.

The poem of Herrick's that perhaps best lends itself to singing at Christmas-time has not, as far as I know, ever been included in a carol collection or set to music. This is his 'The Wassail':

Then may your plants be pressed with fruit,
Nor bee nor hive you have be mute,
But sweetly sounding like a lute.

Next may your ducks and teeming hen
Both to the cock's tread say Amen,
And for their two eggs render ten.

Last may your harrows, shares and ploughs
Your stacks, your stocks, your sweetest mows,
All prosper by your virgin vows.

Alas! we bless, but see none here
That brings us either ale or beer:
In a dry house all things are near.

Erik Routley has commented: 'Perhaps it is the rather surprisingly miniatory last verses, that express the sentiments of waits attending on a teetotal family, that have kept the lines out of the books.'

A Christmas Caroll sung to the King in the Presence at White-Hall

Chor. What sweeter music can we bring
Than a carol, for to sing
The birth of this our heavenly King?
Awake the voice! Awake the string!
Heart, Ear, and Eye, and every thing
Awake! The while the active finger
Runs division with the singer.

From the flourish they come to the song.

1 Dark and dull night, fly hence away,
And give the honour to this day,
That sees December turned to May.

2 If we may ask the reason, say;
The why, and wherefore all things here
Seem like the Spring-time of the year?

3 Why do's the chilling winter's morn
Smile, like a field beset with corn?
Or smell, like to a meade new-shorn,
Thus, on the sudden?

4 Come and see
The cause, why things thus fragrant be:
'Tis He is born, whose quickening birth
Gives life and lustre, public mirth,
To heaven, and the under-earth.

Chor. We see him come, and know him ours,
Who with his sunshine and his showers

Turns all the patient ground to flowers.
The darling of the world is come,
And fit it is we find a room
To welcome him. The nobler part
Of all the house here is the heart.

Chor. Which we will give him, and bequeath
This holly and this ivy wreath,
To do him honour who's our King,
And Lord of all this revelling.

97

WHEN GOD ALMIGHTY CAME TO BE ONE OF US

This is another carol of which I was unaware when I began compiling material for this collection. It was drawn to my attention by Jim Gordon, a Baptist minister in Aberdeen and keen hymnologist, who told me that he regarded it as one of the most original and lively carols to have been written in recent times. I agree with him and am delighted to give it wider circulation by including it in this book.

It was written by Michael Hewlett, an Anglican priest who was born in 1916, studied at Merton College, Oxford, and served in curacies in Brighton and Crawley. From 1956 to 1969 he was vicar of St John's, Malden, from 1972-6 team vicar of Cheriton Fitzpane, and from 1976 until his retirement in 1986 team vicar of North Creedy.

In a letter to me Michael Hewlett recalled that the basic idea for the carol came from someone else's article in a parish magazine:

> The thought was that the Incarnation, if one is to take it seriously, involves the incorporation of the Godhead not merely in a human body but in all the circumstances, contemporary or universal, in which human lives are carried on. So inn-keeper and shepherds, Caesar Augustus and contemporary thinking about the stars, were all involved in making the Incarnation a real event in human history.
>
> 'And they will never be the same again', having been used in this way by God – as indeed one ought to expect. And certainly it does seem to me that there is a certain nuance about the thought (especially) of a carpenter, perhaps also of a shepherd, which springs from their involvement in the strategic purposes of God.

This carol has not made its way into too many hymnbooks, although I am glad to say that the editors of the ecumenical

Australian hymnal, *With One Voice* (1979) did see fit to include it. In Britain, its appearance has largely been confined to publications from the Galliard/Stainer and Bell stable such as *Faith, Folk and Festivity* (1969), *Songs for the Seventies* (1972) *Partners in Praise* (1979) and the *Galliard Book of Carols* (1980). Michael Hewlett was delighted to hear of a carol service in India which finished with the children dancing down the aisle singing it.

The hymn was not written with a particular tune in mind but when the author showed it to a friend, he immediately suggested the melody of the Geordie folk song THE KEEL ROW and that is the tune to which it is invariably sung. Hewlett suggested to the editor of *With One Voice* that it would go well to WALTZING MATILDA 'but he felt that would be thought of as sacrilege – using a sacred Australian anthem for a secular purpose'.

Song and Dance

When God Almighty came to be one of us,
Masking the glory of his golden train,
Dozens of plain things kindled by accident,
And they will never be the same again.
Sing all you midwives, dance all the carpenters,
Sing all the publicans and shepherds too,
God in his mercy uses the commonplace,
God on his birthday had a need of you.

2 Splendour of Rome and local authority,
Working on policy with furrowed head,
Joined to locate Messiah's nativity,
Just where the prophets had already said,
Sing all you tax-men, dance the Commissioners,
Sing civil servants and policemen too,
God in his purpose uses the governments,
God on his birthday had a need of you.

3 Wise men, they called them, earnest astrologers,
Watching for meaning in the moving stars,
Science or fancy, learned or laughable,
Theirs was a vision that was brought to pass.
Sing all you wise men, dance all the scientists,
Whether your theories are false or true,
God uses knowledge, God uses ignorance,
God on his birthday had a need of you.

4 Sing all creation, made for his purposes,
Called by his providence to live and move:
None is unwanted, none insignificant,
Love needs a universe of folk to love.
Old men and maidens, young men and children,
Black ones and coloured ones and white ones too,
God on his birthday, and to eternity,
God took upon himself the need of you.

98

WHEN HE IS KING

This rather lovely and lyrical carol was apparently thought up on a pub crawl through Hampshire in November 1927. Its author, Bruce Blunt, an amateur poet, was desperately hard up and decided that writing a carol for publication might enable him 'to get suitably drunk at Christmas'. The words came to him one moonlit night as he was wending his way between the Plough at Bishop's Sutton and the Anchor at Ropley. Blunt later wrote out the poem and sent it to his friend Philip Heseltine (better known by his pseudonym Peter Warlock) who set it to music and the completed carol was published on Christmas Eve 1927 in the *Daily Telegraph*. In a letter to a friend many years later Blunt recalled 'We had an immortal carouse on the proceeds and decided to call ourselves "Carols Consolidated"'.

Blunt and Heseltine did, in fact, collaborate on several other carols, including 'The First Mercy', which began 'Ox and ass at Bethlehem', and 'The Frostbound Wood' which first appeared in 1930 in the Christmas pages of the *Radio Times*.

Bruce Blunt was born in 1899 and died in 1967. I regret to say that I have been unable to find out anything else about him. Philip Hesletine/Warlock was born in London in 1894 and educated at Eton and Christ Church, Oxford. He wrote over 100 songs as well as choral and instrumental works and spent most of his short life in London where he died in 1930.

'Bethlehem Down', as they chose to call this carol, has a somewhat similar theme to Sabine Baring-Gould's 'Sing Lullaby!' (No. 71), especially in its line: 'Here he has peace and a short while for dreaming'.

Although both the words and music of this carol are very affecting, it has never caught on. Apart from this one, the only other book which I am aware of that includes it is the *New Oxford Book of Carols*.

98 WHEN HE IS KING

When he is King we will give him the King's gifts,
Myrrh for its sweetness and gold for a crown,
Beautiful robes, said the young girl to Joseph,
Fair with her firstborn on Bethlehem Down.

2 Bethlehem Down is full of the starlight
Winds for the spices, and stars for the gold,
Mary for sleep, and for lullaby music
Songs of a shepherd by Bethlehem fold.

3 When he is King they will clothe him in gravesheets,
Myrrh for embalming, and wood for a crown,
He that lies now, in the white arms of Mary,
Sleeping so lightly on Bethlehem Down.

4 Here he has peace and a short while for dreaming,
Close huddled oxen to keep him from cold,
Mary for love, and for lullaby music,
Songs of a shepherd by Bethlehem fold.

99

WHILE SHEPHERDS WATCHED THEIR FLOCKS BY NIGHT

This much-loved and much parodied paraphrase of St Luke's account of the Annunciation to the shepherds came seventeenth in the 2005 BBC *Songs of Praise* poll.

It was the first Christmas hymn to gain official approval in the Church of England when it was included in the 1700 *Supplement to the New Version of the Psalms* which was bound in with the Book of Common Prayer. Until 'Hark, the herald angels sing' was added to the canon of 'approved' hymns in 1782, it was, indeed, the only Christmas carol which was officially permitted to be sung in Anglican church services.

'While shepherds watched' is generally thought to have been written by Nahum Tate. Born in Dublin in 1652, the son of a Church of Ireland clergyman who rejoiced in the name of Faithful Teate, he came to England after graduating from Trinity College, Dublin, and wisely changed his name to Tate. A friend of John Dryden, Tate was a distinguished if somewhat eccentric versifier in his own right, producing the libretto for Purcell's opera *Dido and Aeneas* and re-writing Shakespeare's *King Lear* to give it a happy ending. He was made Poet Laureate in 1692 but despite his most significant work during his period of office being *Panacea – a poem on tea*, he fell victim to excessive drinking and died in 1715 in a debtors' prison.

Together with a fellow Irishman, Nicholas Brady, Tate produced a new metrical version of the Psalms in 1696. This was adopted by the Church of England and superseded the 'old version' produced by Thomas Sternhold and John Hopkins in 1562. Among the Tate and Brady psalms which are still sung today are 'As pants the hart for cooling streams' and 'Through all the changing scenes of life'. Tate's metrical paraphrase of Luke

2:8–14 appeared as the sole Christmas hymn in the 1700 supplement to the 'new version' of the psalms, which was approved by the monarch in council for use in churches. The supplement also included one Easter hymn and three for use in communion services.

Numerous small alterations have been made to the text, the most common perhaps being the substitution of 'swaddling clothes' for 'swathing bands' in verse four. Those responsible for producing the authorized collection of paraphrases for the Church of Scotland in the mid-eighteenth century felt that they could improve on the Anglo-Irish original and north of the border the carol has a completely different opening:

While humble shepherds watched their flocks
In Bethlehem's plains by night,
An angel sent from heaven appeared,
And filled the plains with light.

There are other smaller differences in the Scottish version. In verse two the shepherds are seized with sudden rather than mighty dread and the concluding couplet of verse six runs:

Good will is shown by heaven to men,
And never more shall cease.

Other textual variants sprang up in the eighteenth and nineteenth centuries, including one that begun 'As shepherds watched their fleecy care'. Generations of schoolboys have, of course, sung of shepherds washing their socks by night.

Variations in words are nothing, however, to the number of different tunes to which this hymn has been set. Over a hundred have been identified in printed sources and it is likely that there were more. Because it is in common metre, 'While shepherds watched' could be sung to numerous psalm tunes. It is now almost universally associated with a single tune, WINCHESTER OLD, a psalm tune first found in a book published in 1592. This was included as one of 75 tunes printed in the sixth edition of the *Supplement to the New Version of the Psalms* (1708) as being suitable for the authorized hymns and psalms although 'While shepherds watched' was set in that volume to an early eighteenth-century tune called ST JAMES. The firm linkage of 'While shepherds watched' to WINCHESTER OLD was, like so many enduring marriages of words and tunes, the work of the editors of *Hymns Ancient and Modern* (1861).

Before this particular coupling was effected, there was no clearly recognized favorite among the many tunes to which the hymn was sung. One of the most popular was undoubtedly CRANBROOK, composed by Thomas Clark, a cobbler and precentor at a Wesleyan chapel in Canterbury. It is the same tune which accompanies the Yorkshire song 'On Ilkley moor Baht'at.' Also much used was a tune first published in 1749 by Joseph Watts in *A Choice Collection of Church Musick*. This vigorous fuguing tune, very much in the eighteenth-century west gallery tradition, was clearly well known to Thomas Hardy who mentions it in two of his writings. In *Tess of the D'Urbervilles* William Dewy soothes a savage bull by playing 'the Nativity hymn' on his fiddle. In a poem entitled 'The Dead Quire' its singing brings back to life the long-dead members of the Mellstock Choir who are heard by their drunken successors joining in 'the holy air':

'*While shepherds watched their flocks by night,–*
Thus swells the long familiar sound
In many a quaint symphonic flight –
To, *Glory shone around*.'

The editors of the *New Oxford Book of Carols*, who include seven tunes for this hymn, including one from Cornwall and another based on a soprano aria from Handel's 1728 opera, *Siroe, Re di Persia*, apparently popular in the United States, suggest that a variation of the CHESTNUT tune of 'God rest you merry, gentlemen' may have been the most common of all the tunes sung to 'While shepherds watched' before the present century.

A whole crop of tunes are still sung by the village carollers of

Yorkshire. They include CRANBROOK, LYNGHAM, the vigorous fuguing tune written for a Methodist village choir in Northamptonshire in 1803 by Thomas Jarman, a Baptist tailor and used by Methodists and the odd exuberant Presbyterian for Charles Wesley's 'O for a thousand tongues', LIVERPOOL written around 1786 by Edward Harwood, NORTHROP, OCTOBER and BUCKLEY. Perhaps the most popular of all the tunes used in the South Yorkshire pubs is FOSTER (also known as OLD FOSTER) which is also given in the *New Oxford Book of Carols*. Foster, a Methodist who lived in the mining village of High Green, wrote the tune for Sternhold and Hopkins' 'old version' of Psalm 47, 'Ye people all with one accord' and published it in a collection of his psalm tunes in 1820 where it was scored for choir, organ, strings, woodwind, brass and drum.

The compact disc produced in 1995 of carol singing around the South Yorkshire pubs, *A Festival of Village Carols*, contains 'While shepherds watched' sung to LIVERPOOL and also to a tune called SWEET CHIMING BELLS in which Tate's familiar verses are interspersed with the refrain:

Sweet bells, sweet chiming Christmas bells,
Sweet bells, sweet chiming Christmas bells,
They cheer us on our heavenly way,
Sweet chiming bells.

Those who want to hear just how vigorously this hymn used to be sung (and how staid WINCHESTER OLD is by comparison) are also recommended to purchase another recent compact disc, 'While Shepherds Watched – Christmas Music from English Parish Churches, 1740-1830' issued by Hyperion records in 1996. It has Tate's paraphrase sung to four different tunes: CRANBROOK, FOSTER and tunes by Michael Beesly of Blewbury, Oxfordshire (born 1700) and John Smith (1712-95). For good measure, it also has 'As shepherds watched their fleecy care' and 'There were shepherds abiding in the field'.

While shepherds watched their flocks by night,
All seated on the ground,
The angel of the Lord came down,
And glory shone around.

2 'Fear not,' said he (for mighty dread
Had seized their troubled mind);
'Glad tidings of great joy I bring
To you and all mankind.

3 'To you in David's town this day
Is born of David's line
A Saviour, who is Christ the Lord;
And this shall be the sign:

4 'The heavenly Babe you there shall find
To human view displayed,
All meanly wrapped in swathing bands,
And in a manger laid.'

5 Thus spake the seraph; and forthwith
Appeared a shining throng
Of angels praising God, who thus
Addressed their joyful song;

6 'All glory be to God on high,
And to the earth be peace;
Good will henceforth from heaven to men
Begin and never cease.'

100

WHO WOULD THINK THAT WHAT WAS NEEDED

The notion of the 'God of surprises' is very much a feature of modern theology, not least thanks to the best-selling book of that title by the Jesuit priest, Gerard Hughes. This contemporary carol, the second in this collection from the Iona Community's Wild Goose Worship Group (the other being 'Funny kind of night', No. 23), picks up this theme by presenting Christmas in terms of God surprising earth with heaven.

'Who would think that what was needed' was written by John Bell and Graham Maule and first appeared in the first collection of Wild Goose songs, *Heaven Shall Not Wait*, which was published in 1987. It has since appeared in *Rejoice and Sing* (1991), the new Anglican edition of *Hymns Old and New* (1996) and in rather truncated form, without the third verse and with verses one and two reversed in *Baptist Praise and Worship* (1991). In these books, the phrase 'by-passed strangers' in verse two has been altered to 'passing strangers'. *Rejoice and Sing* also substitutes 'In our search for sense and meaning' for 'While the human lot we ponder' in verse three.

In the preface to his collection, *Innkeepers and Light Sleepers*, Bell has written of his mission to 'grasp the earthiness of the people in the Christmas story as well as the mystery of the incarnation'. This he feels several well-loved older carols have failed to do:

> To say that there is nothing wrong with traditional Christmas carols is to be less than discerning. Some – perhaps the majority – are good. But there are some which tell patent lies about the nativity or about Jesus himself.
>
> There is no biblical evidence to support the theory that 'snow had

fallen, snow on snow' but there is substantial evidence to suggest that Jesus did not 'honour and obey' throughout all his wondrous childhood. What about him running away from his family when returning from Jerusalem?

There is also the temptation to depict the characters in the nativity story as less than full-blooded. Mary tends to be portrayed as anaemic, docile and constantly doting, not the kind of woman who could cope with a pile of dirty nappies. Joseph is sometimes depicted as spineless and the shepherds and wise men, perhaps too closely modelled on their Sunday-school nativity play stereotypes, lack either humour or surprise.

And in the midst of all this, the wonder, the confusion, the conundrum of the incarnation is hid behind the verbal equivalent of Victorian stained glass.

I have to confess to being someone who rather likes Victorian stained glass and loves Victorian hymns and carols, as John Bell knows all too well. While we must agree to differ on that point, however, I am full of admiration for the way that he has stripped sentimentalism and soppiness out of his own Christmas songs and given them a gritty earthiness.

'Who would think that what was needed' was written to be sung to the tune SCARLET RIBBONS. In *Heaven Shall Not Wait* the authors note: 'Scarlet Ribbons is a beautiful melody. The song is especially effective when sung, in a darkened church, as midnight approaches on Christmas Eve.'

God's Surprise

Who would think that what was needed
To transform and save the earth
Might not be a plan or army,
Proud in purpose, proved in worth!
Who would think, despite derision,
That a child should lead the way!
God surprises earth with heaven,
Coming here on Christmas Day.

2 Shepherds watch and wise men wonder,
Monarchs scorn and angels sing;
Such a place as none would reckon
Host a holy helpless thing;
Stabled beasts and by-passed strangers
Watch a baby laid in hay;
God surprises earth with heaven
Coming here on Christmas Day.

3 Centuries of skill and science
Span the past from which we move,
Yet experience questions whether
With such progress we improve.
While the human lot we ponder,
Lest our hopes and humour fray,
God surprises earth with heaven,
Coming here on Christmas Day.

COPYRIGHT ACKNOWLEDGEMENTS

A song was heard at Christmas © Timothy Dudley-Smith
Child of the stable's secret birth Christmas © Timothy Dudley-Smith
Every star shall sing a carol © Stainer & Bell
From heaven you came, helpless babe © Thankyou Music/Adm. By worshiptogether.com songs excl. UK & Europe, adm. by kingswaysongs.com, tym@kingsway.co.uk. Used by permission
Funny kind of night © 1992 WGRG, Iona Community, G2 3DH
Girls and boys, leave your toys © Oxford University Press
Going through the hills © Oxford University Press
It's rounded like an orange © Oxford University Press
Little Jesus, sweetly slept © Oxford University Press
No use knocking at the window (Standing in the rain) © 1963 TRO Essex Music Ltd. Of Suite 2.07, Plaza 535 Kings Road, London SW10 0SZ. International Copyright Secured. All Rights Reserved. Used by Permission
O Tennenbaum © Walter C. Ehret
People look east © Oxford University Press
See him lying on a bed of straw Michael Perry © Mrs B Perry/ Jubilate Hymns 4 Thorne Park, Torquay, TQ2 6RX www.jubilate.co.uk. Used by permission
Sing this night © Oxford University Press
The Virgin Mary had a boy © Copyright 1940 by Boosey & Co Ltd reproduced with permission by Boosey & Hawkes Music Inc.
Unto us a boy is born © Oxford University Press
When God Almighty came to be one of us © Stainer & Bell
When he is king we will give him the king's gift © Copyright

FURTHER READING

Andrew Barr, *The Nation's Favourite Carols* (Lion Hudson, Oxford, 2005)

Ian Bradley, *The Daily Telegraph Book of Hymns* (Continuum, 2005)

Ian Bradley, *Abide With Me: The World of Victorian Hymns* (SCM Press, 1997)

Douglas Brice, *The Folk Carol of England* (Herbert Jenkins, 1967)

Sydney Carter, *Green Print for Song* (Stainer & Bell, 1974)

Glyn Court, *Carols of the West Country* (West Country Books, 1996)

Percy Dearmer, Ralph Vaughan Williams & Martin Shaw (eds), *The Oxford Book of Carols* (Oxford University Press, 1928)

Maurice Frost, *Historical Companion to Hymns Ancient and Modern* (Hymns Ancient and Modern, 1962)

Davies Gilbert, *Some Ancient Christmas Carols* (1823)

R.L. Greene, *The Early English Carols* (Oxford University Press, 1977)

William Henry Husk, *Songs of the Nativity* (John Camden, 1864)

Hymnquest: *A Dictionary of Hymnody* (Stainer & Bell, 1997)

Christopher Idle, *Christmas Carols and their Stories* (Lion Publishing, 1988)

Hugh Keate and Andrew Parrott (eds), *The New Oxford Book of Carols* (Oxford University Press, 1992)

Alan Luff, *Carols of the British Isles* (Guild of Church Musicians Study Guide No.6, 1995)

Michael Perry (ed.), *Carols for Today* (Hodder and Stoughton, 1986)

William Phillips, *Carols: Their Origin, Music and Connection with Mystery Plays* (Routledge, 1921)

Eric Roseberry (ed.), *The Faber Book of Carols* (Faber, 1969)

Erik Routley, *The English Carol* (Oxford University Press, 1959)

Erik Routley (ed.), *The University Carol Book* (EMI Music Publishing, 1961)

Ian Russell, *A Song for The Time Village Carols from the Black Bull, Ecclesfield* (Village Carols, Sheffield, 1987)

William Sandys, *Christmas Carols, Ancient and Modern* (1833)

Richard Watson, *The English Hymn* (Oxford University Press, 1997)

Richard Watson and Kenneth Trickett, *Companion to Hymns and Psalms* (Methodist Publishing House, 1988)
Tyler Whittle, *Solid Joys and Lasting Treasures* (Ross Anderson Publications, 1985)
David Willcocks and John Rutter (eds), *Carols for Choirs 1 & 2* (Oxford University Press, 1960 & 1970)

INDEX OF FIRST LINES

Hymn
Number

INDEX OF AUTHORS, TRANSLATORS AND COMPOSERS